Movie Monsters
of the Deep

Movie Monsters of the Deep

Faith Roswell

WHITE OWL

First published in Great Britain in 2024 by
White Owl
An imprint of Pen & Sword Books Limited
Yorkshire – Philadelphia

ISBN 978 1 39905 295 5

A CIP catalogue record for this book is
available from the British Library

Typeset by Mac Style
Printed in the UK by CPI Group (UK) Ltd, Croydon, CR0 4YY.

Pen & Sword Books Limited incorporates the imprints of After
the Battle, Atlas, Archaeology, Aviation, Discovery, Family History,
Fiction, History, Maritime, Military, Military Classics, Politics,
Select, Transport, True Crime, Air World, Frontline Publishing, Leo
Cooper, Remember When, Seaforth Publishing, The Praetorian Press,
Wharncliffe Local History, Wharncliffe Transport, Wharncliffe True
Crime and White Owl.

For a complete list of Pen & Sword titles please contact

PEN & SWORD BOOKS LIMITED
47 Church Street, Barnsley, South Yorkshire, S70 2AS, England
E-mail: enquiries@pen-and-sword.co.uk
Website: www.pen-and-sword.co.uk
or
PEN AND SWORD BOOKS
1950 Lawrence Rd, Havertown, PA 19083, USA
E-mail: uspen-and-sword@casematepublishers.com
Website: www.penandswordbooks.com

Contents

Acknowledgements   viii

Introduction   ix

Chapter 1   Here be Monsters   1
Mermaids, sharks, tentacled beasts … was a real creature scaring sailors,
or was it just imagination and too much rum? From the mythical
Kraken to the ordinary octopus, what were the earliest water monsters in
recorded history and how did they become movie stars?

Chapter 2   The Big Three   15
The king of the monsters rose from the sea for the first time, an amphibious
man went looking for romance in the wrong place, and two men called Ray
destroyed a lighthouse and created a legacy. These three movies changed
the water monster genre forever.

Chapter 3   *Jaws*   31
The terrifying events that happened years before the movie, its accidental
success, and its disastrous aftermath. If you already know that things went
wrong while filming *Jaws*, you are about to find out just how wrong!

Chapter 4   Claws and Tentacles   47
In a world now terrified of sharks, could any creature knock *Jaws* off the
terror top spot? What else was lurking in the depths of the ocean?

Chapter 5   Making Monsters   61
From jerky stop-motion to high-tech CGI; how do you make a good water
monster? Which movies have contained the best and worst creations, and
which unlikely movie features a terrifyingly realistic attack?

Chapter 6   The Gamechangers   73
The late 1990s brought comedy and some very unexpected twists to the
world of the water monster. As the horror-comedy trend took over the
cinema, could a creature feature ever be scary again?

Chapter 7   The Truth is Down There   87
Our growing understanding of the real-life animals in water monster
movies has affected the way we show them onscreen. Our creatures and
characters now behave very differently, so what makes a good movie
monster now and how can we enter their world as friends?

Chapter 8   Y2: Kaiju   103
Big films, big monsters and big business. A viral campaign introduces
a ridiculous sounding B-movie to millions of people and at the other
end of the scale, a monster versus robot battle gets the Hollywood
treatment. How did one iconic character change the way we talk about
action heroes?

Chapter 9   Are Mermaids Monsters?   119
Far from cute romantic comedies and Disney magic, the world of horror
treats the mermaid very differently indeed. Do mermaids count as sea
monsters? You decide …

Chapter 10   *Sharknado*, or 'hell no!'?   137
How did *Sharknado* become a cult phenomenon? Just why do people love
bad movies? In the age of one-upmanship, how did 'serious' filmmakers
respond to the trend for the ridiculous?

Chapter 11   What's Next?   153
We find out the fate of our lovesick Gill-man from Chapter Two, as
Guillermo del Toro reimagines *Creature from the Black Lagoon* as a love
story! As a new trend emerges, what's the next big thing in the world of
the water monster?

Chapter 12   Movie Monsters of the Deep Awards   171
We are still discovering new species every year! What is still out there,
waiting to be found? Real, imaginary, or unknown; which creatures

appear most in sea monster movies and which have surprisingly not had their moment yet?

Chapter 13   100 Monster Movies from the Deep   185
Good, bad, terrible, true(ish) … How many of these movies have you seen?

Bibliography   199
Index   206

Acknowledgements

Thank you to everyone who has had to hear sea monster and shark movie facts at least once a week since I learned to speak, whether they asked for them or not. Especially …

My mum, who has supported me ever since I first picked up a crayon and scribbled a story. I can't possibly express how grateful I am; for once, I am lost for words, but thank you for everything.

My friends and loved ones who have proofread, offered advice, been there when I've had the inevitable writer crisis of confidence, celebrated with me, picked up way too much information about B-movies by osmosis, brought the coffee round and listened to me – and more importantly, heard me.

Fans of my work in both psychological self-defence and cage fighting, who have shared my excitement and cheered on my progress writing this book through my social media updates.

My publishers (Pen and Sword) and editors who took a chance on a B-movie nerd and her obsession with water monsters.

All of the writers, scientists, researchers, explorers, production companies,* actors, adventurers, directors and crew whose work has made my book possible.

Bruce, the rubber shark; we couldn't have done it without you.

---

* 20th Century Studios, A24, Atlas Entertainment, AV Pictures, BBC Natural History Unit, Chungeorahm Film, Columbia Pictures, Creature Features Productions LLC, Discovery Channel, Element Pictures, Fox Searchlight Pictures, Happinet Pictures, Jerry Bruckheimer Films, Kino Świat, Lionsgate Films, Metro-Goldwin-Mayer Studios [MGM], Netflix, Nippon Herald Films, Showbox Entertainment, Sony Pictures, The Asylum, Toho Studios, Uncork'd Entertainment, Universal Studios, Walt Disney Pictures, Warner Bros. Walt Conti provided the quotes in chapter 5, used with permission. Stan Winston Studio mechanical designer Richard Landon provided the quotes in chapter 6, used with permission.

Introduction

Is there a shark movie that is scarier than *Jaws*? What is the sneaky secret hidden in the Loch Ness monster's name? How did the Gill-man in *Creature from the Black Lagoon* become a romantic hero? Do mermaids count as sea monsters? What terrifying sea creature was discovered to really exist, and just what on earth is a globster?

From Kraken to kaiju, *Open Water* to *The Shallows*, monsters of the deep have fascinated and horrified us for centuries. There is even a name for the fear of deep bodies of water: 'thalassophobia'. Humans have a natural fear of predators in the water and yet we just can't stop thinking about them! There are a lot of deep water monster movies out there; good, bad, strange and 'so bad it's good'. While I cannot feature every single one ever made (and trust me, you don't want me to) I've collected some of the best, worst and most interesting out there to tell you about.

If you ever wanted to know your crocodile from your Cthulhu and find out how they make the monsters come alive, whether you like your monsters in the ocean or in lakes, based on real animals or totally made up, with fins or tentacles, one head or five, if you love your movie monsters of the deep then this book was written for you.

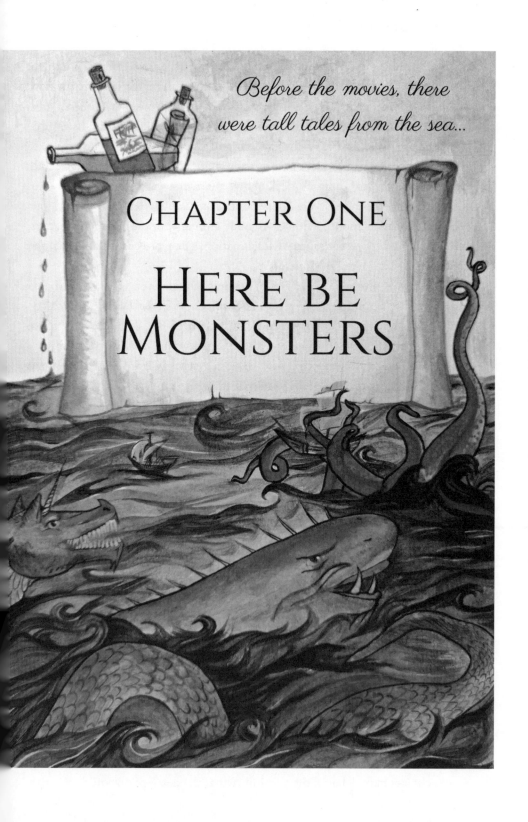

Before the movies, there were tall tales from the sea...

CHAPTER ONE

HERE BE MONSTERS

Asailing ship enters uncharted territory, years before the first complete maps of the world have begun to circulate. The sea is calm, for now. Sailors both veteran and new attend to their work – excited, nervous, terrified beyond belief or a mixture of the three. There is no discernible difference between the sea behind them and the sea ahead. In the best-case scenario, they will discover something exciting or useful but on the other hand, the map left on the captain's desk shows the worst-case scenario: an ocean teeming with the oddest creatures comprising scales, tentacles, enormous teeth or cavernous mouths. Some resemble animals from the land: lions, pigs, bears, dogs and more. Others defy imagination. The words calligraphed in the corner say it all: 'Here be Monsters'.

Though this phrase is well known, it is misquoted. Even Captain Barbossa famously says it in *Pirates of the Caribbean: Curse of the Black Pearl* (2003) mid sword fight with Jack Sparrow. The first time the 'Here be …' phrase was found written down is in the Hunt-Lenox globe dating from the year 1504, but the Latin phrase 'hic sunt dracones' actually translates to 'here are dragons'. Later maps and globes referred to lions and 'tygers'. Still, while the 'Here be Monsters' quote might not have been as popular as many people think, maps from the 1400s onwards often decorated unexplored areas with intricate drawings of fantastical creatures of all kinds.

Monsters of biblical proportions

Almost every culture that has contact with the sea also has legends that tell of monsters of the deep. Even the Bible features them – and multiple times! While the Bible is a collection of writings gathered over centuries and much of it can be interpreted as metaphorical, the descriptions for these creatures had to come from somewhere. Serpents and dragons were sometimes used as a representative of evil and the words were often used interchangeably by ancient scholars. Some think that these biblical monsters were inspired by dinosaurs or not-yet-extinct prehistoric sea creatures. Others think that they were based on animals we would still recognise today.

Three of the most fearsome biblical water monsters:

Leviathan: an enormous serpentine creature associated with chaos according to Christian legend. The Leviathan is usually depicted as a giant snake but some scholars have debated the possibility that the description could refer to a crocodile. According to the Old Testament and in parallel with other cultural myths including the Norse myth in which the god Thor is destined to slay the Midgard Serpent *Jörmungandr*, God destroyed the Leviathan in order to shape the world. 'In that day the Lord with his hard and great and strong sword will punish Leviathan the fleeing serpent, Leviathan the twisting serpent, and he will slay the dragon that is in the sea' (Isaiah 27:1).

Behemoth: a swamp inhabitant and beast of great power. Hippopotamuses are formidable and semi-aquatic, leading some experts to believe that the Behemoth is based on an enormous hippopotamus, which ancient Egyptians were known to hunt. However, the Behemoth is described as having a 'tail like a cedar' and hippopotamuses have short tails, so others have made a compelling argument that the description perfectly fits a sauropod dinosaur, which certainly had the big strong tail and also spent time in swamps.

Giant fish: Jonah 1:17 tells the story of Jonah, a man who tried to escape a mission from God (to prophesy the destruction of the city of Nineveh). As punishment, a storm was sent after the ship he was escaping on and his fellow sailors were forced to throw him overboard. He was swallowed by a giant fish and according to the story he spent three days in its belly. The identity of the fish is usually thought to be a whale or shark but while lobster diver Michael Packard became trapped in a humpback whale's mouth for less than a minute in 2021 and lived to tell the tale, nobody has ever been reported to have survived for even one day in the stomach of a whale, or indeed, a shark.

Water monsters have always captured imaginations in a big way. In Ancient Greece, Homer's epic poem *The Odyssey* was written around the eighth century BC and features a deadly sea monster named Scylla who lived in a rocky cave and waited for passing ships which she would attack, grabbing sailors in her six mouths. In the story, the enchantress Circe warned the hero Odysseus that the sea crossing was so narrow that he would have to choose between its two obstacles: a whirlpool and the monster. Scylla was a threat to six of his sailors while the whirlpool threatened the entire ship and all onboard, so he chose to pass the monster, losing six sailors in the process. Scylla became a recurring character in Greek mythology and while her origins and appearance depended on the individual writers' imagination, she is usually portrayed as a woman with a ring of six snapping dog heads growing from around her waist and the ability to move at lightning speed.

Around the same time Homer was alive, another author was also telling stories of sea monsters. In the poet Hesiod's epic *Theogony*, Gaia (the personification of Earth) and Tartarus (a great prison abyss) had a son together, the sea serpent Typhon. Again, other authors elaborated on his tale and invented their own backgrounds for the character, showing that even the ancient Greeks composed alternative fiction, borrowing each other's work and characters. Today, we'd call it fan fiction.

Travellers' tales and the 'Age of Exploration'

While myths, legends and parables have clearly featured water monsters since the very beginning of recorded history, the earliest known first-hand reports of monster sightings appeared in detailed travel journals kept by Carthaginian traveller Himilco (approximately sixth century BC), the first known traveller from the Mediterranean Sea to reach the north-western shores of Europe. He describes the sea as being difficult for a boat to move in, filled as it was with seaweed and numerous sea monsters. Of course, there is a strong possibility he was exaggerating in order to prevent any Greek rivals from following him but while his records have now been lost to history, they must have been very inspiring, for Roman writers continued to quote his accounts for many years afterward. The poet Postumius Rufius Festus Avienus referred to Himilco's adventures in his own work, the *Ora Maritima* (fourth century AD) '... there monsters of the deep, and beasts swim amid the slow and sluggishly crawling ships'.

The 1400s to 1600s are often known as 'the Age of Exploration'; explorers, sailors and colonizers took to the seas and returned with tales of the ocean's inherent danger, unfathomable vastness and bizarre ship-sinking inhabitants. Many animals they could have encountered have since been tentatively identified as walruses, whales, narwhals and sharks, but along with many other unusual inhabitants of the water, these would have been seen as monstrous by people seeing them for the first time. Still, other descriptions are so outlandish that they do not match any creature we know of today.

The name *porcus marinus* (sea swine) has been used to describe a variety of sea creatures since the age of Ancient Greece, but in 1539 the name was given to one distinctive animal living in the waters of Iceland. Swedish writer, cartographer and clergy member Olaus Magnus created the *Carta Marina* – an intricate and ambitious map of the Nordic countries featuring place names, landscape details and lists of the impressive variety of creatures found nearby. It was the first map of its kind and listed among the creatures was this 'sea swine': a lumbering, grunting, water-dwelling animal that to this day has not been identified. (These are not to be confused with a variety of sea cucumber known as the sea pig.) There is still debate over what exactly sea swine were – some thought their shape resembled the thick body of a porpoise while others believe the comparison to a pig came from the grunting noise reportedly made by the animals, which were also thought to have tusks. We may never know.

The line between real and unreal was a very faint one during the Renaissance period. As the study of marine life was still a very novel and exciting concept, many deep water inhabitants were newly discovered and then drawn by illustrators working from sailors' fantastical descriptions. Many naturalists often listed both mythical and real creatures alongside each other in their books and a popular theory in the 1500s was that every animal on land had an ocean counterpart which is why the horse-headed, fish-tailed and very mythical hippocampus appears in many serious zoology books published at the time. As travel and exploration became more common, the world was becoming a much bigger and more exciting place for people who were adventurers themselves, scholars, or casual but eager readers of the journals and articles detailing new discoveries – no matter how misguided or factually inaccurate some of these new 'discoveries' turned out to be.

Even in the early days of exploration, most sea and water monsters were understood to be members of a larger population of their species and not a one-of-a-kind character straight out of a storybook … with an exception we still know well. Norwegian Bishop of Bergen, Erik Pontopiddan, wrote his *Natural History of Norway* in 1752 with a detailed description of the Kraken – now one of the most well-known sea monsters of all time and still a recognized antagonist in today's movies. Pontopiddan also included descriptions of several other sea monsters including the sea serpent and the mermaid, both of which he passionately argued existed.

A rational explanation?

By the 1800s, as knowledge of the sea and its inhabitants grew, some of the more regular 'monster sightings' were given rational explanations – some were thought to be giant squid, whales or even manatees. In 1892, Anthonie Cornelis Oudemans, then director of the Royal Zoological Gardens at The Hague published a guide which collected the usual reported descriptions of sea monsters, offered possible explanations, and detailed the creatures potentially responsible. His work disproved hoaxes using a scientific approach and is still widely respected today. The guide, entitled *The Great Sea Serpent*, suggested that many reports of sea serpents were actually sightings of a previously unknown giant pinniped (from the same family as the seal and walrus) with a long neck. While the leopard seal comes closest to this description and can be terrifying to look at, there are still many differences between the common sea serpent reports and the appearance of a seal – even a leopard seal.

While some accounts have been demystified to an extent and we may now be more familiar with some of the creatures most likely seen and their behaviour, there are still unexplored areas of deep water and sometimes the more we know about the creatures that call the water home, the more fascinated and terrified we are.

Monsters in the lakes

Water monsters were not only inhabitants of the oceans. One of the world's most famous lake monsters – 'Nessie' of Loch Ness – was first described in the abbot Adomnán's book *Life of St Columba* (sixth century AD), in a tale describing the saint's encounter with the monster. Fortunately for St Columba, he remained calm and simply made the sign of the cross at the advancing inhabitant of the loch until the beast retreated. Easy! Descriptions like these tend to be exaggerated in order to 'prove' a saint's saintliness and must be taken with some scepticism but still, Loch Ness monster sightings have been reported ever since and by people from all walks of life and religious callings.

The water monster thought to inhabit Okanagan Lake in British Columbia, Canada, is often referred to as Ogopogo but it was originally named Naitaka by the nearby Secwépemc and Syilx tribes (or 'n 'x̌ax̌aitkʷ' (n-ha-ha-it-koo) in Nsyilxcən, the Syilx language). The legend was misunderstood by early settlers who thought it described a malevolent entity but in fact the Syilx name translates as 'the sacred spirit of the lake' and it is considered a force of nature rather than a physical being. While people have reported sightings of a creature in the lake as recently as 2018, it may not be Naitaka. What other mysteries could be hiding in Okanagan Lake?

In Australia, a dangerous amphibious creature is said to lurk in the swamps, billabongs, creeks and other inland bodies of water. While European settlers and colonizers reported sightings throughout the 1840s and 50s, the creature had been known to Aboriginal Australians for many years previously, where legend tells of the bunyip – usually translated as 'devil' or 'evil spirit' – although its original meaning and role in Aboriginal mythology may have changed over time due to translation errors and regional variations.

Often thought to prefer the taste of women and children and said to possess a terrifying roar, few accounts agree on what the bunyip looks like though all say it looks very strange indeed. Feathered, flippered, one eye, two eyes, tall and thin, short and wide, egg-laying, dog-like, horse-like, even starfish-like. Barely any descriptions match, leading to the two most common theories identifying the bunyip as either an elephant seal or a cassowary; two of the most different animals imaginable! The bunyip still features in stories all over Australia; it is a nature-protector in some and a vicious man-eater in others. In stories written for children it is usually a benevolent and misunderstood creature, portrayed as either a mischievous prankster or a shy and gentle friend.

Many water monsters that have a long-recorded background in legends also tend to have a following among tourists and monster hunters. Loch Ness monster merchandise has been sold for decades, ever since business owners realised people were making special trips to the loch just to look for Nessie.

By the mid-1900s it appeared that many other lakes were suddenly home to their very own modern monsters, which made prominent appearances in advertisements, articles and of course merchandise aimed at prospective tourists. South Bay Bessie of Lake Erie, Champ of Lake Champlain, Chessie of Chesapeake Bay, Morag of Loch Morar, Mussie of Muskrat Lake and Sharlie of Payette Lake are a few of the more well-known lake monsters today.

Monstrous muses

In the 1800s, with sea monsters featuring in classic Greek myths revered by scholars and students as well as respected natural history texts, the sea and its mysteries began to inspire the fiction authors of the time. Peter Benchley's *Jaws* was still over a hundred years away but a story about another enormous sea monster was keeping readers awake and this one was based on real events.

The whaling ship *Essex* was said to be a lucky ship to sail on. She had already been on many successful voyages and several of the sailors working onboard had been newly promoted. The twenty-one-man crew was highly competent and the planned whaling trip in 1819 was expected to be just as lucky, with many barrels of profitable whale oil expected to return with the ship, but within days it seemed as though the *Essex*'s luck had run out. A squall knocked the ship onto its side, whales were scarce – financially disastrous for a whaling expedition, supplies began to run low, a crewman started a fire as a prank which then burned out of control, another crewman deserted and finally the *Essex* was rammed by an enormous sperm whale and sank in 1820. The twenty remaining crewmen grabbed as many supplies as they could from the sinking ship and set sail in three whaling rowboats, each with a senior crewman in command and two sets of navigation equipment shared between the three boats. They aimed for the South American coast but became disorientated and after nearly a month at sea as well as another whale attack on one of the boats, the men landed on the uninhabited Henderson Island. They soon exhausted the island's supplies of seabirds, crabs and brackish water. A week later, seventeen men set sail again, aiming for Easter Island while three chose to stay behind on the island with a small quantity of rations. Over the following weeks, the seventeen men began to succumb to dehydration, starvation and general ill health. One boat drifted away and was never heard from again. The sailors on the remaining two boats resorted to cannibalism – drawing lots to determine who would be sacrificed. These boats were separated after a squall but were rescued separately within a week of each other. Eight sailors were eventually rescued including the three men who had remained on Henderson Island and Thomas Nickerson – the cabin boy who later wrote and published his account of the sinking of the *Essex*.

The events were widely reported on and the survivors became minor celebrities, though the desperate measures they had taken to survive were understandably played down.

In the early 1800s, a very distinctive albino sperm whale was living in the Pacific Ocean, spending much of his time near Chile and the waters near Mocha Island. Nicknamed 'Mocha Dick', he was reported to have survived over ninety encounters with whaling boats, even sinking some of them. Due to his unusual appearance and long survival, many sailors had made it their personal mission to be the one who caught and killed him. He was eventually killed in 1838, measuring over 21 metres long.

Combining the incredible survival story of the sailors from the *Essex* with accounts of this real-life formidable 'character', Herman Melville wrote and published *Moby Dick* in 1851. The story was advertised as a tale of monsters, though whether the monster is the titular white whale or his obsessive hunter Captain Ahab is for the reader to decide.

Moby Dick, by Herman Melville

In the story, the narrator Ishmael joins the crew of a whaling boat for the first time, gets to know his fellow crew members, learns about the business of whaling and discovers that he and the crew have actually been hired for Captain Ahab's personal mission; to get revenge on the white whale responsible for the loss of his leg and known as 'Moby Dick'. The whale is described as a terrifying, intelligent and ferocious animal, while the sharks devouring a whale carcass are compared to mindless greedy devils and are not portrayed as a particular threat to people – unlike most modern stories in which sharks feature!

Moby Dick has been adapted over ten times in film alone and referenced in virtually every kind of media entertainment in existence including literary, radio and television productions, including a 'lake monster' themed episode of the 1990s television show *The X-Files*, in which main character Dana Scully's dog Queequeg (named after a *Moby Dick* character) finds himself in trouble with something big and mysterious living in the lake. It was previously established that the book has sentimental value to Scully and her family. The cultural impact of this white whale is probably second only to the shark in *Jaws*!

20,000 Leagues Under the Sea, by Jules Verne

Stories have contained elements of science fiction like aliens, other worlds and space travel for centuries. Though Mary Shelley's *Frankenstein* (1818) is usually considered the first science fiction themed novel, Jules Verne's book *20,000 Leagues Under the Sea* (1869) is almost certainly the first science fiction book set under the sea!

The story begins with people sharing reports of a sea monster and an expedition being launched to find and destroy it. Our narrator, marine biologist Professor Pierre Aronnax, joins the expedition but when they find the 'monster' it turns out to be a futuristic submarine named the *Nautilus*, commanded by the mysterious Captain Nemo, who brings Aronnax and his companions onboard. With the sea providing meals and tools for his entire crew, Nemo lives in secret, conducting research on the marine life surrounding the *Nautilus*. The story tells of the many adventures of Nemo, his crew and the men from the original expedition who are told they cannot leave, for fear that they may reveal the submarine's existence. They hunt sharks, encounter 'devilfish' (giant squid) and sink another ship as relations between the crew of the *Nautilus* and its newer passengers grow more tense.

With today's computer-generated imagery [CGI], special effects and underwater filming equipment, a story like *20,000 Leagues Under the Sea* could be brought to life easily but at the time, the world of movie production was very new indeed! Still, that didn't stop directors and writers from adapting the novel using the technology they had available.

The first ever movies were very, very short and compared to today's blockbusters, incredibly boring (e.g. *Grandma's Reading Glass* (1900) which showed a boy and his grandma looking at objects through a magnifying glass), but by the mid-1900s most had simple plots and some even employed the use of camera trickery to create supernatural effects. Even so, making an adaptation of *20,000 Leagues Under the Sea* would be unfathomably ambitious but it appears that in 1905, director Wallace McCutcheon attempted to do just that! Many old films have been lost to history due to unreliable preservation methods rendering the films too damaged to play while others were simply misplaced. This adaptation was mentioned in one film catalogue but there is no other evidence that this movie was ever made. Was it filmed and lost or just planned and never actually made? We may never know....

20,000 Leagues Under the Sea (1916)

The first ever underwater film footage was shot in 1909 and just a few years later director Stuart Paton lost no time in shooting his own adaptation of *20,000 Leagues Under the Sea*, making it the first ever motion picture to be filmed underwater. The story was changed in order to add a subplot about a wild girl and a ghost but it is still recognisably based on Jules Verne's novel.

The underwater scenes did not use underwater cameras. The crew rigged a complex system of watertight tubes and mirrors so that the camera operators could shoot reflected scenes under the water from above the surface. The fact that it was 'filmed at the bottom of the sea' featured prominently on posters and advertisements for the film, along with a large drawing of a shark. Sharks appeared in this adaptation very briefly but like extremely famous actors, if sharks make the smallest of cameos in movies, their appearance is almost always advertised! This adaptation was a silent movie which combined footage with captions, and while one caption claimed that a 'man-eater' is charging the characters, this requires some suspension of disbelief. Actually, a shark swims in their general direction with no apparent interest in them. The scenes involving a man in danger of being eaten by a giant octopus are far more memorable although the special effects (a giant octopus puppet disguised by a large cloud of sand) are not what modern audiences would consider convincing. Still, blurry puppets aside, the film attracted huge crowds, was the highest grossing film of 1916 by far at eight million dollars (the runner-up grossed one million) and was deemed 'culturally, historically, or aesthetically significant' by the United States Library of Congress and selected for its National Film Registry in 2016.

This would not be the last adaptation of Jules Verne's novel and even the iconic Captain Nemo has made appearances as a guest character in his own right in other works of fiction.

Did You Know?
Even if the sea went as deep as the centre of the earth, it would still only be 1592 leagues deep! The title refers to the distance the *Nautilus* travelled under the sea, and not the depth it travelled.

20,000 Leagues Under the Sea **fact file**

Released: 1916
Directed by: Stuart Paton
Starring: Allen Holubar, Jane Gail, Matt Moore, William Welsh, Curtis Benton, Dan Hanlon, Edna Pendleton
Creature: Sharks, barracuda, giant octopus
Effects: Real-life footage and puppetry
Legacy: The first feature length motion picture to be shot underwater and based on Jules Verne's 1869 novel. Over sixteen film and television adaptations and influences, numerous stage plays, video games and audio media. Captain Nemo appears in other productions in his own right.

There are a lot of people out there that like being scared! Some of the first feature length movies ever released were horror movies but while most of the well-known ones feature vaguely human-shaped monsters, *20,000 Leagues Under the Sea* is almost certainly the first ever sea monster movie. Though it was a phenomenal success which would spark a trend and multiple copycats these days, the next popular sea monster movie would not be filmed for another ten years. When it finally arrived, it told a familiar story ....

The Sea Beast (1926)

The first adaptation of Herman Melville's *Moby Dick* was this 1920s silent film. Lead actor John Barrymore had signed a three-film contract with Warner Bros. and due to his long-held ambition to act in *Moby Dick*, insisted that this be the first film he shot. Director Millard Webb reimagined Melville's original tale, giving it a central love story, a happy ending and a new name: *The Sea Beast*. It was a roaring success, becoming Warner Bros. highest grossing film at the time. Technically, the word 'silent' refers to the fact that actors' voices were not recorded, for silent films were still set to music, while dialogue was inserted in the form of text for the audience to read between scenes. As the age of the silent movie ended, it was remade in 1930 with recorded dialogue and starred John Barrymore again.

In an age before the huge leaps in technology and resulting developments that would come to the world of special effects, by necessity most monster movies were carried not by the look of the monster but by the characters and storyline and the acting in *The Sea Beast* received enormous praise. We often consider old movies as tame by today's standards especially when seen in the original black and white and without the use of high-definition camera footage, but the March 1926 issue of *Photoplay* magazine praised John Barrymore's acting in a particularly gory scene 'wherein the sailors cauterize the bloody stump of the leg torn off by the sea beast', describing it as 'too gruesome for the sensitive souls'.

The whale was a large rubber puppet filmed on a lake in California with a miniature ship.

The Sea Beast fact file

Released: 1926
Directed by: Millard Webb
Starring: John Barrymore, Dolores Costello, George O'Hara
Creature: Sperm whale (Moby Dick)
Effects: Miniatures and puppetry
Legacy: Remade with sound as *Moby Dick* (1930). A German-language version, *Daemon des Mers*, was filmed simultaneously but directed by William Dieterle.

The success of *The Sea Beast* meant that in the eyes of producers, inserting a creature of the deep into a film and pitting it against a handsome hero would almost certainly be a recipe for a hit. Immediately after the 1930s 'talkie' version came *The Sea Bat* (1930) featuring a manta ray on a mission of destruction and the horror film powerhouse Boris Karloff, shortly before he would play the iconic Frankenstein's Monster; *Tiger Shark* (1932), a dramatic love story set against a background of tuna fishing – a highly dangerous profession at the time – and featuring some significant shark attack scenes; a nearly two decade break while *King Kong* (1933) and its sequels dominated the monster movie genre, before *Killer Shark* (1950) brought the sea back onto the screen with underwater footage of real sharks … but barely enough to warrant the movie's title! With *Killer Shark* enjoying markedly less success, the sea fell out of favour. For the next twenty-five years 'made-up monsters' filled the gap in the market, but the next time a monster based on a real sea creature starred in a movie, we would never forget about it.

CHAPTER TWO

THE

BIG

THREE

THESE MONSTERS CHANGED THE MOVIE WORLD...

— STARRING —

RAY	RAY	A	THE
BRADBURY	**HARRYHAUSEN**	**CREATURE**	**KING**

Radioactive, genetically modified, giant lizard-like monsters crawling out of their deep ocean lairs, lifting a scaled arm menacingly with one thing on their minds: destruction!

Trends come and go in the film industry and while the craze for movies starring real-life creatures from the deep was quietening down, the rise of bigger, scarier and more imaginary creatures was only just beginning. This trend included some of the most iconic and well-respected monster movies out there, with legacies that continue today – even returning later in this book.

Before Godzilla emerged from the sea to wreak havoc on Tokyo and the Gill-man made his presence known in the Black Lagoon, there was another creature; a rudely awakened dinosaur from 20,000 fathoms below.

The Beast from 20,000 Fathoms (1953)

'*Watch out! The Beast is Coming!*' The film poster boasts a very ominous tagline while the titular 'beast' destroys a building resembling a castle, looming against the backdrop of a yellow-orange sky. It resembles a Komodo dragon (a real-life enormous lizard species) and a mythological dragon as well as several dinosaurs at once but according to the filmmakers it's actually a fictional dinosaur invented for the movie.

Two Rays

In 1951, writer Ray Bradbury published a short story named *The Beast from 20,000 Fathoms*, in which a lonely sea monster hears the sound of a lighthouse's fog horn and, believing it to be the call of another of his kind, leaves the ocean in order to find the other member of his species and his potential mate. Angered by the lighthouse's refusal to move or acknowledge him, he destroys it and retreats back into the ocean.

Around the same time, a movie about a sea monster was being shot with the help of another Ray; celebrated special effects and stop-motion animation creator Ray Harryhausen, who happened to be a friend of Ray Bradbury. The two had bonded over their love of the 1925 film adaptation of Arthur Conan Doyle's novel *The Lost World* and their fascination with the science fiction genre and were hoping one day to work on a dinosaur movie together. This dream was realised almost accidentally when Harryhausen noticed that the movie he was working on was going to feature a sequence involving a lighthouse which closely resembled a scene in Bradbury's story. When Harryhausen brought the similarity to the attention of the producers, they collaborated with Bradbury by buying the rights to the title *The Beast from 20,000 Fathoms*, featuring the lighthouse scene more prominently and crediting his original work as inspiration in the publication materials. The film was not an exact adaptation of the haunting story and so Ray Bradbury would later change the title of his own creation to *The Fog Horn*.

In the movie's plot, the dinosaur 'beast' is no tragic lonely-heart attracted by an eerie call out of the darkness; instead, this sixty-metre monster (named the 'rhedosaurus' after the two Rays) was woken from its suspended animation in ice by nearby atomic bomb testing, and it was apparently not impressed. Rampaging along the east American coastline and destroying everything in sight, it killed, injured, terrified and generally caused chaos. Unfortunately for the rhedosaurus, the military's attempts to stop it do more harm than good. The beast's blood is infected with a deadly prehistoric virus and when its injuries inevitably bleed, this virus causes even more destruction. Eventually, the beast is taken down by a radioactive weapon while it is preoccupied with destroying a rollercoaster.

Modern audiences have been less than thrilled with the movie's pacing. Much of the eighty-minute runtime is spent focusing on a scientist trying with limited success to convince people that he saw a dinosaur rather than the rampaging creature itself. However, it was a major international hit at the time, tapping into the public's growing fear of nuclear war and love of monsters and giving Ray Harryhausen full control over the creature effects in what was a completely new concept for audiences of the time.

Special effects
The Beast from 20,000 Fathoms launched the career of the celebrated Harryhausen. This was the first movie in which he had full control over the technical effects and he spread his wings, metaphorically speaking! He created a technique called 'dynamation' which involved splitting the background and foreground of pre-shot footage into two separate images then 'sandwiching' animated models between the two in order to have them look as though they belonged in the set. Dynamation became a regular strategy for him and most of his films include animated model characters interacting with the set. While modern audiences have often been impressed by hyper-realism in animation, there's an unnerving quality to stop-motion animation that makes it very effective when used to create monstrous creatures. (Harryhausen would later

work on the hit films *Jason and The Argonauts* (1963) and *Clash of the Titans* (1981) before he retired. Both of which feature stop-motion animation heavily.)

Did You Know?
The Beast from 20,000 Fathoms sparked the 1950s trend for giant monster movies in the Western world and started some of the original scenes and tropes we expect from the genre even today. It has even been described as one of the most important monster movies of all time.

The Beast from 20,000 Fathoms fact file

Released: 1953
Directed by: Eugène Lourié
Starring: Paul Christian, Paula Raymond, Cecil Kellaway, Kenneth Tobey
Creature: Rhedosaurus (fictional dinosaur)
Effects: Stop-motion animation
Legacy: Inspired *Godzilla* (1954) and numerous other films. *Godzilla* (1998) features several identical scenes and has been considered an updated remake by some.

Though stories of mermaids, sirens and other human-like water creatures had been quite popular with the public for many years, they were invariably portrayed as beautiful (with one exception being sideshow master P.T. Barnum's 'Fiji Mermaid' hoax involving a fish tail, a dead monkey and some creative taxidermy). The seductive but potentially dangerous half-fish, half-human creatures had up until now starred in films portraying them as whimsical romantic heroines causing varying degrees of mischief with the hero. The first male fish-person movie monster would be no such romantic hero. At least, not for a few decades anyway.

Creature from the Black Lagoon (1954)

Adventurers, explorers and scientists on a geological mission to the Amazon river make an alarming but intriguing discovery: a fossil which could provide the answer to their theories about a possible missing link between land and sea animals. They soon discover the Gill-man; the tall, scaly, living version –

sometimes curious, occasionally enraged, and usually romantic at heart. The latter state was the most terrifying of all for viewers and the poor scientist character Kay, who finds herself the unwilling object of the creature's desire! What will happen in this tale of unrequited love in a foam fish suit?

While the movie itself was a moderate success, its cultural impact and legacy is far greater and further reaching than would be expected for a film that was considered competent but not great. Certainly, the monster is instantly recognisable – a great achievement on the part of his designers. People recognise the creature from the film even if it's in a reference far removed from the original, and the sequence featuring the unwitting leading lady swimming through the lagoon as the Gill-man lurks below her still features in forums and websites dedicated to discussing famous movie moments, as well as image albums designed to trigger thalassophobia: the fear of deep water. Another part of its impact could be the unusual storyline in which the Gill-man could be seen as a tragic figure, even a sympathetic one. The scientists did shoot at him first, after all!

If any potential viewers had managed to miss hearing about *Creature from the Black Lagoon*, the movie would get another wave of attention the following year after a brief cameo scene in the romantic comedy *The Seven Year Itch* (1955). After watching the movie in the cinema, Marilyn Monroe's character would comment wistfully to her date that the Gill-man wasn't bad – he just wanted to be loved.

Sabotage! 'The Beauty who created the Beast'
Before the movie was even released, *Creature from the Black Lagoon* was already horrifying people. Lead actor Ben Chapman made promotional appearances in full costume and the press tours accompanying the movie were reported to have brought both fun and fear to the attendees. The role of the Gill-man was demanding enough that it required very specific casting. The character was played by two actors; towering at just under 2 metres tall, Ben Chapman played the Gill-man in his land scenes while underwater stuntman Ricou Browning took on the role for his water scenes.

The creature costume was an incredibly ambitious invention, designed by Disney animator and aspiring actress Milicent Patrick. After impressing the head of the Universal Studios make-up department, Bud Westmore, with sketches for other movies she had worked on, she became the first woman to work in a special effects make-up department. After designing the costume, she was sent to promote the movie on a press tour dubbed 'The Beauty Who Created the Beast'.

The fact that she was responsible for the iconic monster design has been confirmed by both the costume's sculptor Chris Mueller and actor Ben Chapman; however, for many years the only credit went to Bud Westmore! Westmore felt that Patrick's only job had been to sketch his ideas and he was furious that she had been given credit and publicity for the work. The studio changed the name of her tour to 'The Beauty Who Lives With the Beasts' and gave him sole credit for the design but not appeased enough, Westmore fired her.

Milicent Patrick returned to acting and never worked behind the scenes again. In the 1970s, science fiction writer and magazine editor Forrest J. Ackerman did an eight-page article in *Famous Monsters* magazine documenting Patrick's Gill-man creation as well as her work on other monster movies. Later, Mallory O'Meara also gave Patrick the credit she was due in her 2019 book *The Lady from the Black Lagoon*.

Legacy

Many traditional monster movies have become outdated through either their portrayal of historically distasteful attitudes and prejudices held at the time of filming, or through aging special effects techniques. The story of *Creature from the Black Lagoon* is one a modern audience can still appreciate, even though its sympathies may have changed. To a modern audience, the heroes of the 1950s appear as trampling, littering, loud and ill-mannered men trespassing into the domain of a creature who might have been perfectly content in his lagoon before they all showed up and he fell in love!

The enduring and memorable image of the Gill-man character has cemented his legacy alongside iconic monsters from movies like *Dracula* (1931) and *The Wolfman* (1941) despite one huge difference; in the other movies, the actors playing the characters were recognisable even behind their make-up whether in appearance or voice while the Gill-man has no real voice and a full body suit. All work done to humanise him or at least portray him as a character rather than just an animal required the actor using his body to express himself, resulting in the famous swimming scenes with the lead actress Julia Adams, before he is seen carrying the swooning lady away in a pose more often seen on the front covers of romance novels. These images captured the imagination of creators, including the young Guillermo del Toro who paid his own homage decades later.

The Gill-man's likeness is still used in media from horror-comedy *The Monster Squad* (1987) and Stephen King's *It* (1990) (in which the shapeshifting monster briefly assumes the form of the Gill-man) to quirky animated kids' vampire tale *Hotel Transylvania* (2012). William Winckler's 2005 horror homage *Frankenstein and the Creature from Blood Cove* uses a design inspired by the Gill-man and even The Munsters and Scooby Doo have featured their own versions of him.

Four songs have been written about the Gill-man, from calypso to heavy metal! His image has featured in almost every form of art or pop culture there is, and in a full-circle return to the original premise of the film in which fossil hunters discover his fossilised ancestor, the Gill-man even has his own fossil! Palaeontologist Jenny Clack of the University of Cambridge discovered a fossilised amphibian in what was once a swamp and named it *Eucritta melanolimnetes* translated as 'the true Creature from the Black Lagoon'.

Creature from the Black Lagoon fact file

Released: 1954
Directed by: Jack Arnold
Starring: Richard Carlson, Julia Adams (later Julie Adams), Richard Denning, Antonio Moreno, Nestor Paiva, Whit Bissell, Ben Chapman, Ricou Browning
Creature: Gill-man
Effects: Prosthetics and bodysuit. Originally filmed for 3D screening
Legacy: *Revenge of the Creature* (1955); *The Creature Walks Among Us* (1956); inspired *The Shape of Water* (2017). Referenced in numerous horror films as well as comedy shows, games, comics, songs and more.

Japan is generally considered to be the home of the giant monster movie genre but before Godzilla came to destroy Tokyo in 1954, the Japanese language version of *The Beast from 20,000 Fathoms* was released. It was called *Genshi Kaijū Arawaru*, which translates as 'An Atomic Kaiju Appears'. This is the first recorded use of the word 'kaiju' in a film title, though kaiju as a concept had been part of Japanese storytelling culture for centuries. The word means 'strange beast' and is the name for the genre in which these creatures appear, just as horror is a genre and a 'horror' can also describe a creature.

On his way back from a disappointing mission trying and failing to obtain filming rights for a location, producer Tomoyuki Tanaka had the idea for a giant monster movie, inspired by the reassuringly made-up *The Beast from 20,000 Fathoms* and the horribly real *Daigo Fukuryū Maru* incident, in which a tuna fishing boat was contaminated by nuclear fallout from a nearby thermonuclear weapon test. The boat's crew of twenty-three people suffered acute radiation syndrome but eventually recovered except for the chief radioman, Kuboyama Aikichi, who died – the first victim of the hydrogen bomb.

The success of monster movies (*King Kong* had been a big hit) and inevitable news coverage of anything atomic-sounding appeared to have potential for success. Still, directors turned Tanaka's idea down, struggling to take a giant radioactive monster from beneath the sea seriously. When Ishirō Honda came onboard as the director, he and the team decided that in order to potentially win over film critics they should portray the monster's attack as a real-life catastrophe with the appropriate level of seriousness. They named the monster Gojira- 'gorilla-whale' or, to Western audiences, Godzilla.

Godzilla (1954)

Havoc is wreaked in the ocean when boats begin to disappear and the yield of fish drops to zero. Something strange is going on and one elder blames the ancient sea monster Godzilla, which returns to prove him right, destroying part of Odo Island. The survivors travel to Tokyo asking for disaster relief and a research team is sent to the island. The team find radioactive footprints and conclude that the sea monster has been woken by underwater hydrogen bomb testing. As seventeen more ships are lost at sea, debate rages; should they tell the public?

The film continues with a love story, the discovery that the monster also has devastating atomic breath, the resulting catastrophic and hospital-filling radioactive disaster and a conflict between the people wanting to kill Godzilla and the people wanting to study him.

It turns out that the only way to destroy Godzilla is by using a highly dangerous weapon called the 'Oxygen Destroyer' which disintegrates oxygen atoms, causing all targeted living organisms to die of asphyxiation. Its creator, Daisuke Serizawa, refuses to use the weapon, fearing the prospect of being forced to create more for use in war. Still, after much debate and soul searching, he allows the weapon to be deployed, However, Serizawa also sacrifices himself and all of his research notes in the process, ensuring that such a weapon could never be created again. The film ends with a caution: that if nuclear testing is to continue, another Godzilla may rise from the ocean depths.

If some of the plot points sound familiar, that is because they have inspired countless monster movie creators in the years since *Godzilla* was released!

Allegory

Some films and texts are picked to pieces by reviewers, discussed in schools and studied for years by people looking for potential allegory. *Godzilla* was never so subtle! The creature symbolises a nuclear apocalypse from Japan's perspective. Director, Ishirō Honda, confirmed this saying that had Godzilla been a dinosaur or even just an enormous creature, it would have taken just one cannonball to kill him. On the other hand, people wouldn't know what to do if a monster had characteristics equal to an atomic bomb, so he applied the effects of such a bomb to Godzilla.

The opening scene in which Godzilla destroys a Japanese ship is a reference to the *Daigo Fukuryū Mara* incident. Later, special effects director, Eiji Tsuburaya, and his crew scouted the locations they wanted Godzilla to destroy in the movie and were nearly arrested after a security guard overheard their detailed plans! They were released after showing police their business cards for Japanese film and theatre production and distribution company Toho Studios.

Godzilla is without a doubt the first and only sea monster to be considered culturally significant in relation to war, science and politics. The comparison has been described as obvious, gigantic and unsubtle, and it has even been suggested that this film was a 'cultural coping method'. Its legacy has endured because *Godzilla* is a movie about much more than a sea monster destroying things.

Creature design

The monster took some time to design. The original plan had been for Godzilla to be a giant octopus but after a rethink and some experimentation with gorilla and whale-based drawings as well as a more humanoid design with a head shaped like a mushroom cloud, the team used several dinosaurs for inspiration. Godzilla's rough skin texture was based on the keloid scars seen on the victims of Hiroshima, underlining the movie's horrendous inspiration sources.

Special effects director, Eiji Tsuburaya, originally wanted to use stop-motion animation to create Godzilla – the same technique used in *The Beast from 20,000 Fathoms* – but as such a process would have taken an estimated seven years with the staff on hand, he ended up developing a technique of his own called 'suitmation' in which an actor wears an extremely elaborate and detailed 'creature suit'. While the technique later fell out of favour compared to the newer options offered by CGI, many filmmakers still use these practical effects like creature suits, but with CGI enhancements.

The first Godzilla suit was made of latex and molten rubber over a wire, mesh and bamboo frame. It weighed over 100 kilos and was incredibly physically demanding for the actors to wear. A lighter but still demanding suit was created and a puppet was used for close-up shots, spraying mist and baby powder from its mouth to create Godzilla's atomic breath.

Typically, a fast-moving monster is deemed scarier for an audience; part of what makes sharks and snakes frightening is the fact that you cannot outrun or outswim a bite and many of today's sea monster movies rely on this speed factor to give the audience a jump scare. On the other hand, the slow and deliberate pace set by Godzilla is part of what makes his scenes genuinely disturbing today, especially in the context of the inescapable horror the monster represents.

Legacy

The *Godzilla* franchise is the world's longest running film franchise, with thirty-six films created. The monster is one of Japanese pop culture's most defining symbols and has inspired television, comics, art and videogames. Even the suffix 'zilla' is still used to denote a giant and vaguely threatening thing (though usually comedically, as seen in the UK's 2009 *Oasis* drink advert featuring 'RubberDuckZilla'). Scenes have been tributed, copied and parodied to the point that many have become standard monster movie tropes.

Godzilla's title 'king of the monsters' is apt; no other movie monster from the deep has such a legacy and with another sequel due for release in 2024, his reign continues.

Godzilla fact file

Released: 1954
Directed by: Ishirō Honda
Starring: Akira Takarada, Momoko Kōchi, Akihiko Hirata, Takashi Shimura
Creature: Godzilla
Effects: Suitmation and puppetry
Legacy: Enormous! Over thirty films, five of which are American. Videogames, television, music, toys and guest appearances. Inspiration for quotes, portmanteaus and expressions.

A winning formula had been found! For the next two decades, cinema would be dominated by *Godzilla* sequels and copies of *The Beast from 20,000 Fathoms* just using a different interchangeable monster or giant rampaging version of a living animal. In the following twenty years, there were two *Creature from the Black Lagoon* sequels and thirteen *Godzilla* sequels released.

Over time, Godzilla began to develop a personality and the terrifying monster of the original film became more of an antihero.. *Godzilla Raids Again* (1955) set up the 'Godzilla fighting other giant monsters and kaiju' formula. Some of these monsters would return, others were a one-off nemesis.

Meanwhile, the success of the original *Godzilla* and its nuclear theme captured the imaginations of other filmmakers. None of the various nuclear, atomic, radioactive and otherwise mutated monster movies would come close to having the immense cultural impact of *Godzilla*, possibly because the metaphor and inspirations were closer to the public consciousness in Japan, while repeating the formula in American film studios did not capture the same deep-rooted public fear. *It Came from Beneath the Sea* (1955) starred a radioactive octopus rampaging over the San Francisco coast and featured the special effects talents of Ray Harryhausen but its legacy is limited to a four-book comic sequel, an occasional mention in other films and a title parody in R.L. Stine's 1995 *Goosebumps* series book *It Came from Beneath the Sink*.

The world's first and so far only, lovesick humanoid amphibian returned for the *Creature from the Black Lagoon* sequel *Revenge of the Creature* (1955) with a film poster resembling a romance novel cover, just as the original movie did.

Having survived being shot in his debut outing, this time the Gill-man has his heart set on ichthyology student Helen. Captured and held prisoner in the Ocean Harbor Oceanarium, the unlucky-in-love creature makes his escape... but he can't just leave Helen!

While the film did not impress critics (except for its underwater sequences), it was ahead of its time in some ways, showing the female lead caught between the options of having a career or a husband, and evoking more sympathy for the captured Gill-man. With a small comedic part as a lab technician, it also marks Clint Eastwood's first appearance onscreen, though he is unnamed.

The Gill-man's final outing for a few decades took him further inland; in *The Creature Walks Among Us* (1956), he appears to be mutating. Captured once again, there are notable changes in his physique which make him appear more human than he had previously. Still, when one of the scientists in the facility imprisoning him attempts to frame him for murder, the Gill-man goes on a rampage of righteous anger before heading back to the sea alone. While this movie did little to enhance the legacy of the series and the Gill-man was already a popular and recognisable monster, the final movie in the official series did cement his status as a tragic and sympathetic character.

The world of the deep water movie monster mostly ground to a halt for the next five years. British film *The Giant Behemoth* (1959) was derided as an almost scene-for-scene copy of *The Beast from 20,000 Fathoms* with a radioactive element included in order to attract fans of *Godzilla*. More entertaining than the movie itself are some of its critics pointed remarks. American film critic, Andrew Wickliffe, wrote 'I'm not sure the British are really suited for giant monster movies. No offense to the Brits, but watching a bunch of folks stand around and keep the stiff upper lip while radioactive monsters from the deep attack London isn't too much fun'.

Gorgo (1961)

Two years later, another British giant monster movie arrived onscreen. This monster emerges from the sea and attacks London before being captured and transferred between a scientific research team, a circus, and the Navy, before its irate and enormous mother follows it out of the sea in order to retrieve it. Despite the monster bearing no resemblance to a snake and without a gaze that turns people to stone, it is named Gorgo after Greek mythology's snake-haired death-staring gorgon Medusa.

It might be a little inaccurate of reviewers to call *Gorgo* a *Godzilla* rip-off; after all, the film was originally intended as a direct tribute and plans had even been made to set it in Japan. After considering France and Australia (which was dismissed due to the producers' opinion that there were not enough landmarks that people cared about if the monster destroyed them), England was chosen and the plot changed. There is no radioactive element, though the makers did use a combination of miniaturisation and suitmation; the technique developed while filming *Godzilla*.

At first glance, another giant monster movie is not especially groundbreaking considering the genre's popularity but while the idea was not very original, the special effects used generated great praise – as did the unusual ending in which the monsters survived and escaped rather than dying amid a climactic explosion or similar effect.

The poster shows the monster grabbing at planes in a very *King Kong*-like manner but despite all the clear influences from other movies and Old English folk tales (like *Beowulf*, in which the hero kills a monster named Grendel, only for Grendel's furious mother to come seeking revenge), *Gorgo* inspired a legacy of its own in the form of comic books. One collection was even reprinted as recently as 2021. Other comics took so much 'heavy inspiration' from *Gorgo* that they had to change the name of their titular creature in order to avoid certain copyright issues … giving readers 'Gorga' and 'Kegor'.

Gorgo **fact file**

Released: 1961
Directed by: Eugène Lourié
Starring: Bill Travers, William Sylvester, Vincent Winter
Creature: Gorgo and its mother
Effects: Suitmation and miniatures
Legacy: Paperback novelisation by Monarch books (1961); *Gorgo* comic books by Charlton Comics (1961-1965); three-issue miniseries *The Return of Gorgo* (1962-1964); appearance in the *Spiderman* universe in *Annual #6* with a changed name; numerous re-releases and reprints. Scenes have been used in the background of several movies and a music video by rock band Ash.

Godzilla's enduring legacy is partly due to it being much more than a sea monster movie, but even setting aside this near-the-knuckle phenomenon (which was heavily sanitised before being released to an American audience) the *Godzilla* formula was a winner. Giant monster is awoken by large scale activity, usually human. Giant monster wreaks havoc on a city featuring well-known landmarks. Giant monster is taken down by firepower or ingenious big weapon. For well over a decade, the monster movies released were either standalone creature features which followed this basic plot or were part of the *Godzilla* franchise, which introduced new creatures for the monster to fight or team up with, like the sea monster Manda, the giant mothlike kaiju Mothra and of course, the ape King Kong.

Today, franchise crossovers are relatively common and 'easter eggs' (references to other films and in-jokes) are deliberately planted for the audience, but other than a comedy crossover series in which popular duo Abbot and Costello met monsters like The Mummy, this was a new phenomenon and had not been done on such a scale before. The first *King Kong* crossover was originally intended to be a battle between King Kong and Frankenstein's Monster but after issues with rising costs, copyright red tape and staff disagreements, Universal Studios collaborated with Toho Studios, who had wanted to make another movie in the *Godzilla* franchise. At the time, King Kong was thought to be the bigger 'star' out of the monsters and so he was written as the winner of the fight. After a brief underwater battle, Godzilla does not emerge. While many reviewers were unimpressed, *King Kong vs Godzilla* (1962) was a hit, with the highest box office attendance figures of any *Godzilla* film to date in Japan!

The person least impressed by *King Kong vs Godzilla* was Willis O'Brien, the animator for the original stop-motion Kong character. His idea for a Frankenstein's Monster vs King Kong movie had been taken on by producer John Beck and over time and negotiations the idea had changed beyond recognition. O'Brien tried to sue Beck but lacked the funds to do so and when Merian C. Cooper, producer of the original *King Kong*, tried to stop distribution of *King Kong vs Godzilla*, believing that he owned the sole legal rights to the character, he found that this was not the case. He wrote a scathing letter to a friend describing the 'man in the gorilla suit' which he had always been opposed to, preferring stop-motion animation.

Son of Godzilla (1967) was the first *Godzilla* movie to feature a female writer; Kazue Shiba collaborated with Shinichi Sekizawa on the movie's screenplay and as other *Godzilla* films had already introduced fun and humour to the franchise, the studio made couples on dates their target audience and created Minilla – a cute baby monster. *Son of Godzilla* showed Godzilla acting like a proud but exasperated father and added slapstick comedy elements. Minilla was played by former professional wrestler and actor 'Little Man' Machan (real name Masao Fukazawa), hired for his ability to do flips and other athletic moves while inside the creature suit. The movie was seen as a fun and friendly parody of the *Godzilla* series and received praise for its special effects.

By this point, *Godzilla* was a powerhouse series all its own with copycats and rivals springing up in pop culture across the world and while the titular monster began life (and many of the movies) in his natural habitat deep beneath the sea, the devastation and giant kaiju battles usually took place out of the water. For now, the full potential for a deep water monster movie had gone untapped.

The element of water is dangerous enough on its own without even considering the creatures that call it home but add something huge lurking beneath the surface and it's an instant generator for the fear factor. Humans have several rational fears built into our bodies; the fear of deep water and the fear of being eaten are two of them that are extremely easy to combine.

There was an entire ocean out there and the potential to evoke genuine terror with a predator ready to attack had gone untapped … until a shark terrorised the little town of Amity and changed the creature feature movie genre forever.

When everything
was going wrong,
what went right?

Chapter Three

JAWS

STARRING 'BRUCE'

Almost everyone

Sharks

It seems incredible that most people were once unaware that sharks were or could be dangerous to humans, but before 1916 they barely crossed the mind of the average swimmer. Sometimes referred to as 'sea dogs' in old sailing manuscripts and reports, tales of shark attacks were treated with the same level of scepticism that more modern audiences treat the biblical story of Jonah and the Whale. It was considered a hint of reality in an exaggerated tale, although lovers of art might have known about an attack in Havana Harbor in 1749 because the unfortunate swimmer, cabin boy Brook Watson, not only lost a leg but later commissioned popular artist John Singleton Copley to paint the encounter. The painting, entitled *Watson and the Shark* (1778) was painted from sketches and descriptions, for Copley had never actually seen Havana – or a shark! He hides most of the gore underwater, showing the rescue effort in the aftermath of the injury while the shark advances once more; enormous, with orange eyes and slit catlike pupils. Copley produced three versions of the painting and Watson bequeathed one to Christ's Hospital in West Sussex, with the hope that it would prove 'a most usefull Lesson to Youth [*sic*]'. Unfortunately for us all, he did not provide much insight on what lesson he felt a painting of a shark attack in Havana would teach young people in a British hospital.

In 1891, American businessman and multimillionaire, Hermann Oelrichs, offered a reward of $500 (around $16,300 today) for any man, woman or child who could prove that they had been attacked by a shark in the temperate waters north of Cape Hatteras, North Carolina. Nobody came forward so scientists remained convinced that sharks were harmless outside of tropical waters, and so did the general public. As most shark bites would have happened out at sea away from hospitals, and in an age when emergency healthcare was far less advanced than it is today, and often in warmer climates in which infection could take hold more quickly, it is no wonder that shark bites (even exploratory ones as we now know most are) were generally too fatal for the potential recipient to claim the reward.

By the time Oelrichs died in 1906 (of reasons unrelated to sharks), the reward had still not been claimed. Had he stayed alive for another ten years, he would have had to pay up, and quite spectacularly.

The Jersey Man-Eater

In the early 1900s, scientists had a very limited understanding of sharks and many of the known 'facts' of the time have since been proven wrong. Both zoologist, Henry Weed Fowler, and curator, Henry Skinner, of the Academy of Natural Sciences in Philadelphia stated publicly that even the largest great white shark lacked the jaw strength to snap a human bone. As we now know, this is extremely false information! A great white shark can bite with a force of over 18,000 newtons, which can sever a limb easily. For comparison, the average dog bite has a force of around 250 newtons. Many scientists and zoologists had thought that sharks were shy creatures and this is mostly true but it does not mean that they will not bite under the right circumstances.

In July 1916, a series of shark attacks terrorised people living along the New Jersey coast. The shark attacked five people, killing four of them and changing the public and scientific view of shark behaviour over the course of just twelve days.

The attacks began in the charmingly named Beach Haven; a resort town on the New Jersey coast. On 1 July 1916, Charles Epting Vansant went for a quick swim in the sea accompanied by a dog that had been playing nearby. Soon after he entered the water he began shouting; he had been bitten on the leg. Some bystanders thought he was calling to the dog but when lifeguard, Alexander Ott, realised that he was hurt, he attempted to rescue him, making him the first lifeguard in American history to rescue somebody from a shark attack. Vansant died soon after being rescued and witnesses reported that the shark followed them to shore, refusing to let go of his leg.

News of the attack was treated as an oddity and authorities decided not to close the beaches. It was summer, high tourist season and the media downplayed the incident, only reluctantly admitting that a shark could have been involved at all. Reports talked of a fish which was only 'presumably' a shark and proposed the theory that the dog Vansant was swimming with had been the true target of the attack. Even the local sea captains' reports of seeing a large shark in the area were dismissed and the beaches remained open, though with newly installed shark nets.

On 6 July 1916, another attack happened, this time at the resort town of Spring Lake, 72 kilometres north of Beach Haven. Charles Bruder was swimming in the sea when he was bitten and the situation was so unexpected that spectators did not realise what they were seeing at first. One woman informed two lifeguards that a canoe with a red hull had capsized! The bite severed Bruder's legs and he died before he was taken to the shore. This time, the media response was fast and sensational with shark stories featuring as front-page news in multiple papers. Press conferences were held and lifeguards patrolled in response to the events, and yet not all resort towns forbade swimming, instead advising people to stay near the shoreline. Even then, many could not believe that a shark was responsible for the deaths, blaming everything from orcas and sea turtles to German boats. The one voice of reason appeared to be Dr William G. Schauffler, one of New Jersey's most respected medical doctors. On examining the bodies, he stated that 'there is not the slightest doubt that a man-eating shark inflicted the injuries'.

The next two attacks took place in the partially tidal inlet of Matawan Creek. Matawan was not a beach resort and relied less on tourism than the towns along the New Jersey coast did. It was also an incredibly unlikely location for a shark attack; the creek was far inland for a start, and freshwater. Still, sea captain, Thomas Cottrell, reported seeing a shark over 2 metres long in the creek, but he was dismissed by authorities who claimed that heatstroke had caused him to imagine things. Later that day, a group of local boys and a pet dog were playing in the creek and saw what they at first assumed to be an old, weathered log, but they realised the truth when a dorsal fin appeared in the water. The boys and dog scrambled for the shore and all made it except one: Lester Stillwell, who disappeared under the water.

Even then, the idea that a shark could be in Matawan Creek was so unbelievable to locals that when the boys ran for help, they assumed that Stillwell —- known to have epilepsy – had suffered a seizure rather than a shark attack. Several people, including local businessman Watson Stanley Fisher, dived into the creek to search for him, finding his body soon afterward. Before they could all reach the shore, the shark attacked again. Fisher lost his grip on the body while attempting to fight the shark off and return to shore, and he too was bitten, severing his femoral artery. He died in hospital, and Stillwell's body was eventually recovered.

The shark bit its final victim just thirty minutes after the attacks in Matawan Creek. 12-year-old Joseph Dunn was bitten on his left leg but his brother Michael reacted quickly and after a gruesome tug-of-war with the shark, Dunn was loaded onto Thomas Cottrell's boat and taken to hospital. He was released two months later, having made a full recovery.

After the attacks on Stillwell, Fisher, and Dunn, residents attempted to use dynamite to deter the shark and there was a $100 reward (around $2,500 today) issued for capturing and killing the shark in Matawan Creek. Still no sharks were captured or killed in that area. Away from Matawan Creek, the hunt for the 'Jersey Man-Eater' would later be described as the largest-scale animal hunt in history, with hundreds of sharks being killed along the coasts of New Jersey and New York. Michael Schleisser, animal trainer for the infamous Barnum and Bailey sideshow (the one showing the 'Fiji Mermaid'), caught a juvenile great white shark which was found to have nearly 7 kilograms of human remains in its belly! Many other people brought dead sharks for consideration but it was never definitively proven which, if any, was the Jersey Man-Eater.

The International Shark Attack File lists a great white as the species responsible, though there is a compelling argument for the bull shark too. Great white sharks are an oceanic species and unlikely to survive for long in water with a low salt content, while the notoriously aggressive bull shark often enters creeks and other freshwater areas. Bull sharks are thought to be behind many of the attacks attributed to great whites.

The fear and bad press following the Jersey Man-Eater attacks is estimated to have cost New Jersey resort owners an estimated $250,000 ($6,200,000 in 2021) in lost tourism. Even sunbathing declined by as much as seventy-five per cent in some areas!

Scientists and other experts admitted their errors in underestimating sharks in the months following the events at Matawan Creek and as the world wars progressed, bringing an increase in the sinking of naval ships, sharks were attracted to the resulting bonanza.

Mass attacks like the one on the USS *Indianapolis* in 1945 (the deadliest mass shark attack of all time with a death toll of between sixty and one hundred and fifty sailors, involving up to six different species of shark) added to the fear, but in general most people still did not place sharks highly on lists of the things that gave them nightmares. The film industry also reflected the moods of the time, featuring romances (often set against a war background), patriotic movies involving heroic feats and propaganda, and light-hearted comedies.

In the early 1970s, freelance writer, Peter Benchley, was pitching two book ideas at once to publishers: one, a non-fiction book about pirates and the other about a man-eating shark terrorising a small town. The latter was more appealing to his publisher and in 1974, *Jaws* was published:

In a small beach town resort named Amity (meaning 'friendship'), a series of shark attacks proves devastating. But when will the people in charge of the beach take action? After one death? Two? More? Frustrated, three men set out to destroy the shark themselves.

Benchley had been inspired by his interest in shark attacks and the feat of celebrity fisherman, Frank Mundus, in catching a great white shark weighing an estimated 2,063kg off the coast of Long Island. And although many plot points in the novel bear a striking resemblance to the 1916 Jersey Man-Eater attacks, specifically the appealingly named locations and delayed reactions of the beach town authorities involved, Benchley always insisted that he was not inspired by this event.

Universal Pictures producers Richard D. Zanuck and David Brown had heard about the upcoming book from a magazine article, ordered preview copies which they each read in a single night and the pair bought the film rights before the book was even published, and for $175,000 (over a million dollars today!). The novel stayed on the bestseller list for forty-four weeks.

Jaws (1975)

Jaws was the first major motion picture to be shot on the ocean, credited with starting the 'summer blockbuster' phenomenon and, in 2001, it was selected by the Library of Congress for preservation in the United States National Film Registry as a 'culturally, historically, or aesthetically significant' work.

Filmed partly from the shark's perspective and offering occasional glimpses of a fin and bloody water, the audience finally gets a proper look at the shark at around an hour into the movie; the halfway point. Director, Steven Spielberg, was praised for this unusual approach, relying on suspense and an unforgettable theme tune. It is often described in reviews, articles and podcasts as a film that would never have been made today as modern audiences have been deemed too impatient; they simply would not wait so long to see the shark!

Actor, Richard Dreyfuss, who played Hooper commented that when filming began, they had no script, no cast and no shark. Some of the sequences were so difficult to capture that David Brown would later say that if he had read the book twice, he would not have agreed to make the film in the first place. Due to the ambitious scale of the project and some unpredictable elements like malfunctioning props, an 'often-drunk' main star, parts uncast until the last minute, no script and a director who wanted to be somewhere else, it is a wonder the film was made at all.

What went wrong?

A reluctant director

It would be the film that put director, Steven Spielberg, on the map, but he didn't want the job. While he had been very keen to take over after the previous director, Dick Richards, was fired for repeatedly referring to the shark as a whale (yes, really!), Spielberg grew concerned that *Jaws* was very similar to his earlier film, *Duel* (1971), which also featured an everyday hero doing battle with a large and unstoppable beast (though in *Duel* the 'beast' was a truck). He requested he be moved to another project in development, a romantic drama named *Lucky Lady*. Universal vetoed this and with fifty-five days in which to shoot, Spielberg was left to get on with it.

Script issues

Peter Benchley's original novel was complex, with many subplots and tangents including an affair between oceanographer, Hooper, and Chief Brody's wife, Ellen. Benchley was hired to write the screenplay for the film (in part to avoid being delayed by a proposed writers' strike as he was not a member of any union) but by the time he had presented his third and final draft, insisting that he was 'written out' and could do no more, Steven Spielberg and the production team were still not happy, feeling that the characters were unlikeable and not as well-rounded as they could be. By the time Spielberg brought writer, Carl Gottlieb, on board as the new primary screenwriter they were under pressure and running out of time. Gottlieb had to finalise the script for each scene the night before it was going to be shot. The cast and crew had dinner with Gottlieb and Spielberg each night and many of the resulting conversations and brainstorming sessions made their way into the movie. Some of the dialogue was based on the actors' improvising lines together at dinner, other lines were added in the middle of shooting and most of the subplots were removed, keeping the 'shark terror' story as the core plot point.

No cast

Even the actors were cast at the very last minute. Spielberg had always wanted to cast relatively unknown people so that the shark would be the main star but the producers had specifically requested he hire known actors for the central roles of Chief Brody, Hooper and Quint. As a compromise, he looked for actors with experience but who were not instantly recognisable, in order to give the impression that the events in the film could happen to absolutely anyone. Even with a wide range of actors to choose from, just nine days before production was due to start, neither Quint nor Hooper had been cast.

Richard Dreyfuss originally turned down the part of Hooper when it was offered to him, but reconsidered after seeing his own most recent film called *The Apprenticeship of Duddy Kravitz* (1974). Dreyfuss *hated* it! Disappointed in his own performance and afraid that nobody would ever hire him again, he called Spielberg and accepted the role after all. Spielberg and Gottlieb rewrote the character to fit the actor better and 'film Hooper' became so different to 'book Hooper' that Spielberg asked Dreyfuss not to read Peter Benchley's novel before filming began.

Mishaps on set

When producers suggested Robert Shaw for the role of Quint, it was the actor himself who needed to be convinced because he did not like the book. He took the role but got into a prank war with Richard Dreyfuss on set, which quickly got out of hand. Quint's character was an arrogant daredevil and whether Shaw was method-acting by channelling some of Quint's personality is unclear but Shaw taunted Dreyfuss for his mannerisms and dared him to do increasingly dangerous stunts like climbing up the mast and jumping into the ocean. Shaw's issues with alcohol were known and the actor began drinking both during and behind the scenes. In the famous scene aboard the *Orca* boat during which the men get drunk and compare scars and stories, Shaw got so paralytically drunk in real life that he blacked out and the footage was unusable. After calling Steven Spielberg later that night to ask if he had done anything embarrassing, a stone-cold sober and very apologetic Shaw returned to set early the next day and completed the scene in one take.

The shark broke

People working on movies have sometimes been known to make bizarre demands and the producers working on *Jaws* were no exception. Their first idea for creating a realistic and frightening monster of the deep was ... to train actual great white sharks! When informed that this was dangerous to try and impossible to achieve, the team moved onto Plan B: animatronic sharks. Big animatronic sharks. Outrageously expensive animatronic sharks. To be specific, three animatronic sharks measuring over 7 metres long and costing $250,000 each, all named 'Bruce' after Steven Spielberg's lawyer, and each of them malfunctioning for most of the time. It might have been easier to try and train the great white sharks!

Believing that the atmosphere he wanted to create could not be achieved anywhere else, Steven Spielberg was determined to shoot in the real ocean rather than using a Hollywood studio water tank. This led to other unforeseen issues: sailboats drifted around in the background; cameras got damaged by the salt water; the three Bruces frequently malfunctioned, for reasons ranging from bad weather and pneumatic hoses taking on salt water, to getting tangled up in seaweed; and the 'non-absorbent' neoprene foam used for the outside of the sharks turning out to be very absorbent indeed, causing them to balloon. Even the boat *Orca* once began to sink, with the actors onboard. Spielberg later calculated that during the twelve-hour daily work schedule, only four hours on average were actually spent filming.

Understandably, the atmosphere on set was not always at its friendliest or most relaxed. Amid the on and off-screen rivalry between actors Shaw and Dreyfuss, the challenging conditions and the tedious waiting around caused by the many problems on set, tensions often ran high. The movie was intended to be shot in 55 days but the production finally wrapped at the end of a gruelling 159 days, after which Spielberg stated that he did not believe he would ever work again. He was not even present on set for the final scene in which the shark is blown up by Brody as he was certain that at the end of the shoot the crew intended to throw him into the sea. The production was such a frustrating challenge that the crew nicknamed it 'Flaws'.

What went right?

Creating suspense

Due to the constant malfunctioning of the mechanical shark, Spielberg was forced to get creative in order to make things work. Instead of showing the monster early and using visual horror as the compelling attraction, he used camera tricks and the power of suggestion to create suspense. Tactics such as filming events from the shark's point of view, showing just a dorsal fin, intercutting footage of real sharks in the wild and filming attacks from the surface of the water, forced viewers to sit helplessly like the rest of the onlookers as the shark claimed victims. When the shark finally appeared, he used forced perspective and camera angles to emphasise its size, dwarfing the boat. The results were far more disturbing and frightening to viewers than he could have imagined. After all, many shark attack victims do not see anything until the shark makes its presence known. Spielberg would eventually say that the malfunctioning shark had been a godsend, forcing his direction to become more like Alfred Hitchcock (known for his suspenseful films) as opposed to Ray Harryhausen, whose talents in special effects were now widely respected.

Excellent casting

The occasional rubbery appearance of the shark can be forgiven by the memorable and extremely good acting from the human stars. As Spielberg said: the worse the shark looked, the better the acting had to be! Shooting the film in as naturalistic a manner as possible and showing the impact of the shark attacks happening to ordinary people rather than action stars was a decision in part inspired by the king of the monsters himself, Godzilla.

A happy accident

Even one of the characters' dramatic escapes was not so much a result of clever direction but a happy accident. Ron and Valerie Taylor were filming real great white sharks in the wild for later use in the film and the plan had been to place a very short actor in a shark cage in order to make the shark appear enormous beside him. Frank Rizzo, a 1.2m tall stuntman, waited in the cage for the shark to pass by but the shark attacked the boat, sideswiping the cage and ripping it free where it sank to the bottom of the sea with Rizzo still inside.

When casting the role, Rizzo was offered the job on the spot having arrived at an audition straight from a car crash without even cleaning up the blood covering his face! Still, as gutsy as he was, risking being attacked by a shark in real life was not in the job description and as the shark went to town investigating the cage, he escaped to safety. However, this meant that there was a problem with the footage of the shark attacking the cage which, at the time, was supposed to hold a doomed Hooper. 'Hooper' was not in the cage. In order not to lose the chilling footage, Spielberg rewrote the story, allowing Hooper to live having escaped in the same way as Rizzo – by squeezing past the shark.

Powerful writing and quotability

The identity of the writer behind Quint's iconic monologue about his experience on the USS *Indianapolis* is unclear. Spielberg credits a collaboration between playwright, Howard Sackler, who had offered to do an uncredited rewrite of Benchley's original draft; screenwriter John Milius; and Quint actor

Robert Shaw himself, who was also a playwright. Tired, very much sober and with a desire to prove himself, his feat of completing the scene in one take not only produced a mesmerising result but became film legend, though still pretty embarrassing for Shaw!

Getting the opinion of a test audience sometimes changes the course of an entire film, as it did for a later film in this book. While the test audiences loved *Jaws*, watching their reactions allowed Spielberg to make a few changes, resulting in some of the most quotable scenes. Chief Brody's famous line 'you're gonna need a bigger boat' had occurred immediately after the first appearance of the shark's head and was drowned out by the resulting screams from the audience. Spielberg extended Brody's reaction, allowing the audience to recover before Brody says his line, which was ad-libbed by actor Roy Scheider as a joke! The cast and crew had a small support boat for the much bigger barge that carried props and equipment, and many had complained that this boat was too small. It had already become a running catchphrase among the cast and crew after anything went wrong.

That jump scare…

Deciding to make the audience scream one more time, Spielberg reshot the scene during which the missing fisherman Ben Gardner is discovered (well, what's left of him, anyway). Having overshot by one hundred days working on a production that appeared to have gone wrong in any way it could, Universal Studios, fairly understandably, refused to pay for this, so Spielberg used $3,000 of his own money and shot the scene in editor Verna Fields's swimming pool, which he filled with powdered milk and covered with a tarpaulin in order to give it a dark and murky feel. The sudden appearance of Ben Gardner's head gives one of the movie's most gruesome jump scares.

The score

The distinctive two-note theme music is recognisable even to people who haven't seen the film but when composer, John Williams, played the notes on a piano as a demonstration for Steven Spielberg, the director thought he was joking. Still, the music (thought by some to suggest the shark's heartbeat and by others to evoke panicked human breathing) has a counterpart: silence. In most scenes during which the shark attacks, the music abruptly cuts off into silence once the shark has bitten. Watch the movie again and you will notice the music is not present in a scene when a prankster floats a fake dorsal fin through a crowd of swimmers. Those two notes have become a musical synonym for suspense and having won over Steven Spielberg with his idea, Williams won an Academy Award for the movie's score.

The real-life Quint

From the character's introduction in which he brings a room to silence by scratching his nails down a blackboard to his gory demise toward the end of the film, Robert Shaw's performance as Quint is intense. The often-made comparison to *Moby Dick*'s Captain Ahab is not coincidence: Quint's introduction in the original novel shows him emptying a cinema by laughing uproariously at a screening of *Moby Dick* and his death came from being dragged under the water by a harpoon – the same fate as Captain Ahab – and not from the shark. The character is larger-than-life, not always likeable, and yet unapologetic. He is also based on a real person.

Fisherman, Frank Mundus, began his career as a shark hunter before becoming a shark advocate and conservationist, as many people involved in the production of *Jaws* did. His methods were considered flawed even by the standards of the time, killing whales for use as chum (meat, bone and blood used as bait, especially for attracting sharks) and harpooning sharks, which is outlawed today. Chumming alone is a practise heavily criticised and now illegal in many places.

People were attracted to his business of 'monster fishing' as he called it, partly for the allure of seeing the sharks and partly for his colourful character. Even his feat of capturing a great white shark weighing over 2,000kg proved controversial; some said the shark had been feeding very well at the time of capture and was therefore heavy with its meal, but the International Game Fishing Association ruled that the catch was legitimate. Still, rulings rarely negate controversy!

Mundus's shark is still listed as the largest fish of any kind ever caught by rod and line. Having accompanied him on shark hunting expeditions, Peter Benchley credits his feat for inspiring the book and Mundus himself for inspiring the character, but interestingly he is not credited in the film.

Joe Gaviola, a Montauk businessman, was quoted in an article in the East Hampton Press: 'He is Quint. If you read the book, he was everything Frank was. Benchley spent weeks fishing with him. Give me a break. He is Quint'.

The eccentric Mundus, also known as 'The Monster Man', painted his toenails and wore a hoop earring, an ostentatious hat and of course a large shark tooth necklace.

Jaws is not just about a shark

This seems an odd thing to say about a film which helped to spark a global fear of sharks but although Steven Spielberg has insisted otherwise, critics and audiences have argued that *Jaws* is very pointedly not about a shark.

Under the apparent calm of activity on the surface is an unknown danger, one that the townsfolk could not have possibly imagined. There is an unstoppable force that has potential to devastate the ordinary everyday lives of fishermen, swimmers and other fun-seekers. It does not discriminate. It is not the shark; it is the horrendous decision of the authorities, especially the town's mayor, to keep the beaches open and to keep the townsfolk ignorant of the danger. The character of the mayor (played by Murray Hamilton) has been the subject of many articles. He is designed to infuriate people with a combination of smugness, privilege and utter incompetence. He is the authority figure that everyone knows and hates a version of. His refusal to take responsibility for his decision to prioritise profits over people represents a very specific mindset, one that has been demonstrated by many leaders throughout history.

The shark itself is terrifying, but what is worse is the fact that many of the attacks could have been preventable. The townsfolk were at the mercy of a force other than the shark: corporate greed. This is a theme that people can relate to, from the downplaying of the 1916 Jersey Man-Eater attacks, to the 1990s exposure of a contamination cover-up by citizen Erin Brockovich (later made into a film starring Julia Roberts), to the controversial actions of government officials during the COVID-19 pandemic. It is a theme that is likely to continue to resonate, making *Jaws* stand the test of time.

Later copycat films tended to focus only on the central monster, with an occasional few minutes of screentime dedicated to a subplot. While the horror genre relies on scares, many subsequent monster movies would leave out other themes in favour of bigger monsters with more teeth, but a monster is just a monster. One reason for the enduring success of *Jaws* is that the shark is only part of the story.

The *Jaws* Effect

Watching *Jaws* in the cinema was said to have caused a single case of cinematic neurosis: a condition in which a person experiences mental health disturbances after seeing a film. Other horror movies have been associated with the condition and while advertisers and promoters have used this potential link to increase hype around their movies, The *Jaws* Effect was a well-documented and proven phenomenon. Dr Christopher Pepin-Neff of the University of Sydney researched the fear of shark attacks, local policy on dealing with 'rogue sharks' and the watching of *Jaws* and movies like it and found that the focus on shark attacks increased fear of sharks. It also gave an unrealistic perception of the danger sharks pose to humans and as a result, allowed the implementation of unscientifically sound culling programs, which led to a dramatic decline in shark populations. He called this phenomenon 'The *Jaws* Effect' and in his 2015 paper he cited three specific instances in which the Western Australian government's policy was rooted in the '*Jaws* mindset'; that shark bites are always intentional, always fatal and the fault of a 'rogue shark which must be hunted down'.

Though reports of shark attacks had been increasing steadily throughout the twentieth century, the language used when describing sharks had changed. 'Shark-infested waters' was a phrase that appears to have come into use from around 1916 onwards according to the *Collins English Dictionary* website and yet, we rarely speak of 'bee-infested meadows', 'cow-infested fields' or even 'hippopotamus-infested rivers', even though all of these creatures are responsible for more human deaths per year than sharks are. Cows kill an average of twenty-two people per year while sharks killed just eleven people in 2021, but the fear of sharks taps into two of the human brain's most primal fears: deep water and being eaten. These fears may be understandable and sensible but the problem is, the overreaction post-*Jaws* was terrible news for sharks! After the movie aired, shark hunts became popular again. Reports of galeophobia (fear of sharks) increased dramatically and in the US alone, there was a fifty to ninety per cent decline in shark populations shortly after the movie was released.

This significant change drew the attention of marine biologists. The decline in their population amid the phenomenal success of *Jaws* led to a greater interest in the study of sharks and their behaviour. There was a demand for knowledge and real-life footage of the creatures, requiring funding which scientists and videographers asked for and got. We have never grown tired of this interest, leading to spectacular footage of sharks behaving normally in their natural environment (for example in the award-winning *Planet Earth* TV series presented by David Attenborough) and eventually, tireless conservation efforts from some unexpected protectors.

We're sorry, sharks

Imagine feeling responsible for the decline of an entire species! This is the position that Peter Benchley found himself in, after being made aware of The *Jaws* Effect.

Benchley's fascination with sharks had been an ongoing part of his life but around fifteen years after the release of *Jaws*, he saw the bodies of de-finned sharks lying at the bottom of the ocean; victims of the shark fin soup trade. He called it one of the most horrifying sights he had ever seen and by 1995 he was loudly campaigning for shark research and conservation.

After his death in 2006, his widow Wendy said that her husband's novel had inadvertently tapped into people's greatest fears and that the disturbing sight he saw on the dive had fed into his own fear that he may have contributed to this destruction. He would speak out many times about the fact that he could not have written the same book twenty years later without casting the shark as more of a sympathetic character and certainly not the monster fish of his original story. Using money that he had earned through writing *Jaws*, Peter Benchley funded a shark conservation movement which he would promote and champion until his death.

Benchley was not the only member of the *Jaws* team to become an outspoken advocate for shark conservation and preservation. Valerie Taylor, formerly Australia's leading female spear fisher, shot footage of real great white sharks for use in the movie but after a similar change in perspective to that of Peter Benchley, she and her husband Ron became vocal shark advocates after a trip in which they watched multiple sharks being hunted and killed.

Richard Dreyfuss (Hooper) also spoke out against the killing of sharks, headlining a panel at SharkCon 2018 and stating his opinion that the way to save sharks is to portray them as protagonists rather than monsters.

Did You Know?

After serving on the police force since 1986, in May 2022 Jonathan Searle, the child actor playing the fin-wearing prankster, became police chief for Martha's Vineyard; the movie's principal filming location!

Later movies would present their monsters in different ways- both sympathetic and not so much, but for a good two decades after the release of *Jaws* the 'monster shark horror' genre prevailed.

Jaws fact file

Released: 1975
Directed by: Steven Spielberg
Starring: Roy Scheider, Robert Shaw, Richard Dreyfuss
Creature: Great white shark
Effects: Animatronics, real-life footage
Legacy: Beyond measurable. *Jaws* changed the movie world, public perception of sharks and influenced countless other films and is even referenced in movies for children, like *Shark Tale* (2004) and *Finding Nemo* (2003). Sequels were *Jaws 2* (1978), *Jaws 3-D* (1983) and *Jaws: The Revenge* (1987). Documentary *The Shark is Still Working* (2012), stage play *The Shark Is Broken* (2019), Universal Studios theme park ride.

Jaws put a face and teeth to our most primal fears, giving the green light for virtually every other water monster horror movie that was in discussions at the time while changing the way we approach the genre entirely, from concept all the way to marketing. While no other deep water monster movie has been quite as memorable, the genre was about to get very fun indeed!

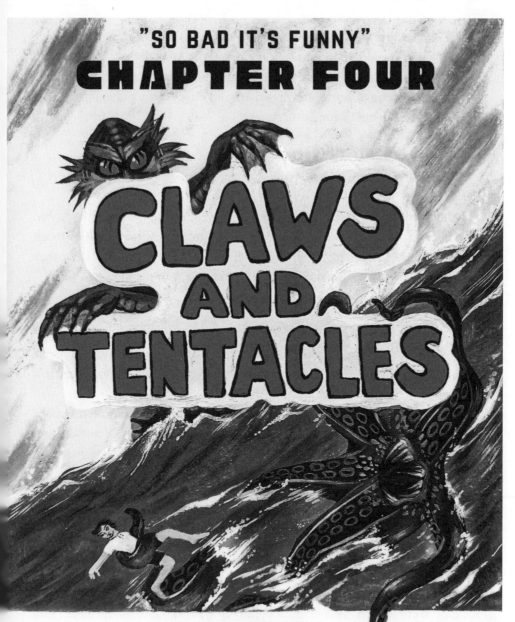

"SO BAD IT'S FUNNY"

CHAPTER FOUR

CLAWS AND TENTACLES

STARRING

"HADDOCK WITH DENTURES"
A PARTY IN AN IRISH PUB
A RELUCTANT HERO
THE KRAKEN

T he world of the creature feature had been rocked by *Jaws*, a movie that was not only genuinely terrifying but critically acclaimed, with a legacy that included triggering shark phobias people didn't even know they had! In its wake, horror movie writers and directors scrambled to find the next big terror using two main strategies:

Number one, make *Jaws* again, but featuring a different sea creature.
Number two, make *Jaws* again.

The results ranged from unexpectedly entertaining to downright terrible. While films that are considered 'so bad they're funny' now have their own cult following and fandom, most of these could not claim that status ... but they sparked reviews that were often more entertaining than the movies.

Tentacles (1977)

Tentacles holds the rare distinction of a zero per cent critic score on the movie rating website Rotten Tomatoes, alongside a ten per cent audience score. It is described as being utterly, shockingly bad.

For readers interested in the plot: people start going missing in an idyllic seaside resort town. A reporter discovers that the culprit is a giant octopus and while a marine biologist attempts to stop the monster octopus's rampage before more people die, it appears that the truth is even more disturbing; a large corporation may be involved and trying to cover up what they know. Does this sound familiar to anybody?

Tentacles contains a scene involving characters drinking around a table while discussing the monster and there is even a jump scare involving a dead person's head that suddenly appears with an eye sticking out. Both of these closely resemble some of the most famous scenes in *Jaws*.

One scene which pushed the boundaries of taste and should have been truly shocking for its rarity, even in today's movies, is the death of a baby. A distracted mother turns away from her baby in its pram before looking back to find that the baby is now nowhere to be seen, but its fate is hinted at when the movie cuts to a scene showing the pram floating in the water. The mother's face reflects surprise and a little bit of disappointment, as though she had found her cat pushing ornaments off a shelf, or unexpectedly run out of coffee, rather than losing her child. The scene cuts and the movie continues, making these very disturbing few minutes unintentionally hilarious for just how disproportionate the reaction to such a scenario is.

Reviews spoke of wasted talent, terrible acting and an unoriginal story. Tom Milne of *The Monthly Film Bulletin* had one of the most scathing reviews of all, describing the finale as 'grotesquely maudlin'. While reviewer, Marjorie Bilbow, of *Screen International* gave the special effects mild praise, these effects mostly consist of a very tight close-up shot of a model octopus, a puppet and shots of a real octopus.

The movie's special effects resembled those from *Jaws* in another key way; just as the animatronic sharks famously malfunctioned, the giant and expensive octopus puppet created for use in *Tentacles* sank.

Tentacles fact file

Released: 1977
Directed by: Ovidio G. Assonitis
Starring: John Huston (father of actress Anjelica Huston), Shelley Winters, Bo Hopkins, Henry Fonda (father of actress Jane Fonda), Cesare Danova
Creature: Giant octopus
Effects: Puppet, real-life footage
Legacy: Absolutely none.

Orcas: Dodging a bullet!

The movie monsters featured in this book range from excellent to utterly, comedically awful. Still, in hindsight and with our current knowledge about sharks, their usual lack of threat to humans and their important role in the ocean's ecosystem, perhaps it is a good thing that since *Jaws,* no movie has changed the reputation of a creature so effectively!

When film producer, Dino de Laurentiis, called up fellow producer, Luciano Vincenzoni, in the middle of the night with the request to 'find a fish tougher and more terrible than the great white', many would have considered the request impossible; the great white shark may well be the toughest fish in the ocean. With the strongest bite of all fish, a distinctive look and a fearsome reputation, they have just one predator: the orca. Orcas (aka killer whales) are the largest members of the dolphin family. They hunt in formidable packs, have their own language systems, are extremely intelligent with advanced problem-solving abilities and they can and do attack and eat sharks, including the great white. They may be tougher than the great white shark, but they are far from terrible and are definitely not fish!

Vincenzoni's brother, Adriano, had an interest in zoology and pointed him in the direction of the orca as an alternative to a fish. The resulting movie, *Orca: The Killer Whale* (1977), told the tale of an orca's revenge on a boat captain for killing its family but did not bring anything new to the movie world other than some icebergs. The writing and plot were described as soggy, nonsense and riddled with oceanic clichés, but the underwater camerawork was praised and the special effects were apparently so realistic that trucks transporting the rubber orcas to the set were blocked by animal rights activists believing them to be real! Fortunately for the orca, the movie was a critical flop and the reputation of the animal, which has been known to ram boats in recent years but has never been documented to kill a human being in the wild, was safe.

In preparation for the 'summer blockbuster' season, two movies were being shot at the same time. One of these was a monster movie featuring genetically modified piranha being kept in a tank in a private military complex. *Piranha* (1978) involved a cheerful summer camp, great threat to children, fairly terrible special effects and a military cover-up. It is a horror-comedy provoking as many laughs as screams and would later become a cult hit. Even Steven Spielberg referred to it as his favourite *Jaws* rip-off and while some studio executives were reportedly ready to take legal action due to the movie's plot similarities, it is rumoured that Spielberg himself told them that *Piranha* was a parody and that they should allow the filming to go ahead. It received commercial success despite mixed reviews but might have enjoyed a better reception at the box office if it had not been overshadowed by the other movie, released just a few weeks afterward.

Jaws 2 (1978)

A new hotel opens on Amity Island and while life for the townspeople appears to be getting back to normal after the events in the original movie, Chief Brody can't forget his experiences. When people who thought it was safe to get back in the water begin dying under mysterious circumstances, he is afraid that it's the work of another great white shark. Surprise: it is! Brody has his family to look out for, but teenage boys have minds of their own and Brody's son has taken a boat, his brother, and several of his friends out onto the water.

Roy Scheider performed well in his role of the 'everyman turned hero' and Carl Gottlieb returned as a writer. Still, this production was also plagued by issues.

'Here we go again…'

Steven Spielberg once told the San Francisco Film Festival in 1975 that he felt sequels were cheap carnival tricks, so he was most definitely not interested in directing *Jaws 2* at the time (though later added that he would have worked on the sequel if the original production had been less troubled.) Still, Universal Studios wanted a sequel almost immediately and the producers took on the project in order to stop other companies stepping in. Steven Spielberg wanted nothing to do with it, Richard Dreyfuss declined to reprise his role as Hooper because Spielberg wasn't involved, Robert Shaw's character Quint had been killed onscreen in the original movie and this left Roy Scheider.

But Scheider did not want to be there; his presence in the film was the result of a compromise with Universal Studios in order to end a three-film contract that he had signed. After walking out of his role in *The Deer Hunter* (1978) due to creative differences before filming even began, the studio agreed to release him from his contract on the condition that he appear in *Jaws 2*. Scheider reluctantly agreed but said he felt that there was no new ground to explore and that people would now be coming to see the shark and not him.

Creative differences and personality clashes

The proposed plan had been to write a prequel based on Quint's account of the USS *Indianapolis* shark attack. While the studio liked the idea, they wanted another action film; specifically, a summer blockbuster and preferably a repeat of the lasting effect the original movie had on the general public. Of course, this is not a formula that can be repeated to order. The director John D. Hancock clashed so intensely with executives that he was fired. The studio was not a fan of the darker and more subtle direction that he was planning to take, though Hancock claimed a contributing factor was the fact that he had fired an actress who turned out to be the girlfriend of one of the executives. Though several people volunteered to direct (even Spielberg considered returning), Jeannot Szwarc was chosen, though he and Roy Scheider did not get on. The production was given a total overhaul, many actors were fired, roles were redeveloped and yet again Carl Gottlieb was hired at the last minute to rewrite the script! Szwarc bought Gottlieb time by filming extended action sequences while he worked on the new and more light-hearted script.

Shark problems

It was never going to be possible to replicate the suspense created in the original film; the audience already knew what the shark looked like, so Szwarc made the decision to take the opposite approach and show off the shark as much as he could, distinguishing it by giving it a scarred face and a 'plausible' desire for revenge (though in reality sharks are not vengeful creatures). The original animatronics were no more, having rotted from the understandable lack of care in storage as nobody thought that a giant malfunctioning shark prop would be wanted again. The tube frames making up the basic shark shapes had been rescued and three new sharks were built for the movie, using the same body mould but with a much more ambitious design.

One criticism of *Jaws* is the rubbery looking shark; another reason it rarely makes an appearance on camera. Part of the problem was attributed to 'pinching' in the neoprene around the shark's jaw which created the look of a hinge, so sculptor Chris Mueller created an entirely new head to disguise this. The sharks were officially known as 'Bruce Two' but in the same tradition as the original movie, they were known on set as Fidel and Harold (the latter named after producer David Brown's lawyer).

Shooting on water is always a challenge for prop makers and the salt water began to corrode metal elements in the sharks … again. Hancock blamed the mechanical shark for contributing to his departure from the project, telling a newspaper that the shark still didn't swim or bite and broke every couple of shots. As the mechanical sharks did not move in the way real sharks would, production worked with Ron and Valerie Taylor again in order to obtain footage of sharks in the wild for use in the film.

Did You Know?

While filming, a group of hammerhead sharks took an interest in the teen actors supposedly marooned on a boat and in distress. The crew thought their calls for help were just good acting, and nobody realised their situation or genuine terror until later! While real-life sharks are not generally aggressive, they are curious animals.

Success?

Except for many of the core cast, crew and producers, people believed in *Jaws 2*. Big brands like Coca-Cola offered merchandising and sponsorships, there were souvenirs for sale, such as shark tooth necklaces and associated products, including a novelisation of an earlier screenplay draft, and Martha's Vineyard newspapers reported on the return to filming with an excited and positive tone.

After its release, *Jaws 2* steadily received mixed reviews, placing it at around sixty-one per cent positive on the Rotten Tomatoes film rating 'tomatometer'. The common consensus is that it never could have lived up to the original movie's success but when compared to the following two sequels it is a good, solid film with competent acting.

On the other hand, critics have been cutting. Roger Ebert described the film as 'pure trash' and Tom Pulleine of *The Monthly Film Bulletin* criticised the characterisation of the mayor, who acknowledged the events in *Jaws* but still refused to take Brody's warnings seriously, making him look like a fool and in Pulleine's opinion, sabotaging the potential for serious dramatic interest. This interpretation could have been changed had an earlier deleted scene been kept, in which the mayor is the only person to vote to save Brody while he is threatened with the prospect of being fired.

Of course, the star of the show has been subject to the most criticism. Many reviews refer to the dreaded monster not as 'the shark' but as 'the mechanical shark', illustrating just how inescapably fake it really looked. While Spielberg's original decision to hide the shark was made out of necessity, a little more restraint could have been used in order to invest the audience before the long close ups of what is, after all, a machine, and a machine that the critics could not, would not and did not believe in.

For a short period of time, *Jaws 2* was the highest grossing sequel ever made. It was beaten almost exactly a year later by *Rocky 2* but taking into account the cast reluctance, personality clashes and disparaging words on the subject of sequels from Spielberg, you have to wonder what kind of success it could have been if the original cast had all been on board, or what Spielberg could have done with the idea for a film about the USS *Indianapolis* mass shark attack.

Jaws 2 **fact file**

Released: 1977
Directed by: Jeannot Szwarc
Starring: Roy Scheider, Lorraine Gary, Murray Hamilton
Creature: Great white shark
Effects: Animatronics, real-life footage
Legacy: Merchandise of all kinds; sequels *Jaws 3-D* (1983) *Jaws: The Revenge* (1987); and arguably one of the greatest taglines ever used: '*Just when you thought it was safe to go back in the water...*'

While *Jaws 2* was considered a moderate hit, it did affect the influx of monster movies of all kinds trying to replicate the success of *Jaws* – and there were many! Even aside from the unashamed copycats featuring sharks just as mechanical and unsuccessful as the Bruces, but without the stellar acting and team to carry it, most still featured a wilfully ignorant council or other authority figure, or even a more sinister cover-up like the one in *Piranha*. Most either showed the monster as little as possible but without the subplots or compelling characters of *Jaws* or relied on jump scares and showing the monster consistently without much consideration to plot, characters or pacing.

Eventually, the market grew saturated and it was time for another monster trend to take over for a while. After Ridley Scott's multi-award-winning *Alien* (1979) was released, space became the newer, more popular setting for monster movie and directors had a new source of inspiration.

Away from horror, a different genre brought sea monsters back to the screen in a movie with a story that appealed to both adults and children, with a team made up of proven stars. Special effects megastar Ray Harryhausen's last film proved that stop-motion animation was still an effective strategy in the monster world; it was time to unleash the Kraken.

Clash of the Titans (1981)

Greek myths have featured deep water monsters for centuries; sirens, Scylla, Typhon, the whale-like Cetus ... even the sea god Poseidon has been known to behave monstrously. The film *Clash of the Titans* is a loose retelling of the myth of the Greek hero Perseus, who had many adventures, including rescuing the princess Andromeda from a sea monster. *Clash of the Titans* treated its monsters as named and known characters, just as the original Greek myths did. The monsters here are more than just animal predators, they're intelligent and aware, and all the more frightening for it.

Ancient Greek mythology resembles a modern-day soap opera, with each character embroiled in intrigue, exploits and complex relationships with many others. The movie simplified many of these interwoven tales of gods, mortals and monsters in order to tell the story more neatly, without leaving loose ends: The princess Andromeda of Joppa is betrothed to Calibos, the cruel and rebellious son of the sea nymph, Thetis. When Calibos is cursed and deformed by Zeus (king of the gods) for destroying most of his flying horses, Andromeda's mother, Queen Cassiopeia, looks for alternative husbands for her. Unfortunately, the vengeful Thetis has decided that if her son cannot marry Andromeda, no man will. She curses Andromeda, forcing her to ask her suitors a seemingly impossible riddle. If the suitor can answer it then he can marry her, but if he cannot then he will be executed. Andromeda is both beautiful and a princess, so the curse is not as off-putting as Thetis and Calibos might have hoped for and our hero Perseus solves the riddle, but his problems are just beginning. At the wedding, Cassiopeia's boasting offends Thetis, who takes revenge by demanding that Andromeda be sacrificed to the Kraken. It is up to Perseus to save both the princess and the city of Joppa.

'Charmingly archaic'

Respected special effects creator Ray Harryhausen was a co-producer and MGM Studios allowed budget increases in order to hire bigger name stars. Fans of the epic tale loved the nostalgic 'swords, sandals and sorcery' tale while those that did not enjoy the film saw it as a dusty relic. This became the last feature film to showcase Harryhausen's stop-motion animation work, though he was nominated for a Saturn Award for Best Special Effects.

As a new age of computer-assisted effects was on the horizon with movies like *Star Wars: Return of the Jedi* (1983) showcasing the newest technology available, Harryhausen's work has been described in the Rotten Tomatoes consensus as 'charmingly archaic'. While some film fans have found the once cutting-edge effects outdated, Harryhausen has been respectfully described by other fans and magazine articles as 'the real Titan'.

The Kraken

Originally described as an enormous sea monster with many horns or arms and distinctly different from a sea serpent, the Kraken was first mentioned in a travelogue by the adventuring priest and travel writer, Francesco Negri, in 1700. Then, in 1734, explorer and missionary Hans Egede contributed a detailed description of his own, comparing the creature to the Icelandic sea monster *hafgufa*. Egede claimed that the creature was as tall and bulky as the ship, with a snout, paws, a spout like a whale and a lower body like a sea serpent. Egede may not have been familiar with the creatures of the sea but it is agreed that he must have seen something interesting, based on his observant reputation. Egede has been described as 'a truthful, pious, and single-minded man, possessing considerable powers of observation, and a genuine love of natural history; his statements are modest, accurate, and free from exaggeration' (Oudemans, 1892, p.113).

In 1753, Norwegian bishop, Pontoppidan, updated the descriptions given by Negri and Egede, becoming the first person to describe the Kraken as an octopus, though he did not necessarily recognise his own description, suggesting an enormous crab or starfish could also be the Kraken's true species. Around that time there were studies investigating the possibility of giant octopuses existing and based on Pontoppidan's description, the Kraken was usually thought to be a giant octopus or squid, and the image of monstrous tentacles rising out of the water and wrapping themselves around ships was firmly cemented into the public imagination. In the movies of the 1910s and 1920s, the Kraken was portrayed as a real-life octopus, and filmed in a bathtub interacting with a toy ship. *Clash of the Titans* was the first movie that portrayed the Kraken as something completely different.

Ancient tales of Andromeda's rescue from sacrifice portray the monster as a different character: the sea monster Cetus. In Greek art, ceti are depicted as serpentine fish. While most tales and illustrations show Cetus to be a sea serpent, the name we give to whales, dolphins and porpoises – cetaceans – still come from this character! Harryhausen replaced Cetus with the Kraken and discussed his creation at length in an interview for *ASC Magazine*. The design was his own but he combined various sea monster legends and artistic license, giving the Kraken disconcertingly human elements, like arms. This humanity made the Kraken more of a character as opposed to just an animal. He explained that he felt giving it four arms rather than eight would add to its grotesque appearance, joking that the number was definitely not due to the same budget problems he had suffered from when working on *It Came from Beneath the Sea*, in which a six-armed octopus attacked the Golden Gate Bridge! Harryhausen's Kraken also has a human-like torso, a monstrous head slightly resembling *Creature from the Black Lagoon's* Gill-man and a long tail with fishlike scales and fins.

This design didn't make its official film debut until 1981 but the image had been very much on Harryhausen's mind. He sketched it for the *Imagination!* comic book cover in 1938 and contributed an evolved version for the cover of *Voice of the Imagi-Nation* in 1942. Nearly twenty years later, a real-life sculpted stop-motion version emerged in the 1957 movie *20 Million Miles to Earth*. Clearly, he had quite an attachment to this particular creature design and just like many artists who experiment with reusing an idea, he wasn't done with it until he was officially 'done with it'! The Kraken was released for the final, painted, perfected, technicolour time in *Clash of the Titans*.

Despite the scenes involving the snake-haired, death-staring Medusa generally being considered the best parts of the movie, many of the movie posters featured the Kraken instead. Sea monsters just have that extra allure!

Clash of the Titans fact file

Released: 1981
Directed by: Desmond Davis
Starring: Harry Hamlin, Laurence Olivier, Judi Bowker, Maggie Smith, Burgess Meredith, Ursula Andress
Creature: Kraken
Effects: Stop-motion animation
Legacy: A four-issue comic book miniseries named *Wrath of the Titans* (2007) continued the story five years after the events of the movie in a partial tribute to the work of Ray Harryhausen. Remake *Clash of the Titans* (2010) and its sequel *Wrath of the Titans* (2012)

The early 1980s are widely considered to be the golden age of practical effects and even in the 2020s, many filmmakers have been returning to practical effects techniques as they tend to withstand the test of time better than pure CGI which quickly looks dated. Still, for every director that stuck to practical effects, e.g. John Carpenter's *The Thing* (1982), others looked for the cutting edge of computer technology, e.g. *TRON* (1982), the first live-action film to extensively use 3D and CGI (before refusing an Academy Award nomination as the public felt the computer technology was 'cheating'). With so many new and exciting developments in the world of special effects, directors and designers alike were finding their own styles and trademarks ... and creating some truly terrible flops too, many of which have been given their spotlight either in incredulous YouTube reviews or by becoming cult hits; a respectable alternative achievement for many monster movies.

The audience watching *The Loch Ness Horror* (1981) could have been excused for thinking the film was a deliberate spoof, using a puppet head for the creature and setting it in Scotland while shooting it in California (which has a very different landscape!), but they may have had higher hopes for *Jaws 3-D* (1983), the sequel that should have been a spoof.

Jaws 3-D (1983)

A baby great white shark infiltrates an aquarium theme park and appears to be killing the employees. The park's lead marine biologist, Kay, and her boyfriend, Mike Brody (chief Brody's son, played by Dennis Quaid who admits to being high on cocaine in every single scene) realise that the baby must have been followed in by its gigantic mother, who is still loose in the park. With the help of two performing dolphins, they save the aquarium and save the day.

It had been pitched as a spoof by its very own producers, David Brown and Richard Zanuck, who had also produced the first two movies. The planned title, *Jaws 3, People 0* had even been publicised, with film critic, Gene Siskel, praising the producers for not taking themselves too seriously. But it appeared that the studio was having precisely none of this and put forth ideas of their own which the writing team despised and occasionally very reluctantly agreed to, such as including Brody's son as a main character. As for Brody himself, Roy Scheider ran from the project as fast as he could, signing up for action film *Blue Thunder* (1983) immediately to ensure that he was unavailable to reprise his role.

Even now, the 3D element has never quite taken off in cinema. Occasional 3D screenings are sometimes offered for mega action or superhero movies but the trend still appears to come and go. Of all the film genres though, creature features with their jump scares and predatory monsters appear to be the obvious choice for using this effect and at the time the third instalment in the *Jaws* series was being filmed, there was a revival of interest in 3D.

This was Joe Alves's directorial debut and, thinking that this renewed interest would get his movie extra attention, he took great measures to ensure that it was shot and shown in cinemas to the best of 3D quality of the time. The franchise name and 3D treatment certainly attracted audiences with some cinemas reportedly making more money per screen from *Jaws 3-D* than from the latest *Star Wars* movie *Return of the Jedi* (1983), but the film was considered a failure in comparison to the groundbreaking original and competent first sequel. The plot was described as cheesy, the 3D approach as gimmicky and the dolphins as irritating characters better suited to a children's film than a blood-soaked shark horror. It also contained what is now widely considered one of the worst special effects scenes of all time: the 'glass smash' in which the shark breaks through a glass wall into the underwater control room. It barely moves a muscle except for a very slow opening of its mouth, is clearly outlined against the background, was lit completely differently to the rest of the set, advances painfully slowly and stops when it is supposed to hit the glass, as the actors in the room all react in slow motion and very, *very* dramatically.

The good news for *Jaws 3-D* is that it was nominated for five awards. The bad news is that all five were The Golden Raspberry Awards, also known as the Razzies. This parody of the Academy Awards nominates the worst movies made each year and *Jaws 3-D* was nominated in the categories for Worst Picture, Worst Supporting Actor, Worst Director, Worst Screenplay, and Worst New Star (a joint nomination shared between the 'shrieking dolphins' Cindy and Sandy). It did not win any of these awards. On the other hand, a Golden Raspberry special award for Worst Career Achievement was given to 'Bruce, the Rubber Shark from *Jaws*' in 1987.

Jaws 3-D fact file

Released: 1983
Directed by: Joe Alves
Starring: Dennis Quaid, Bess Armstrong, Simon MacCorkindale, Louis Gossett Jr
Creature: Great white sharks
Effects: 3D, composite imaging, animatronics
Legacy: Another sequel, *Jaws: The Revenge* (1987)

Although *Jaws 3-D* performed well at the box office it is considered a flop but remains an official part of the franchise, while another box office success, *Great White, aka The Last Shark* (1981) faced a court battle regarding copyright. Unconnected to the franchise in any way, yet with a very similar plot and some scenes almost exact duplicates of ones in *Jaws*, it was pulled from screens by judge David V. Kenyon, who deemed it far too similar to the original shark horror.

There would be no standout sea monster movies for some years but the amount of middling-to-terrible creature feature films released provided fuel for witty critics and many subsequent reviews were quotable in their own right. In his book *The World's Worst Movies*, Tim Healey's review of *Piranha* sequel *Piranha 2: The Spawning* (1981) described the bloodthirsty shoal of fish as resembling 'haddock with dentures'!

CHAPTER FIVE

MAKING
MONSTERS

I n today's age of virtual reality, high-definition [HD] TV, hyper-realism, smoother-than-ever graphics, 4D cinema effects and other futuristic-sounding developments, many people from professional film critics to tech bloggers have reported feeling that audiences have become detached from movies. That monsters have been over-designed and airbrushed to the point that they have lost their realism. Some have said that audiences can no longer suspend their disbelief because unlike real-life creatures, the newer creations are so 'perfect' that they no longer seem tangible. Who would have thought that we'd have the same complaints and observations about movie monsters that we do about photoshopped supermodels in magazines! So, is there a winning formula to creating a good monster of the deep? In swamps, the ocean, lakes, shallow seas and other bodies of water, with the limitless potential for finding and creating monsters living within them, how have our most successful water monsters been brought to life? Can we bring the realism back, and will we ever be afraid again?

Models and miniatures

Building miniature sets had been a staple strategy for early visual effects artists and miniatures are still used in movies today, providing a more budget-friendly alternative to building enormous, time-consuming, and expensive full-size sets. Over time, these miniatures have become more elaborate and filmmakers often use overlaid computer effects to enhance and change them, rather than creating the entire set digitally, which may quickly start to look outdated.

As high definition has become more popular and super-fans can notice and analyse every single detail in a scene, the pressure to make sets as believable as possible even before any action takes place is immense. A miniature set still gives a tangible appearance and for scenes involving destruction of the environment or object, provides a much more easily reset alternative to blowing up multiple real-life cars, cities or planets. The *Harry Potter* film series, *Lord of the Rings* trilogy and *Titanic* (1997) have all used miniature sets.

Still, miniatures are not the solution for every movie. A static set stands out when we expect a lot of movement in a turbulent environment, for instance underwater where we notice small details that add to realism, like the movement of bubbles and plants. Making every single bubble take direction is impossible, so films like *Aquaman* (2018) that have extended underwater sequences tend to rely on creating an entire background set using CGI rather than miniatures, paying attention to the tiny micro-movements of the environment that we'll probably never fully appreciate while watching the film – but we'd notice their absence!

Puppetry and animatronics

Ray Harryhausen never hid his disdain for what he called the 'man in a suit' strategy and throughout the 1950s and 1960s, the monsters he created and animated from both his own imagination and existing stories usually looked more sophisticated than the costumes actors wore at the time. The quality of creature suits has improved dramatically since Harryhausen's work dominated the special effects world, as has puppetry in general. Some filmmakers don't even like the word anymore as no matter how technically complex, just the word 'puppet' can make many of us think of low-quality sock puppets with button eyes, marionettes on strings and B-movies in which ridiculing the terrible special effects is part of the fun. Many creators at the world-famous Jim Henson's Creature Shop have said in interviews that they struggle to consider the projects they have worked on to be mere puppets because the creations are so believable as characters that it is easy to forget that they are operated by people.

Out of the water, most of the beloved characters in *The Dark Crystal* (1982) and *Labyrinth* (1986) are technically puppets but the artists bringing them to life are credited as operators or creature performers, not puppeteers. The iconic alien in *E.T. The Extra Terrestrial* (1982) was a cross between a creature suit and an animatronic. Designed by Carlo Rambaldi, the character was played by three different actors depending on which actions were being performed, while a team of operators controlled his facial expressions. Less endearing and more terrifying, the most successful animatronics ever created are probably those made for *Jurassic Park* (1993) which have stood the test of time and are still effective at impressing audiences of all ages today.

The production of *Jaws* highlighted many of the problems with using animatronics in the water but years later the makers of the 1999 science fiction shark horror *Deep Blue Sea* would try using shark animatronics with new and improved technology. Director, Renny Harlin, felt that since the release of *Jaws* and its copycats, the expectations of audiences had changed; they wanted to see the monsters and be impressed! Instead of taking the minimal approach used in low budget films, Harlin specifically wanted realistic, high-quality sharks that could be seen and shown off. The answer was a mixture of CGI and very convincing animatronics. By today's standards, the CGI used in *Deep Blue Sea* appears outdated, even cartoonish according to critic Roger Ebert, but its animatronic sharks remain eerily realistic. There had been significant progress in the field, with many creations becoming fine-tuned machines that could move in the same way a real animal would. By the time *Deep Blue Sea* was filmed the technology had advanced so much that shark effects supervisor, Walt Conti, and his team were able to build sophisticated robots even capable of swimming.

In order to replicate the way sharks move, the special effects team spent eight months working on the animatronics and in particular the unusual way sharks' jaws are constructed. Conti explained in the films production notes: 'Sharks' jaws actually float in their skulls, giving them a specific kind of motion. As far as I know, we're the first animatronics team to totally mimic the multifaceted jaw of the shark'. The team used technology more commonly used in aeroplanes in order to build four and a half sharks, some of them remote controlled swimming units with over 1,000 horsepower engines, weighing over 3,600kg and capable of reaching speeds of 30 miles per hour. In a later interview, actor Stellan Skarsgård admitted to being fooled for a minute, thinking one was a real shark.

The world of models and animatronics has moved on so far that even horror prop stores can now sell machines more realistic looking than poor Bruce for around $2,000. Still, while the movie industry may sometimes be able to spend hundreds of thousands of dollars on state-of-the-art animatronics, not all filmmakers choose to, and there are so many other options available.

Stop-motion animation

The jerky micro-movements of creatures like spiders have unsettled many people for centuries and stop-motion animation can resemble this way of moving. When it comes to horror, disconcerting creepiness is often the goal. Modern audiences may consider the work of Ray Harryhausen to be outdated but many reviews even by modern writers still list the emergence of his *Clash of the Titans* stop-motion Kraken as extremely disconcerting.

Outside of the 'so bad it's good' genre, bad visual effects can break a film but when an old approach is used precisely for its power to give us the creeps, directors can get terrifying results. Stop-motion animation is still used today, it has just been updated.

Guillermo del Toro pushed the boundaries of stop-motion animation for his recent film *Pinocchio* (2022) featuring the sea monster Monstro from the original story, which has been described as a dogfish, a whale and other more fantastical creatures depending on the writer or director bringing the story to life. Del Toro's monster is credited as a dogfish but resembles a mixture of creatures, with the general shape of a whale, rows of teeth found in a shark's mouth and a blowhole that resembles a long spout rather than anything found on a whale or other cetacean. He has said in interviews that he has always seen *Pinocchio* as a horror story and this appears to be an opinion shared by many. Even the 1940 Disney adaptation features several scenes which still disturb modern audiences; for once, overshadowing the sea monster! (Usually, a sea monster will steal the show no matter how small its role is!)

Still, with stop-motion movements being so jerky in general, this is not a visual effects style that naturally represents the fluidity, flexibility and effortless speed of many creatures of the deep. While stop-motion animation has its place in horror, that place is not necessarily in the water.

Compositing and green screen

This strategy can be seen in some of the first feature length films and has evolved into today's much more sophisticated visual effects. The world of CGI and advanced compositing is now a very technical process with terms like 'rotoscoping' and 'chroma keying' appearing in film credits and visual artist portfolios, but technology is moving at such a fast pace that we can now create many of these effects at a basic level using social media and phone filters.

Green screen:
Also known as a chroma key, a green screen (and blue screen) works by providing a colour that does not appear anywhere else in the frame, allowing it to be digitally replaced with a different setting or image. Using green screen technology, entire backgrounds can be replaced, or smaller details adjusted. Charlize Theron wore a green glove to play the character Furiosa in *Mad Max: Fury Road* (2015), whose arm had been amputated and replaced with a mechanical prosthetic. The team then digitally removed the part of her arm covered by the glove, leaving the prosthetic in place. The distinctive bright green is usually used as it is absent from human skin tones.

Rotoscoping:
This is a technique that began in animation. Animators would project video clips onto a glass panel and trace over them by hand, frame-by-frame, which took a very long time! It is still used today but mostly done using computers. For example, visual effects artists working on *Guardians of the Galaxy* (2014) photographed and drew a real raccoon in order to create the basic designs for the character Rocket, who resembles an anthropomorphic raccoon.

In early film, characters were 'placed' into background sets and in the most technologically advanced of these, these characters could interact with objects, as in *Godzilla*. Now, big-budget filmmakers regularly use compositing and green screen technology in partnership with other effects, and though we usually think of movies like *The Avengers* (2012) and *The Hobbit* trilogy which use compositing to place their characters in front of digitally added backgrounds, the process can be done in reverse, putting animated or computer-generated characters in a real-life setting. *Who Framed Roger Rabbit* (1988) is probably the most easily identifiable example of this being done but the *Game of Thrones* TV series, *Harry Potter* film series and many other movies have done the same thing. Shark survival movie *The Shallows* (2016) did both, filming lead actress Blake Lively in a tank, then digitally inserting both the background and the shark.

Very simple compositing is often the domain of the B-movie which may not have the budget to create advanced animatronics but instead will add a digital monster into a real set. Filmmakers pursuing a 'so bad it's funny' review often make no attempt to make the creature look as though it belongs there. Compositing alone can, in the B-movie world, lead to hype, interest and a 'you won't believe they went there' factor.

From the Depths (2020)

Shark attack survivor Liz suffers from both survivor's guilt and hallucinations. Ever since she survived the shark attack that killed both her sister and her boyfriend, she has been plagued by visions of the shark responsible in the most unlikely of places.

Using the *Jaws 2*-inspired tagline 'just when you thought it was safe to stay home', in a move that appears to be a feature length film first, the movie *From the Depths* (not to be confused with sea monster movie *Up From the Depths* (1979)) uses compositing to place a computer-generated shark into a setting most would think would be safe: a person's home. It's a fascinating premise and *From the Depths* has all the things we expect from a creature horror movie: jump scares, gory moments, red herrings and even an unexpected twist ending. This is not a movie that performed well with critics, attracting some generally terrible reviews online but the success of *From the Depths* may depend on how seriously the viewer takes it. Liz's hallucinations can occur at any time in any place, meaning no body of water is safe; swimming pools, puddles, even an innocent glass of drinking water! Her hallway isn't a shark-free zone either; she hallucinates the shark swimming down it at one point in the movie. One ten-out-of-ten review listed on the Internet Movie Database [IMDB] claims that the acting, plot and special effects were terrible, but the film was hilarious as a result. Another reviewer praises how 'unintentionally funny' *From the Depths* was ... but was the comedy really unintentional? Considering it was written and directed by Jose Montesinos, co-director of the very self-aware B-movie horror *5-Headed Shark Attack* (2017), this seems doubtful!

Possibly unintentional comedy and what has been described as 'Halloween zombie makeup' aside, *From the Depths* is unpredictable, ambitious and there is a central same-sex relationship between two main characters which is shown to be happy and supportive. This may not be a movie first but in the creature feature horror genre it is still currently a rarity.

From the Depths was shot in just seven days with a budget of $30,000 and the brief 'make a shark movie'.

From the Depths fact file

Released: 2020
Directed by: Jose Montesinos
Starring: Angelica Briones, Terra Strong, Marissa Godinez, Liz Fenning, Taylor Jorgensen
Creature: Shark
Effects: CGI
Legacy: None... yet

Computer Generated Imagery

This is a very, very broad term and entire books can (and have) been written just on the use, history and development of CGI. The first full-length entirely CGI movie was *Toy Story* (1995), a Pixar film about the secret lives of the toys in a child's room. The groundbreaking technology was the shiny new plaything for filmmakers and animators and they rushed to copy the 'new look for animation'. Now many of those scenes look stiff and texture-less.

CGI is used to create and add textures to objects and characters, age or de-age actors, capture motion in order to use an actor's movements and expressions as the basis for a character design (*Lord of the Rings* produced one of the most impressive examples with actor Andy Serkis playing the character Gollum), create entire characters and much more. In fact, it is very difficult to find a deep water monster movie that does not use CGI in some way.

James Cameron's *Avatar* (2009) was the first film to gross two billion dollars at the box office. It was at the cutting-edge of CGI technology, featuring almost all possible uses and applications for CGI in film making and while the story has been criticised many times for being derivative and for its outdated character stereotypes, the visuals were almost universally praised.

Now, with the release of the sequel *Avatar: The Way of Water* (2022), the franchise is again showing innovative use of CGI; this time blending underwater filming with performance capture technology, a feat that had not been accomplished before. It took the visual effects team a year and a half to develop new technology in order to achieve the effects they wanted and many of the actors involved learned to free dive for their roles, including Kate Winslet, who reportedly held her breath for over seven minutes underwater!

Reviews have again been mixed, but almost all have overwhelmingly praised the visuals as well as the new enormous underwater creatures that at first glance resemble a whale, a plesiosaur and a gharial crossed with a dragonfly.

Of course, not all CGI is created equally...

Outdated or badly rendered CGI can look so unsettling that it becomes off-putting to an audience. The film *The Polar Express* (2004) was shot using computer animation effects that were considered the pinnacle of CGI achievement at the time. Now, the expressions on the characters faces are described as disconcertingly blank, glazed, and lifeless, producing the phenomenon known as the 'uncanny valley' effect. This is a term coined to describe the revulsion people can feel when shown something that appears very humanlike but is not human (e.g. a doll or robot). Beginning from a basic robot shape, tests have shown that the more humanlike this robot is made to appear and behave, the more appealing it seems to an audience ... until suddenly it isn't, it's the opposite! There is a cut-off point at which the robot becomes realistic but not *quite* human and the effect is perceived to be creepy and disturbing. This point is known as the uncanny valley. Most of the time, the uncanny valley effect is something filmmakers want to avoid, especially when the goal is to create a charming family movie, but horror movies have often embraced it!

The love affair between B-movies and bad CGI is a long-established relationship and the most successful ones in the genre have a self-awareness that ensures the audience is laughing with the creators rather than at them (or even a bit of both)! In 2019, Matthew Ellsworth, Jason Ellsworth and Matteo Molinari (collectively known as MaJaMa) wrote, starred in and released a film called *Bad CGI Sharks*, which parodies the shark horror genre and especially the terrible CGI often used. [You can read more about this in Chapter Ten]

Found footage

This is a filming approach which usually comes with an effective marketing campaign and clickbait which can last for years. For example, 'The last horrendous moments of his life were captured on the one thing he left behind: his camera'. Leaving a video behind is the modern-day equivalent of the classic 'message in a bottle'.

The found footage subgenre has historically been sparing with its use of CGI as it was originally a clever solution to a lack of budget or filmmaking technology, allowing new filmmakers to be inventive with the tools at their disposal. In a found footage movie, the majority of the runtime appears to have been filmed by the actors themselves in a home video, independent documentary or phone camera format. Even people with nothing but a phone and an idea can make a movie in this style. *The Blair Witch Project* (1999) began a trend for the found footage concept and by the time rampaging monster horror *Cloverfield* (2008) came along, the budget 'home movie' technique was combined with CGI effects, making the format a director's choice rather than a clever solution to a budget problem. Many water monster films have contained a found footage element using dive cameras and characters who are never far from their phones, though while this plays a significant role in *The Shallows*, the videotaped parts do not make up the entirety of the movie.

Casting unknown actors in a film with a found footage element helps to suspend the audience's disbelief, but the movie needs to be plausible for the majority of the runtime. The actors were listed as missing at the end of the *Blair Witch Project* and the cast of the cult horror *Cannibal Holocaust* (1980) had to make public appearances to prove that they were still alive, adding to the movie's hype and attracting curious audiences. There is a time and a place for a 'real-life found footage' marketing campaign. *Frankenfish* (2004), for example, is not it.

Real-life footage

We're back to the movie equivalent of those glossy magazine pages and the controversial dialogue around 'retouching'. How much is too much? Film students, makers and reviewers are often quick to discuss 'the death of' a particular visual effects technique as new technology takes its place, but is that always a bad thing? It matters when the everyday images that we are told should look just like us look nothing like us, but when the subject is a gargantuan tentacled toothy monster rising from a swamp to devour unfortunate boaters, does it matter whether it was made in a computer or not? Cameras and diving techniques have improved over time but one favourite filming technique that has, with the exception of welfare improvements, not changed much is using footage of real animals.

Black Water (2007) is an Australian creature survival horror based on the real story of two young quad bikers who had to spend a freezing night huddled in a swaying tree while the enormous saltwater crocodile that killed their friend waited below. More action scenes were added for the movie and the protagonists were changed from friends to a woman with her husband and sister, but the team filmed saltwater crocodiles in the wild and inserted the footage into the movie for added realism.

As the producers of *Jaws* were quickly told, sharks cannot be trained ... but they make great footage anyway! *The Reef* (2011) is based on the true story of sole survivor, Ray Boundy, and it is believed to be the first Australian-made shark movie. Writer, director and producer Andrew Traucki (who also made *Black Water*) commented on the fact that 'sharks' is a very popular Google search term within Australia, then wondered why the formidable natural wildlife of Australia had not been shown off more. *The Reef* was filmed using real footage of great white sharks.

The story covers a group of friends whose boat capsizes. They decide to try and swim for a nearby island but are attacked by a great white shark who keeps returning. The possibility of sharks is on their minds from the beginning and at first making the choice between staying with the boat or swimming for the island is already tense and unsettling for the characters, and for the audience to watch. For the people who decided to swim, small waves start to look like fins and the water is not clear enough for a good view in any direction. As one character keeps putting goggles on and checking the water beneath, we are all waiting for a jump scare that never comes. Instead, the dim shadow of a shark comes into view. It is footage of a real shark, several metres away and doing nothing except being a shark ... and when you're adrift or abandoned in the ocean, that is a scary enough idea. There is no ominous dorsal fin or snap of threatening jaws when it first appears; it swims, turns a little, and disappears into the blue, leaving the group hysterical and the viewer on edge. In that situation, stranded and treading water in the open ocean, that would be a more common sight than the ones often depicted in 'shark attack' films, and while the attack eventually comes, *The Reef* is all the more frightening for the uncertainty.

The movie *Open Water* (2003) is also based on true events and takes the same approach, favouring realism over exaggerated jump scares. It is filmed on a hand-held camera, though not by the two main actors. Interestingly, despite the heavy use of sharks to provide the scares, some of the film posters rely on the vast size of the ocean to show the couple's predicament rather than the sharks that take one of them. It is the water in many shades of blue and ominously dark underneath the couple that is used to trigger our primal responses and fear of deep bodies of water rather than our fear of sharks. In *Open Water*, just as in *The Reef*, the producers wanted it to feel real. While there are movies with bigger spectacles, more gore and more dramatic jump scares, the strategy of using real footage of the 'monsters' helps to evoke a specific fear; the knowledge that the events have really happened, and there's a chance that they could happen to you. (Though in reality, we do not actually know what happened to the couple that the events in *Open Water* are based on; See Chapter Six for more about this real-life horror story.)

Absolutely nothing

Based on the 1996 book by Alex Garland, *The Beach* (2000) features one of the most disturbing shark attack related scenes of all time, but it is technically not a shark movie! It is not even a deep water monster film; *The Beach* is a drama, thriller and study into human behaviour, but there are two scenes involving sharks and one is blood curdling. This may be the first film since *Jaws* to combine gore with an effective minimalist approach to the 'monster' and do it well.

Richard (played by Leonardo DiCaprio) is given secret directions to a hidden beach paradise and decides to visit and join the community there. He and his two companions are reluctantly but quickly absorbed into beach life … but there's a sinister side to the community.

In the first shark-related scene, Richard is telling the group a tall story in which he fights and kills a shark. Richard is an unreliable narrator here and we cannot be certain whether his version of events actually happened or not, but he describes it as a big fish and its final death scene is played for comedy. The next scene involving a shark is gory, unexpected and in direct contrast to the scene in which he tells his funny story.

Amid a furious Gameboy gaming session (in which the game he is playing looks very like Godzilla), Richard hears screaming from outside his hut. A man is staggering out of the sea toward the beach, carrying another man over his shoulder and dragging a third. They are screaming about a shark. There's blood in the water. Lots. Both injured men are laid on the beach as an attempt to help them is made. Some of the community argue while others watch helplessly. There is no adequate medical treatment on the island. One man is missing a bite-shaped chunk from his leg and has also been bitten on his side. The second man has been bitten on the leg. The camera shows the gore in great detail. Blood and viscera are pouring out of the deep gouges. The first man dies within minutes, while the other man dies slowly, alone but for Richard, who is in shock and has lost his bravado, joy and confidence altogether. The bloody aftermath, the fear and the pain are played very, very seriously. Unlike monster movies in which the attack is used to make the audience jump before an inevitable moment of bloody water and a missing limb, after which the plot needs to move on quickly, this scene is memorable and horrific … and at no point do we ever see the shark.

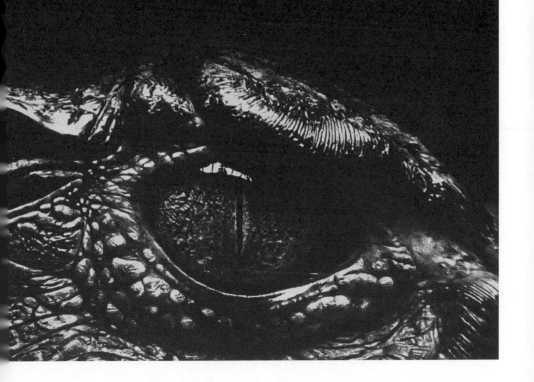

A HUGE **CROCODILE**   BETTY **WHITE**   CHAPTER **SIX**   SAMUEL L. **JACKSON**   CLEVER **SHARKS**

THE
GAMECHANGERS

EVERYONE HAS A PLAN UNTIL THEY GET BIT

Horror and comedy have had a seemingly unlikely partnership for years; many of us use black comedy and gallows humour to cope with bad sights and experiences, and horror-comedy movies have existed since the 1920s. The first well-known and commercially successful horror-comedy film was *Abbot and Costello Meet Frankenstein* (1948), in which the famous comedians play dim-witted porters who find that both Frankenstein's Monster and Dracula have arrived from Europe, and now their brains are in danger. The two would continue to star in other similar films, meeting a variety of recognisable monsters. Most of the early horror-comedies have been confined to the land or at least the swamp, where filming is easier and creating a creature can be done with makeup and next to no budget. When things just didn't look scary enough for a potential monster movie's audience, increasing the silliness and rebranding it as a comedy was the next best strategy. The first horror-comedy to feature a deep water monster was *Creature from the Haunted Sea* (1961) in a *Creature from the Black Lagoon* parody involving a monster suit made from two tennis balls, a wetsuit, Brillo pads and a lot of moss.

Imaginary creature based horror-comedies from the 1980s like *Gremlins* (1984) and *Critters* (1986) enjoyed success and later became cult movies, though they were generally less popular than the movies in which the creatures were able to communicate clearly with people, like vampires, werewolves and 1970s crossdressing aliens from Transylvania.

Still, by the end of the 1990s, goofball horror-comedies shone in the cinema. While increasingly ridiculous features involving monsters of the deep would later become as interchangeable as the *Jaws* copycats of the 1970s, the legacy of the horror-comedy gave the deep water monster genre a shake-up. Filmmakers were now pursuing the accolade of 'enjoyable horror' and with a raging moral panic about gory 'video nasties', the public attitude towards gore appeared to change. Crowds either wanted films to evoke genuine terror and carry an 18 certificate (or R-rated in the US) or be funny, mostly bloodless and aimed at teenagers on dates.

In the world of the deep water monster, after a parade of blood-splattered sequels, even cult ones like *Piranha II: The Spawning* (1982), samey thrillers like *Leviathan* (1989) and transparent attempts to promote a theme park ride but earning a resulting zero per cent review on Rotten Tomatoes, like *Jaws: The Revenge* (1987), the late 1990s brought creativity to the theme. Here was a genre full of material to spoof and creatures to demonise or invent and in 1999 two cult water monster movies came along in the same month!

The first contained something dangerous that was not to be messed with; a formidable creature hiding in plain sight in an unlikely and picturesque location: Betty White. There was also a crocodile.

Lake Placid (1999)

A fish and game officer is carrying out research in the murky water of a beauty spot known locally as Lake Placid, when he is bitten in half by an unseen creature. New York City based palaeontologist, Kelly, is sent to get to the bottom of the mysterious death but gets off to a bad start, having a personality clash with the local officials. When Kelly's crocodile-worshipping oddball colleague arrives with an insane sounding theory, the local team cannot understand how a person could possibly believe a crocodile is living in the lake, but could he be right? (Spoiler: he's right.)

So far, so cliché – and virtually every expected creature horror trope is hit; the gory initial death, the jump scare with body parts appearing, the disbelieving locals ... but what made *Lake Placid* into a cult film was its humour and, since *Jurassic Park* upped the game in the world of scaly beast creation, the excellent animatronics. Most of the characters are quite unlikeable, their methods unorthodox and their one-liners perfectly timed, whether it's a ridiculous line delivered with all the gravity of a eulogy or one of Betty White's devastating takedowns.

The crocodile

Visual effects creator, Stan Winston, started working on the crocodile before the film had even been given the go-ahead. The problem was it had been turned down by multiple studios. Fortunately for the production team, it was this animatronic crocodile that impressed investors, who then agreed to invest in *Lake Placid*. The working crocodile not only looked realistic but its jaws could open and close, its eyes could move and it could shake its head as though it was attacking something.

Its 'big reveal' in the movie came in comedic fashion; the team hear something and realise they're being stalked. As we prepare for the crocodile to emerge from an unexpected angle in a predictable jump scare, instead an enormous brown bear comes bolting out of the wood ... and is immediately taken down by the crocodile.

The largest crocodile recorded in captivity only measured 6 metres but this one measured over 9 metres, had a moving head, tail and jaws, would function underwater and was made by the Stan Winston Studio – the same team behind many of the *Jurassic Park* dinosaurs as well as the monsters in *Alien*. They began by making mock-ups; carefully painted and a fifth of the size the full crocodile would be, before making a full-sized version out of foam. Hydraulics were created in order to make the crocodile move in the ways required, then set in waterproof housings and inserted into the crocodiles, which were coated in waterproofed skins, then finally painted.

In an attempt to avoid the crocodile being another broken Bruce, the team dropped it in a lake to test it. Mechanical designer, Richard Landon, who stated his motto when it comes to animatronics and water is 'Water Always Wins' headed the mechanical crocodile design team and explained 'Its head left/right and tail left/right functionalities were enough to make it propel itself through the water'. When it needed to be shown moving fast, the crocodile was pulled by boat.

By the end of the movie, its penultimate gag is the existence of tiny baby crocodiles, implying that the lake's troubles are only just beginning. As the budget was running out, director, Steve Miner, explained that he and Stan Winston had a disagreement over how best to create the miniature crocodiles. Winston wanted the challenge of building tiny animatronics, while Miner wanted to try filming the scene with borrowed baby caimans. The caimans arrived and the scene was completed in one take. (The final gag involves a motorway, a police escort and a very large trailer.)

Reception

Lake Placid got very mixed reviews, even from respected critics. Roger Ebert's one-star review criticised the film's multi-faceted approach which included horror, comedy, sarcasm, unlikely friendship, gore and more, claimed it was wrong the entire way through and described the crocodile as looking like it has been bought from the factory that makes Barney toys. Ouch! On the other hand, Andrew Collins from *Empire* magazine noted that *Lake Placid* spent four weeks in the USA 'Top 20 Movies' list, praised the witty scriptwriting talents of David E. Kelley and described the animatronic crocodile as 'magnificent'.

It became a cult hit and the presence of Betty White certainly helped it claim its place as one, as well as dial up the camp and sarcasm ready for its inevitable sequels, though Betty did not appear in these.

Lake Placid fact file

Released: 1999
Directed by: Steve Miner
Starring: Bill Pullman, Bridget Fonda, Oliver Platt, Brendan Gleeson, Betty White
Creature: Crocodile
Effects: Animatronics, real creatures
Legacy: *Lake Placid 2* (2007); *Lake Placid 3* (2010); *Lake Placid: The Final Chapter* (2012); *Lake Placid vs Anaconda* (2015); *Lake Placid: Legacy* (2018)

The other deep water monster feature that came out within two weeks of *Lake Placid* also has its funny moments, but unlike the former, the horror wins over the comedy. Just. The science in the late nineties hailed sharks as virtually immortal; ageless, constantly healthy creatures that if studied in the right way could have a significant benefit to humankind. Although *Lake Placid* has its much smaller nature-related subplots, this movie began with a larger message and more than a few commentaries on messing with nature for human gain; a common theme for many creature features but this one was rooted in the 'facts' of the time.

Deep Blue Sea (1999)

Under the tagline 'Bigger, Faster, Smarter, Meaner', *Deep Blue Sea* promised to deliver more than *Jaws* on all four counts, without mentioning the movie at all; a running joke used by the marketing team.

In an isolated and sinister marine laboratory, we are introduced to the movie's protagonists – misguided scientists searching for a cure for Alzheimer's Disease, and antagonists – the disgruntled genetically engineered mako sharks used in the laboratory. In order to extract protein from their cortexes for use in the treatment of Alzheimer's Disease, the scientists justified increasing the size of the lab sharks' brains which would increase the supply of protein but came with a side effect: higher intelligence. When the hyper-intelligent sharks go on a rampage in the flooded facility, a fight to not only escape but outwit them ensues.

The unexpected

In 1960, Alfred Hitchcock's film *Psycho* did the unthinkable, killing its protagonist less than halfway into the runtime. It was a gutsy move (pun intended). From then, the audience did not know what to expect next. Anything could happen! However, once done, such a move loses its shock factor and can't be replicated ... can it? It appears that it can if filmmakers wait for around twenty years. *Alien* (1979) killed its most recognisable actor in its infamous 'chest bursting' scene and after nearly two decades of 'killer shark' films featuring largely interchangeable plots, characters and sharks, director Renny Harlin was inspired by the approach in *Alien* and would use the same strategy.

Around halfway into the movie and in the middle of a rousing speech at the point of extreme danger, Samuel L. Jackson – the most famous actor in the cast – is bitten in a jump scare which, even now, places in lists comprising the most shocking movie deaths of all time. According to VFX supervisor, Jeff Okun, Jackson ranked the *Deep Blue Sea* shark interruption as his favourite of his own movie deaths.

Inside jokes

Deep Blue Sea is very self-aware. Harlin wanted to make a serious horror movie but knew that any shark film would be compared to *Jaws* so rather than actively trying to avoid similarities, he placed in deliberate differences, like the choice to use the speedier mako sharks rather than great whites (shortfin mako sharks can travel at 32 kilometres per hour and jump around 9 metres) and tributes like pulling a number plate from inside a tiger shark, the same one used in a similar scene in *Jaws*.

Harlin goes further still, adding what could be considered in-jokes or friendly teases toward *Jaws* and its creators. Bruce measured 7.6 metres, so Harlin commissioned animatronics measuring 7.9 metres, taking things just a little further. Even Samuel L. Jackson's infamously unfinished speech is similar in tone to Quint's account of the USS *Indianapolis*, before its gory (and, on later viewings, rather comedic) end.

It seems that Harlin did not achieve his aim. While he aspired to a create a horror movie attracting the same critical acclaim level as *The Exorcist* (1973), the test audiences did not react as expected. There were as many laughs as screams and they detested the original ending in which a character they saw as a villain survived against the odds. The ending was hastily reshot. While *Deep*

Blue Sea has not claimed a place among timeless horror classics like *The Omen* (1976) and *Psycho* (1960), it achieved cult success and is still considered one of the better shark films precisely because it is not true horror. The campy and tongue-in-cheek nature of *Deep Blue Sea* not only made the film memorable but sparked a new wave of creativity in the way writers and directors approached the shark movie. Amid this unsuccessful attempt to join the ranks of respected horrors, *Deep Blue Sea* became the shark film that changed the game.

The winner of the 'second best shark film of all time' place is still undecided, but articles in *Cultured Vultures* and *Den of Geek* and many *Ranker* listicles give *Deep Blue Sea* the highest honour a shark film made after *Jaws* was released could achieve: second place.

Is it true? The science in *Deep Blue Sea*

The premise explored in *Deep Blue Sea* was loosely based on the opinions held at the time. Sharks were thought to be incapable of suffering from cancer, never-aging and ever-moving with no need for sleep.

While sharks are fascinating and mysterious creatures which have existed for over 400 million years, none of the above is true. Sharks can get illnesses, including cancer. Great white sharks have been found with tumours and in early 2022 a dead Greenland shark was washed up on a UK beach and found to have meningitis – a world first! Sharks may not need to sleep in the way familiar to humans and most mammals but they do need periods of rest. Some sharks need to move constantly for water to flow past their gills, others have spiracles that force water over their gills allowing them to remain still when resting.

In *Deep Blue Sea*, the mako sharks also develop the ability to swim backwards, which is impossible. In fact, sharks are thought to be the only fish that cannot swim backwards.

Deep Blue Sea fact file

Released: 1999
Directed by: Renny Harlin
Starring: Saffron Burrows, Thomas Jane, LL Cool J, Jacqueline McKenzie, Michael Rapaport, Stellan Skarsgård, Samuel L. Jackson
Creature: Mako shark (genetically altered)
Effects: Animatronic, real footage, CGI
Legacy: Two sequels, *Deep Blue Sea 2* (2018); *Deep Blue Sea 3* (2020)

It was around this time that American studios started working on various remakes of *Godzilla*. While Godzilla's origins are in the sea where he tends to sleep, and it is impossible to write a book about sea monsters without mentioning the enormous influence the king of the monsters had on the genre, most of the action in later *Godzilla* movies takes place on land so this book will not be following them as closely as movies in which more of the action takes place in the water.

With realistic or even semi-realistic effects now being readily achievable for most filmmakers, the love of genetically engineered monsters and enormous creatures, occasionally with some plot thrown in for fun, was at an all-time high. Many directors had been filling every other minute of their movies with action as though in fear that the audience would walk out unless the dramatic attacks and the gore kept coming. The high-tech animatronics, jump scares, grisly spectacles and constant action had become the expected norm in the creature horror genre. Between the years 2000 and 2005, there were over twenty-eight monster themed movies released and later, seven crocodilian themed movies would be released in the year 2007 alone! Even the world of the 'mockbuster' (budget B-movie remakes of well-known features) would get some attention and 'so bad it's good' appeal, like *Mega Piranha* (2009). While the horror-comedy genre had entered into the mainstream world by casting accomplished actors and being self-aware to the point of self-parody, ensuring audiences laughed with the makers rather than at them, and another kind of deep water monster film was emerging – one which would veer away from the cinema silliness and into the horrific.

People have been stranded in deep water in a variety of circumstances since time began and it was only a matter of time before the creature horror and the survival film were merged. Survival films have always been a respected genre, with the visuals approached in many different ways from the realism of *Castaway* (2000) to the fantastical *The Life of Pi* (2012). Amid the usual noise and spectacle offered by creature horror, the movies that began to come out were the cinematic equivalent of negative space; using the environment to tell the story instead of elaborate special effects. At once featureless and ever-changing, being trapped in the sea and unsure of what to do for the best is a terrifying situation for anyone involved, but when we are reminded of the unseen predators beneath that could take a limb off with a single exploratory bite, the tension becomes nearly too much to bear. The sea survival (or non-survival) movies to emerge were less violent but more frightening than the horror-comedy cinema summer blockbusters. These were movies to watch from the safety of your home, in the knowledge that your footing is secure beneath you while the characters are waiting for the sea surface to break. And if the film could boast the line 'based on true events' before the title appeared, even better!

Open Water (2003)

Based on true events...

A couple are on a scuba diving holiday together and as the members of their group dive return to the boat, there is a mix-up with the head count resulting in the two of them being counted as present on the boat when in fact they are still under the water. The boat leaves without them and the two find themselves abandoned in the ocean with nothing but each other and nobody realising that they are missing. At first, they believe that the boat will soon return to collect them but as time goes on, they begin to realise that they really are all alone.

It sounds like the plot for a horror movie in its own right; two people being made helpless through another person's incompetence, but surely nobody could make *that* grave an error? Surely by the end of the day or when the next scuba diving group board the boat for their turn, somebody will realise the mistake and the couple will be found and saved at the last minute? *Open Water* is not that kind of a movie. As the couple's relationship begins to fray under the strain of their predicament, the sharks come to investigate.

Director Chris Kentis's aim was to show sharks authentic behaviour, instead of the monstrous murder machines depicted in most horror or thriller films. Besides, the real-life situation the movie was inspired by is frightening enough.

What really happened?

Thomas and Eileen Lonergan are an American couple who disappeared in January 1998 on a scuba diving trip in Australia's Coral Sea. At the end of the dive there was a mistake with the head count and they were thought to be back on the boat when they were actually still in the water. They were not discovered missing until two days later when a bag with their belongings inside was found on the boat. An enormous search was mounted and they are presumed dead but their bodies have never been found.

While there have been theories that this couple committed suicide or faked their own deaths, this was deemed highly unlikely as their bank accounts were left untouched and pieces of their dive equipment washed up on shore, including a message with a plea for help written on a dive slate. Based on the state of the dive jackets recovered, experts believe the couple succumbed to dehydration and exhaustion rather than an animal attack but the exact cause of their deaths is still unknown.

Filming

Open Water was filmed using a handheld digital camera to give the visuals a realistic, voyeuristic and disturbing effect. Around 120 hours of footage was filmed, with the two lead actors, Blanchard Ryan and Daniel Travis, spending much longer in the water between takes. Sharks were tempted towards the camera with chunks of tuna and in order to give them protection against bites, both actors wore chain mail under their wetsuits (which didn't stop Blanchard Ryan from being bitten by a barracuda on the first day of filming – though a minor injury and both Ryan and Travis getting stung by jellyfish).

Blanchard Ryan discussed the misconceptions around shark behaviour in an interview with *blackfilm.com*, saying that the team tried to portray them in a more realistic way, that sharks don't immediately rush up to tear you apart when you enter the water. 'That's just not how it happens', Ryan said. She stated that while she was aware that people would call *Open Water* a 'shark movie' because there are sharks in it, she did not believe that label was accurate, saying that sharks were fascinating creatures in her opinion; 'They're not out to eat people'.

The actors spent just two days filming with the sharks, which cost around half of the film's $120,000 budget due to the hiring of experienced professionals including shark wrangler Stuart Cove, in order to ensure the safety of the team involved.

Open Water **fact file**

Released: 2003
Directed by: Chris Kentis
Starring: Blanchard Ryan, Daniel Travis
Creature: Caribbean reef sharks
Effects: Real-life footage.
Legacy: Two films, following the same basic premise but with different characters and unrelated to the original. *Open Water 2: Adrift* (2006); *Open Water: Cage Dive* (2017).

Amid the reused and recycled monster movie formulas being shown around the same time, *Open Water* was a very frightening and intriguing change which earned positive reviews almost across the board.

Any new trend tends to start with one standout movie which influences directors, sparking copycats and similar movies before the market is oversaturated and the new ideas begin to go in a completely new direction. This new, realistic, and minimalistic direction worked well for horror, reminding directors that there is an entire ocean, sea, murky river or deep lake to take ideas from: the realm of the 'based on a true story' story.

These words, appearing onscreen at the beginning of a film are always designed to chill, but 'based on' can be a loose term. As in, any looser and it would drop off, and no matter what dramatic liberties directors take in order to change the pace of a true story for a cinema audience or exaggerate it for dramatic effect, the public can tend to forget that a 'based on' credential is not generally the same as a faithful retelling. Still, there are more than enough real-life horrifying encounters with monsters of the deep to provide material for movies for years, even decades, to come.

Did You Know?
Three of the seven crocodile movies made in 2007 were based on real events!

Rogue was based on a real 5-metre-long crocodile famed for being cantankerous enough to attack boats and dinghies, but unlike in the movie, this crocodile never claimed the life of a person. His name was Sweetheart and he was captured alive but then drowned after becoming tangled with a log in transit. His mounted body is on display in The Museum and Art Gallery of the Northern Territory in a Darwin suburb. *Rogue* was a critical hit with a cast that included Radha Mitchell and Sam Worthington but did not do as well as expected in the box office.

Another crocodile-related 'based on a true story' movie is *Black Water*, mentioned previously in Chapter Five. The events that led to people being trapped up a tree while an enormous saltwater crocodile waits underneath has been reported on many times due to the unusual circumstances and survival terror factor, so the fact that only one film adaptation has been made from the story is surprising.

Primeval was very loosely based on the identity of a scarred man-eating Nile crocodile named Gustave who lived in Burundi and there is more information about this movie in Chapter Seven.

The 'based on a true story' concept can be disturbing for reasons other than the creature itself. *The Host* (2006) was inspired by a true event and features a nameless amphibious creature, first seen in the Han River but then emerging from the water to hunt and chase the protagonists through sewers while they hide in drainage systems to escape. *The Host* is one of those rare films that has been inspired by many others but is not a direct copy and created with enough design, imagination and skill that it becomes a success on its own; in this case becoming the highest grossing South Korean movie of all time.

The Host (2006)

After an American military pathologist orders his Korean assistant to dump a significant quantity of formaldehyde down a drain leading into the Han River, the fish in the river die off and mysterious sightings of a strange creature in the water begin. When the creature emerges and kidnaps a man's daughter, her attempts to escape and his attempts to rescue her with the help or hindrance of the people he meets along the way form the plot for the movie.

Godzilla, the city-destroying monster out of water climbed buildings and terrorised Tokyo. Here, the creature was given no name though director Bong Joon-ho said in an interview that he had considered giving it a name because we name other natural disasters like storms and hurricanes. The monster is smaller than people expect when watching *The Host* for the first time. Not being a fan of long suspenseful scenes with an unsatisfying pay-off when the monster is revealed, Bong Joon-ho deliberately steered away from film cliché in which the monster is hidden for most of the movie. In *The Host*, it is seen early on and visible in bright daylight for long stretches of time- quite an unusual move.

Just as many monster films involve incompetent governments or conspiracies, *The Host* is no exception, but there's a very interesting added layer here, taking into account both the complicated political history of South Korea and the filmmakers choice to parody its government, as well as making the event the fault of less-than-moral actions of the American military, who are usually cast as heroes in monster movies.

'Based on a true story'

Yes, really! In the year 2000, a Korean mortician came forward to give his account of an event in which the American military in Seoul ordered him to dump a large quantity of formaldehyde down the drain. (For reference, the correct way to dispose of formaldehyde is to contact your local hazardous waste disposal company for them to collect and recycle it safely.) The completion of this act takes place in the movie's first scene and later the chemical used to combat the monster is named 'agent yellow' in reference to 'agent orange', the dangerous chemical compound used as a weapon by US forces in the Vietnam war.

Throughout the film, the US military is portrayed as mechanically emotionless while the South Korean government are satirized, appearing incompetent and uncaring. *The Host* was described as 'monstrous political satire' in *Hollywood Gothique* magazine while Bong Joon-ho made the point that a large part of his movie is satire – not just the government scenes – and denies that the film is anti-American, but freely admits the use of reference, remarking on the tendency of American films to villainize other countries and governments. North Korean authorities were rumoured to have loved the movie, which is unusual – or possibly understandable – given the reported tension between North and South Korea.

Despite the potential controversy over its 'message' and depiction of the American military, *The Host* was a critical and public success, winning numerous awards in South Korea and further abroad, and appearing on many top ten and significant film lists, even notably praised by Quentin Tarantino.

The creature

An article by David Ehrlich in *Indiewire* magazine describes *The Host* as 'The Defining Monster Movie of the 21st Century'.

Bong Joon-ho took inspiration from stories he had read about a deformed S-shaped fish caught in the Han River. As his creature was intended to be the result of extreme pollution, he wanted it to have a mutated 'not quite right' look. It has front limbs like those of an amphibian, while other smaller limbs dangle uselessly and its fishlike fin looks ragged. It is only about the size of a truck. The modelling was done by New Zealand-based Weta Workshop (known for its work on the *Lord of the Rings* trilogy). While deliberately choosing to show the creature vividly and for long periods of time, Bong Joon-ho felt that an audience's imagination often fails when a creature's face is seen, and so he made the decision not to show its face clearly and to go against the usual approaches used in films when revealing a monster, like hiding it in shadows, revealing it for seconds at a time or having it only hunt at night. This approach was praised by critics and the audience and there is now a statue of the creature on the bank of the Han River, though it has reportedly been unpopular with members of the public!

The Host fact file

Released: 2006
Directed by: Bong Joon-ho
Starring: Song Kang-ho, Byun Hee-bong, Park Hae-il, Bae Doona, Go Ah-sung, Oh Dal-su
Creature: Mutated amphibian
Effects: CGI
Legacy: A promised sequel, remake and videogame, though none have appeared yet … and a statue, which has.

Part of *The Host*'s appeal is the fact that it does not base its premise on over-dramatising or editing the real event that inspired the movie but continues the timeline in a 'what if' manner. Even its obvious influences are tributed rather than outright copied and *The Host* remains one of the more intriguing water monster movies out there.

While few trends ever truly disappear or go out of fashion – after all, the creature feature genre is probably home to more B-movies and cult hits than any other film genre except perhaps for horror in general – the fact remains that every trend moves on at some point, making room for the next.

The trend for 'based on a true story' movies, shot with minimal camera trickery and favouring real-life footage over computer generated monsters appeared to die down shortly after the release of *The Reef.* This time when the 'next big thing' in monster movies emerged, it took an unexpected, almost indescribably ridiculous turn.

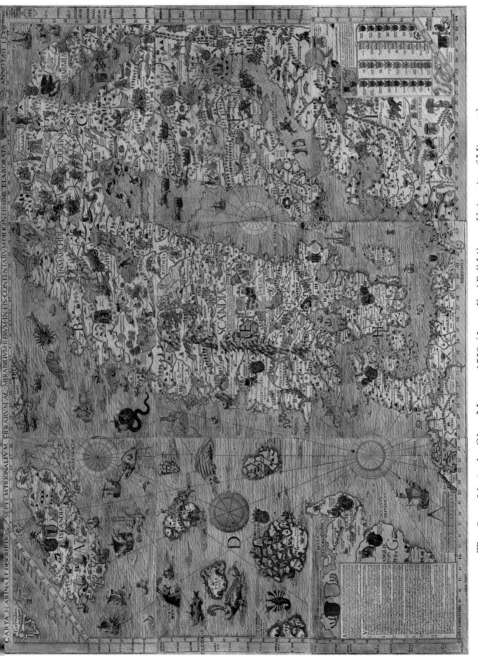

The *Carta Marina* by Olaus Magnus. 1539. *(James Ford Bell Library, University of Minnesota)*

Sculpture: *A Sea Monster*, second quarter 16th century. Artist unknown, created in the workshop of Severo da Ravenna. (*Samuel H. Kress Collection, courtesy National Gallery of Art, Washington*)

Etching: *Hippolytus and the Sea Monster*, published 1676. Artist: Jean Lepautre. (*Courtesy National Gallery of Art, Washington*)

Watercolour and gouache: *Plate 2: Sperm Whale, Sturgeon, Shark, and Other Fish*, late 1500s. Artist: Joris Hoefnagel. (*Gift of Mrs. Lessing J. Rosenwald, courtesy National Gallery of Art, Washington*)

Watercolour and gouache: *Plate 9: A Great White(?) Shark, Two Seals, and Two Fish*, late 1500s. Artist: Joris Hoefnagel. (*Gift of Mrs. Lessing J. Rosenwald, courtesy National Gallery of Art, Washington*)

Creature from the Black Lagoon poster recreation. (*Image: © Willrow Hood; Adobe Stock*)

Godzilla statue displayed in Tokyo. (*Photo: © vacant; Adobe Stock*)

Mysteries of the Nautilus attraction at Disneyland Paris (Les Mystères du Nautilus). (Photo: © Acento Creativo; Adobe Stock)

Oil painting: *Watson and the Shark*, by John Singleton Copley, 1778. (*Ferdinand Lammot Belin Fund, courtesy National Gallery of Art, Washington*)

The formidable jaws of a great white shark. (*Photo: © Pieter De Pauw; Adobe Stock*)

A thalassophobia-inducing sight! (the fear of deep bodies of water). (*Photo: © Oliver Sjöström; Pexels*)

"*The Kraken, as seen by the eye of imagination.*" (*Illustration from John Gibson's* Monsters of the Sea, *1887, made by Edward Etherington*)

Movement capture and a green screen. (*Photo: © Gorodenkoff; Adobe Stock*)

Green screen and stop-motion animation. (*Photo: © Iryna Imago; Shutterstock*)

A more realistic and less aggressive view of a great white shark. (*Photo: © wildestanimal; Adobe Stock*)

CGI octopus robot monster. (*Photo: © Bisams; Shutterstock*)

Crocodilians regularly star in deep water monster movies. (*Photo: © pongpol; Adobe Stock*)

The formidable leopard seal has only appeared as a danger in kids films … so far. (*Photo: © Stanislav; Adobe Stock*)

The sea otter is probably the least likely creature to star in a monster movie! (*Photo: © Vladimir Wrangel, Adobe Stock*)

The octopus has changed its image recently with the help of award-winning documentaries. (*Photo: © Henner Damke; Shutterstock*)

Bronze statue displayed in Copenhagen: *The Little Mermaid* (*Den Lille Havfrue*) by Edvard Eriksen. (*Photo: © C1 Superstar; Pexels*)

Bad CGI sea monsters – so bad they're good? (*Image: © MR1805; Canva*)

The modern shark, created with a computer. (*Image:* © *virtosmedia; 123RF.com*)

H.P. Lovecraft's creation Cthulhu; the next big star of the water monster movie? (*Photo:* © *ArtBank64; Shutterstock*)

A version of Cthulhu created using CGI. (*Image: © Warpaint; Shutterstock*)

Chapter Seven

Real entertainment or real ethics? It's time to find out...

THE TRUTH IS
DOWN THERE

The sea has washed up bizarre things for people to examine and debate ever since water creatures and humans have shared the planet. Most unidentified carcasses have been historically recorded as 'monsters' or 'beasts', until British biologist Ivan T. Sanderson referred to them as 'globsters' in 1962 and the name stuck. Many of these have since been identified as rotting whale carcasses.

The 1990s science fiction TV series *The X-Files* claimed that the truth was out there and at the time the show aired it was said that we knew more about space than we did about the sea. After the technology boom of the late 1990s, we've been able to explore more of the deep water world than ever before. With our growing awareness of the dangers our changing climate poses to the natural world and our interest in many of the at risk or badly represented species out there, the way we approach monster horror has changed.

Just as there are people who can write a story, invent a monster, and direct a film, there are people who can show us the truth that really is out there; creating groundbreaking documentaries like the *Planet Earth* series. Now, we're listening....

When things went wrong:

A hunter on the deck of a ship, ready for an oncoming sea creature – a harpoon in his steady hand. The crew look at him with respect for his poise, his fearlessness, and his dedication to the crew's goal: kill the creature. Once it is dead, everyone can get a good look before the carcass might be sold to a travelling show as an exhibit, or if it is too large for any travelling fair, be measured and documented before being thrown back. The hunter might take a part of it to wear; perhaps a tooth that he can wave around in taverns and get a few free drinks in exchange for his story.

When tales of the deep water and its resident monsters were gaining traction, making their way around the world from the decks of ships, this man would have been the hero of the story. He was one of the daring 'gentleman explorers' who set out to conquer the world by disposing of and displaying its creatures, unravelling its mysteries by dredging the water and seeing what came up in their nets, and by assigning unpleasant personalities to the creatures they pursued in order to get their rapt audience on their side.

There were people who held unusual or unpopular points of view for the time, especially the idea that killing animals for display purposes was wrong and that animals in their habitats would behave like people rightfully protecting their home and therefore shouldn't be demonized for doing so, but these viewpoints were in the minority for many years. One of the earliest voices raised in defence and understanding of animal behaviour was the much respected Saint Francis of Assisi (born 1181 or 1192) who according to legend persuaded a village to regularly feed a wolf rather than killing it for preying on people and livestock out of necessity and was later named patron saint of animals and ecology.

Concerns over the sustainability of forests and teak in particular were raised in the early 1800s, with conservation programmes being implemented in India; the first ever case of state management of forests. Air pollution had long been recognised with the London Clean Air Act being introduced in 1956 to present the thick London 'pea soup fogs' often mentioned in Victorian novels and *Sherlock Holmes* stories. For many years though, the idea that human activity could damage the environment on a larger scale was considered impossible and while campaigns to keep local rivers free from pollution were underway, marine conservation was not given global recognition until 1970. Entering a new age of ocean discovery, both explorers and scientists were recognising the diversity and importance of species in the ocean, while computer technology was used to aid these investigations into life under the sea.

Still, the sense of connection we have to specific creatures in the sea was being developed and sea monster movies were portraying many creatures as dangerous, mindless adversaries. The *Jaws* Effect of 1975 is still being undone today and in the 1970s, action and monster movie heroes followed a particular character type. Director William Grefé had an idea for a film that told an unconventional story involving sharks, but as the film's underlying message showed an unpopular viewpoint, he could not get his idea funded until after *Jaws* was released and the promise of splashing shark attacks proved an audience-grabber. The following story of possible psychic powers and unlikely heroes is one of film's clearest examples of the right idea being executed in the wrong way!

Mako: The Jaws of Death (1976)

After being given a medallion by a Filipino shaman, Sonny Stein discovers that he has a connection with mako sharks (the same species used in the film *Deep Blue Sea*). He is protected from them while swimming among them as a marine salvager and over time he in turn becomes their protector, setting out on a revenge mission against anyone seeking to harm them, as well as other particularly unpleasant human beings. The movie casts Sonny as the joint hero alongside the sharks, while most other human characters were shown to be the villains.

Many reviews claim that over time Sonny develops the ability to telepathically communicate with the sharks, but this is never clearly shown or spelled out in the movie.

This 'sharks as victims' role reversal plot was the exact opposite to the stories told in all the other similar films of the time. Following one of the most influential horror movies ever made, a director choosing to tell a story that went entirely against the public mindset was a move nobody could have predicted. The controversy alone was virtually guaranteed to sell tickets! Showing a shark acting harmlessly onscreen was one thing but portraying them as the real victims had never been done before outside of educational documentaries.

The idea of a sympathetic shark movie was fascinating and an idea well ahead of its time, but was *Mako: The Jaws of Death* really that sympathetic? The poster art featured either a hand waving desperately above the water or a person looking terrified, along with a gigantic shark, mouth gaping open, teeth fully on display. This could have been the poster for any number of monster movies but certainly not a movie aiming to show the shark as a victim of human brutality rather than the other way around. Instead of a witty comment or note about the film's unusual alternative viewpoint, the tagline told the audience that the movie was made without the protective measures that most movies with sea animals would be and promised 'SHEER TERROR'. This sounded like a rather snide dig at the more safety-conscious makers of other shark movies and still didn't do much to promote *Mako: The Jaws of Death* as a story about a heroic man acting in defence of animals.

The actors and cameramen worked without adequate protection and the production team appeared to have no concern for the safety of the sharks either; in fact, as it was not the most successful or critically acclaimed film, the sharks that died in its making probably outnumber the ones that the movie might have managed to save. There are a *lot* of dead sharks, specifically killed for the making of this movie. We see many killed onscreen, seemingly no regard for the welfare of either living sharks or crew and while the characters thrown to their deaths were indeed considerably vile, the ending was not a positive one, the protagonist was portrayed as crazy and in fact nobody came across particularly well to the audience.

The absence of mako sharks is a small detail in the grand scheme of things, but while the word 'mako' is right there in the title *Mako: Jaws of Death* (also not particularly trust-inspiring) most of the sharks in the footage captured are either the mostly harmless nurse sharks, or tiger sharks, one of the deadliest species in the world!

Filming

Considering the age of the movie (and lack of health and safety measures back then) this film truly does have audiences gritting their teeth. The sharks are real, the film was shot without using anything resembling stock footage, the lack of cast and crew protection was used as a selling point and this meant people were in the water with sharks, many of which were either sedated or dead. The first few seconds of the film show a special note from producers thanking the underwater crew for 'risking their lives'. This is not an exaggeration.

Hypocrisy

While in some ways, *Mako: The Jaws of Death* was ahead of its time in offering audiences a new perspective – giving sharks a protector while highlighting the brutality inflicted upon them – in others it reflected the same mindset sparked by the release of *Jaws*: that hunting sharks is a good thing.

In one scene, the lead character furiously and violently reacts to the sight of dead sharks being butchered, but they wouldn't be dead at all had they not been caught and killed for use in that particular scene! In another scene the plot called for a woman to be attacked so rather than having a shark attack her in real life (it seems there *was* a line the filmmakers wouldn't cross), the decision was made to use a dead one while the crew stood just off-camera and waved it around her, simulating a vicious attack. In order to procure the shark, the production team took one from the water and beached it, leaving it to die before taking its teeth out for use as souvenirs. When they put the 'dead' and toothless shark into the water tank, it immediately revived and latched onto the actress's leg!

It's hard to believe that a point could be made so badly or that such an apparently well-intentioned idea could have been executed in this way. An equivalent would be to make a movie about the dangers of drunk driving ... by putting drunk people in cars and filming the resulting crash.

Mako: The Jaws of Death **fact file**

Released: 1976
Directed by: William Grefé
Starring: Richard Jaeckel, Jennifer Bishop, Buffy Dee, Harold Sakata
Creature: Miscellaneous sharks
Effects: Real-life footage
Legacy: None, just an example to learn from.

A story of conservation and revenge with footage of shark diving and a 'protector' character would probably be received quite well by today's audiences but repeating the way *Mako: The Jaws of Death* was filmed would be unthinkable. As our knowledge of shark behaviour has increased, we understand that they tend to be given an unfair portrayal in creature features, known as 'sharksploitation'. Repeatedly casting them as villains to overcome, or even vengeful and persistent monsters to eventually be killed in a 'me or it' scenario, is a trope that occurs in virtually every fictional shark movie in existence. This may be why the realistic way sharks have been portrayed in films like *Open Water* was so lauded.

Basing the more realistic movies on true stories makes it less easy to claim the animal involved has been exploited, but sometimes artistic license is nowhere near as compelling as the true story.

A Nile crocodile named Gustave was said to be responsible for the deaths of over 300 people from the banks of Africa's Ruzizi River and Lake Tanganyika. He was about 60 years old, measured about 6 metres long and was still growing; people could only estimate his size and age as there had been no successful attempt to capture him. He was, understandably, a greatly feared local legend.

Just like a tough character from a children's movie, Gustave had scars; three from bullets and another deep scar on his shoulder from an unidentified source. None of his scars had ever been explained; it is unknown how he got these injuries but it is thought that they made him slower, which is why he had to choose slower prey: humans.

A documentary named *Capturing the Killer Croc* was filmed in 2004 and followed an attempt to capture Gustave and relocate him to a safer place for both him and the people living in his neighbourhood. Multiple different kinds of traps were set, but none captured Gustave.

It is rumoured that he had been killed in 2019 but so far, no evidence has been brought forward.

In 2007, the 'year of the crocodilian' in which seven films starring killer crocodilians were released, Gustave became a film star ... sort of. Originally named *Gustave* but later retitled *Primeval*, the movie's tagline appears designed to mislead; referring to Gustave as 'the most prolific serial killer in history'. As the story is about a team of American journalists who plan to capture Gustave and film him, presumably without harming him, describing the animal as a serial killer seems an odd move.

Burundi has a complex political history and combining a gory crocodile movie with the heavy-handed political commentary included in *Primeval* drew a lot of understandable criticism. The movie was critically panned and described as a *Blood Diamond* (2006) rip off. Its outdated racial stereotypes of the 1980s and 1990s were unpopular and it drew scathing criticism from naturalist and Gustave expert, Patrice Faye, who contributed his opinion for an article in *National Geographic Adventure* magazine, describing the movie as an insult to Burundi, portraying its people as 'savages, barbarians, thieves and murderers'.

In the fifteen years since *Primeval* was released, while there's still work that needs doing on the representation and characterisation of not only people but countries and cultures too, we are growing to understand the importance of seeing a wide range of characters from different backgrounds on our screens. That a Native American character can be a geeky geologist rather than an old mystic with an ominous warning. That casting Black actors to play characters who are no more than wisecracking cannon fodder does a disservice to literally millions of people. That women's roles should have more versatility than those of 'femme fatale' or 'damsel in distress'. In the hands of a knowledgeable director and diverse cast, perhaps one day justice could at last be done to Gustave's impressive story.

Are *we* the bad guys?

Virtually every time a new monster movie based on a real-life creature is released, multiple articles, listicles telling people where to find more of the same, think pieces and educational features are published in response. Many people still like the thrill of a scary movie but at the same time are very much aware that they tend to be less than factual and that humans are increasingly likely to be cast as the villains of the story.

In many deep water monster movies from around the 1990s onwards, we humans are uncomfortably held accountable! We're investigating nuclear power and awakening hibernating kaiju, we're playing with dangerous chemicals and causing mutations, we're fishing too much and drawing sharks in, we're experimenting with biology and genetics that we do not understand and are surprised when it all goes wrong, or we are entering another animal's territory and then condemning it for defending its home.

Unlike our hunter with his harpoon and trophy monster tooth, most of us are now willing to admit that sometimes nature fights back and that blaming the creature of the moment for acting like itself isn't the best strategy. Now, rather than a simple quest to kill, most deep water creature features are a tale of survival; the plot either boils down to a 'last man standing' situation and the human character does not always win, or the creature is never found or harmed, like in many of the more recent shark movies. It's a start....

Watching the seas...

Even since the 1950s when oceanographer, inventor and filmmaker, Jacques Cousteau, made some of the first ever underwater documentaries using technology he co-invented, and Sir David Attenborough starred in a show called *Zoo Quest* (the first major programme to feature the narrator), a steady demand for wildlife documentaries grew. However, they didn't generally have the riveting 'did you see it' factor that got people talking about them the next day at work.

For years, documentaries had not enjoyed the trendiest of reputations. Based on viewing statistics, they were popular but often associated with middle age than with fashionable young people and their families, but by the 1990s as filming technology improved and production companies responded to the increasing demand, kids' TV shows like The *Really Wild Show* became popular. Vibrant personalities like Steve Irwin and Michaela Strachan presented nature in a less scholarly and more accessible way, fictional kids' movies starring sea creatures from orcas to mermaids showed an ocean full of life, and suddenly every pre-teen wanted to be a marine biologist.

The Blue Planet (2001)

The DVD cover describes it as 'the first ever comprehensive series on the natural history of the world's oceans'. There were already long running television series based around natural history but this miniseries spent eight episodes focusing on marine life, filming species and behaviour that had never been captured on camera before. Funny colour-changing walruses, spawning coral filmed in minute detail, a pod of orcas problem-solving together, the newly discovered and cute 'dumbo octopus', deep sea life as alien seeming as, well, aliens. Finally, people were talking about episodes the next day, while families were making time to sit down and watch together. Even today, YouTubers and writers publish compilations and listicles featuring the best moments from *The Blue Planet* series.

Filming

The series took over five years to make, visiting over 200 filming locations and using the best technology available to capture footage. Blue whales were given radio tags and then tracked by air so the crew could follow their migration route. The crew followed particular species in the hope that they would lead them to others, a strategy that usually worked, and a submersible (the same one that was used to explore the wreck of the RMS *Titanic*) was sent over a mile down into the San Diego Trench to film the feeding behaviour of deep sea creatures. Some of the behaviours captured by the team were not only new to the viewers; they were new to science!

The series was narrated by Sir David Attenborough who by this time was the most well-known and widely trusted voice in natural history.

'The natural order of things'

The Blue Planet didn't shy away from the more brutal aspects of life in the water. Orcas were filmed separating a whale calf from its mother before killing it, sardines are shown being herded into panicking masses and eaten by a variety of predators, a leopard seal kills an emperor penguin, turning the water red as its flippers stick out of the water, and the award winning first and second episodes film the slow decay of a huge grey whale carcass which came to rest on the ocean floor and over the next year and a half feeds strange creatures never seen before.

The inclusion of sights like this is often controversial and debated. How much violence will make an audience change the channel? When does a show aimed at families become 'too much'? Attenborough has addressed this dilemma in interviews, saying that documentaries risk becoming fairytales if too much of the reality is removed and sanitised, and that producers cut out far, far worse scenes than the ones they include.

Real life or real ethics?

At what point must 'real footage' be sacrificed in order to prioritise welfare? If realistic animal behaviour is captured in an artificial environment, is it still realistic behaviour? There isn't always an easy answer to questions like this, and *The Blue Planet* team were criticised for filming lobsters in aquariums rather than in the wild. Series producer, Alastair Fothergill, said publicly that around two per cent of the series has been filmed in aquarium tanks. He argued that to capture the same behaviour in the wild would disturb the lobsters and that the ethical way to depict it was by filming the lobsters exhibiting the exact same behaviour in Anglesey Sea Zoo in Wales.

Awards

Despite controversy over the lobster filming strategy, *The Blue Planet* won two Emmy Awards and three BAFTA Awards and was nominated for seven other awards. It is still considered one of the most influential nature documentary series of all time.

The Blue Planet fact file

Released: 2001
Produced by: Alastair Fothergill
Narrated by: Sir David Attenborough
Creature: Many!
Effects: Real-life footage
Legacy: *Deep Blue* – a theatrical version of *The Blue Planet* (2003); concert tour – *The Blue Planet Live* (2006); *Blue Planet II* (2017)

The television series *Walking with Dinosaurs* combined the style of a wildlife documentary with technology used in high budget movies, recreating dinosaurs using both CGI and animatronics made by Crawley Creatures, then depicting them as living animals as though in a documentary series. It was one of the most expensive television projects ever to be made, costing over £37,000 per minute! *Walking with Dinosaurs* was the first in a new genre of documentaries in which extinct animals were brought back to life, or alien creatures were invented, as in Netflix's *Alien Worlds* (2020). Sea monsters had been created with animatronics and CGI for years but the sequel to *Walking with Dinosaurs* would be the first time that it was done for the purpose of a factual big-budget documentary. This would be *Sea Monsters: A Walking with Dinosaurs trilogy*.

Aired in 2003, 'time travelling zoologist' Nigel Marven visits the shallow seas and oceans in different time periods, sometimes appearing to be swimming with the more harmless prehistoric creatures, while in a shark cage for his protection from others (like the megalodon). Armed with a cattle prod just in case any of the creatures get too close for comfort, Nigel finds enormous sea scorpions (which puncture his dinghy), fends off an ichthyosaur and visits Hell's Aquarium (aka the Cretaceous Sea), thought to be the deadliest sea of all time due to the abundance and variety of predators in the water.

Reviews were polarising; people tended to either love the fun, adventurous approach which placed a human alongside prehistoric animals for a size reference the audience could relate to, or they found it patronising and over dramatic to have a presenter onscreen acting as though the extinct creatures were really beside him. Others questioned the accuracy of the information as a lot of knowledge about prehistoric eras is still technically scientific guesswork. The makers of *Sea Monsters* have strongly contested this, having consulted palaeontologists, zoologists and other sources in order to keep the information as accurate as possible. Designs had even been revised on the advice of professionals. Bristol University palaeontologist and sea scorpion expert, Simon Braddy, said in an interview that he felt the design and behaviour of the creatures had been depicted as accurately as possible.

The presenting style on *Sea Monsters* may not have appealed to everybody but the show has an impressive legacy. Some palaeontologists today have credited *Sea Monsters* as their inspiration, sparking a passion that turned into a career. When researcher, Jack Cooper, published his study of the megalodon, he cited its appearance in the show as the beginning of his fascination with the creature.

The dramatic presenting style in some of the popular documentaries may not have appealed to everyone but the inclusion of a little drama is not always a bad thing. By the time the Attenborough-narrated, Fothergill-produced *Planet Earth* series aired in 2006 using the same production team as *The Blue Planet*, many documentaries had become anticipated must-see family viewing. The first episode was watched by more people than any natural history programme since *The Blue Planet*, and it would outperform it, attracting 11.4 million viewers, holding a ninety-five per cent positive score on Rotten Tomatoes.

As far as monsters of the deep go, *Planet Earth* showed 2-metre-long giant salamanders, the largest amphibians in the world; a battle of nerve between mugger crocodiles and a family of smooth-coated otters; Nile crocodiles exploding from the water to take down unwary wildebeest; an unlikely alliance between sea snakes and goatfish; great white sharks leaping fully out of the water to catch Cape fur seals; and some of the creatures living in the deepest parts of the sea, including the vampire squid.

Behind the scenes featurette *Planet Earth Diaries* showed red-bellied piranha feeding frenzies (and some impressive scars on fishermen), and the technology used by the camera crew to film great white sharks, which would make a split-second long attack last thirty seconds, allowing the audience the chance to get a good look … and goosebumps.

Did You Know?

While *Jaws* is thought to have had a devastating effect on the treatment of shark populations, it also piqued interest in the species. In 1988, in an attempt to dispel misconceptions, educate the public and undo some of the damage done, *Shark Week* was created. Now an annual occurrence, the phenomenon grew and it is now the longest running cable television programming event in history.

The rise, fall and comeback of *Shark Week*

It began with ten episodes spread out over a week and many were educational, like *Sharks: Predators or Prey*. It was wildly successful and continued with *Jaws* author, Peter Benchley himself, hosting the 1994 *Shark Week*, with famous naturalist, Nigel Marven (of *Sea Monsters*), hosting it between the years 2000-2002. This tradition of bringing on fun and knowledgeable hosts continued and over the next decade *Shark Week* would be hosted by Adam Savage and Jamie Hyneman of *Mythbusters*; Les Stroud, host of *Survivorman*; Craig Ferguson; Eli Roth; and more. By the mid-2010s though, *Shark Week* was drawing controversy.

Accidental effect on shark reputations aside, the movie *Jaws* was at least a respected piece of cinema. The copycat films that followed were sensationalist but they got viewers in seats and over time, the *Shark Week* programme took a similar approach, prioritising shock factor over education. Increasing the general population's fear of sharks was as far from the original aim of *Shark Week* as it could possibly be, and yet the event was beginning to branch out from the success of its documentaries and interviews by promoting programmes filled with pseudo-science, unproven theories and fictional shows presenting as fact.

Though *Shark Week* was losing its way, there were now several specific concentrated efforts to preserve and save the shark populations of the world from finning, hunting and other threats, with The Shark Trust being founded in 1997. People were also getting indignant, speaking up on the sharks' behalf, whether as experts or as passionate supporters. The last thing that enthusiasts wanted was another surge of ecologically unsound and sensationalist shark tourism. People were not happy, including actor and science advocate, Wil Wheaton, and with the airing of the mockumentary *Megalodon: The Monster Shark Lives* in 2013, which was a work of fiction presented as a factual documentary, they had had enough. This 'documentary' was the most watched show in *Shark Week* history but a great deal of this is thought to be curiosity due to the immense backlash it generated. Though some knew that the information could not possibly be based in fact, for others finding this out came as a shock and when it was discovered that the producers had even cast actors to pose as scientists, the audience felt cheated and ridiculed, many boycotting the network in protest. Real scientists gave their opinions freely to magazines including *Discover*, in which assistant professor at Nova Southeastern University, David Kerstetter, said that he and his colleagues were spending too much time debunking claims like the existence of mermaids and megalodons rather than educating the public with real research.

By the year 2015, new president of the Discovery Channel, Rich Ross, promised to discontinue this trend, stating that he believed it was not the right direction for the channel.

While there was still considerable controversy over a 2017 episode showing a fake swimming race between Olympic swimmer, Michael Phelps, and a computer generated great white shark swimming at the average speed for its species (Phelps was given enhanced swimming gear and lost by two seconds, for the curious), from 2015 onwards the vast majority of the shows aired over *Shark Week* have either been factual documentaries or very self-aware silliness. This included movies with titles like *Zombie Shark* (2015) and the cult phenomenon *Sharknado* (2013).

In 2018, in an attempt to regain audience trust, an updated documentary featuring real scientists returned to the world of *Megalodon: The Monster Shark Lives*, with an updated documentary: *Megalodons: The New Evidence,* which attracted similar viewing figures to the original but was considerably better received.

Shark Week still attracts the occasional controversy as advertisements for the show still rely on viral footage, misleading messages and the fear factor. In general, the audience is assumed to be in on the joke, though one year fake footage of a model shark swimming in Lake Ontario had to be refuted and clarified in the run up to the show. Even so, *Shark Week* has been a force for good on occasion; raising awareness of issues resulting in fans petitioning their lawmakers into making changes. Nine-year-old Sean Lesniak's letter to his state representative, David Nangle, resulted in a bill making the possession and sale of shark fins illegal being signed into parliament. Even scientists have not ruled out the possibility of returning to the show based on the change in direction taken by producers and program makers, which can only be a good thing. *Shark Week* 2022 was hosted by Dwayne 'The Rock' Johnson, and included specials involving All Elite Wrestling and a feature called *Stranger Sharks* which focused on some of the more unusual species out there, with Noah Schnapp of Netflix's *Stranger Things* joining an expedition.

When things go right:
The documentary *Blackfish* (2013) addressed the consequences of keeping captive orcas at Seaworld and other marine parks, and revealing what appeared to be a cover up on the part of Seaworld concerning multiple trainer deaths from orca attacks. While participants in the documentary have reportedly had mixed feelings about the final cut, *Blackfish* ensured that greater attention was paid to the possibility (and some might argue inevitability) of trauma-induced behaviour on the part of orcas, which have never been known to kill human beings in the wild but have shown extremely aggressive behaviour in captivity.

The format for both *Planet Earth* and *The Blue Planet* was incredibly successful, striking the right balance between drama and realism for most audiences. The production team returned with the similarly formatted and presented *Frozen Planet* (2011) which focused on life at the North and South poles. The seventh and final episode dealt with climate change and its effects. There was uncertainty over which television networks would choose to air this episode as it was offered as an optional part of the series. The US was not expected to air the episode as climate change is still considered a politically sensitive issue but the Discovery Channel surprisingly chose to show it in full, reaching millions more viewers.

The popularity of these documentaries can raise awareness of both well-known situations like the climate change crisis, but also of other issues that viewers may not have been aware of.

Canadian documentary *Sharkwater* (2006) featured the tagline 'the truth will surface' and exposed corruption in the shark hunting industry amid an increasing demand for shark fin soup in Asia, threatening mass shark extinction. The film received thirty-one international awards. Writer and director, Rob Stewart, was working on the Kickstarter crowdfunded sequel entitled *Sharkwater: Extinction* when he died of accidental drowning. In tribute, the Academy of Canadian Cinema and Television renamed its annual award for Best Science or Nature Documentary Program or Series 'The Rob Stewart Award', including an additional large cash bonus. Stewart's team finished the sequel and it premiered in 2018.

Planet Earth II was released in 2016. It has been described in reviews as the greatest documentary to date, won multiple TV awards and holds a one hundred per cent positive rating on Rotten Tomatoes. The next year, (after four years of filming and literally thousands of dives), *Blue Planet II* (2017) aired, achieving the highest viewing figures of any television show in the United Kingdom that year. While the best way to combat the issue of plastic in the ocean is being hotly debated (e.g. banning plastic straws and charging consumers for plastic bags versus petitioning the companies responsible for over three quarters of the ocean's plastic waste etc.), awareness of the issue as a whole was greatly increased after *Blue Planet II* aired. This was dubbed 'The *Blue Planet* Effect'.

The internet, particularly social media like TikTok and YouTube, has fed us information about everything from film analysis to indigenous traditions in bitesize chunks, promoting a wider range of voices for us to listen to. This also teaches viewers about the original names for places, animals and concepts, allowing them to choose to use these names – for instance referring to the Lake Okanagan cryptid by its indigenous name of Naitaka rather than the later-bestowed 'Ogopogo'. Moving away from former prejudices, modern viewers are seen to value a wider range of voices, perspectives and stories.

So, what do nature documentaries have to do with movie monsters of the deep?

Ignorance on the part of filmmakers and audiences can have devastating consequences for the animals portrayed in monster movie horror. The enormous popularity of documentaries like *The Blue Planet* might give us goosebumps by showing us the power of apex predators like sharks and leopard seals, but they also share the facts with us, reiterating that most of us are not in any danger. Water creatures of all kinds are fascinating and monster movies are fun to watch, but knowing the line between fact and fiction allows us to be entertained while respecting the stars of the show, giving them their space which keeps us – and them – safe.

UNLIKELY HEROES:
YOUR TIME HAS COME

CHAPTER EIGHT

Y2:KAIJU

W hile the trend for horror-comedy was still going throughout the 2000s-2010s (with a few memorable and disturbing outliers set on land, like Stephen King's psychological monster horror *The Mist* (2007), filmmakers were looking for something new – a movie that would make people talk. What they said was almost irrelevant....

Mega Shark vs Giant Octopus (2009)

Starring 1980s pop singer Debbie Gibson, the title says it all. In the same self-explanatory manner as the 2006 horror-comedy hit *Snakes on a Plane* (in which Samuel L. Jackson of the infamous shock *Deep Blue Sea* death refused to take part unless they kept the working title), *Mega Shark vs Giant Octopus* features ... a mega shark versus a giant octopus. That fact alone is generally enough to attract the interest of monster movie fans but for the less passionate, the viral trailer did the rest.

For those interested in the plot, irresponsible humans spark a chain of events which result in a giant iceberg cracking open to reveal two frozen prehistoric creatures mid-battle: a mega shark and a giant octopus. They thaw and go their separate and rampaging ways while scientists and the military argue predictably over whether to kill them or study them while musing on human nature and wondering what will happen when the ice caps eventually melt.

Realising that the creatures must be natural enemies, an oceanographer and scientist use their mutual attraction and resulting encounter in a utility closet as inspiration for a strategy (yes, really!). They decide to use pheromones to bring the shark and octopus face to face again in the hope that unlike the oceanographer and scientist, when these creatures rush toward each other they'll fight to the death.

Before the infamous *Sharknado* could run (or fly round and round in circles), other films had to walk. This is one of them.

That viral trailer

Depending on opinion, The Asylum (the film company that made *Mega Shark vs Giant Octopus*) is either a one-trick pony, excellent at churning out sillier and sillier schlock films, or a well-oiled machine of marketing genius using the most bizarre concepts to sell films on audience curiosity alone. In fact, the studio has stated before that they generally break even at around three months post-release and have never once lost money on a movie.

Making the decision to show the movie's most ridiculous scene in the trailer ensured that people would tune in out of sheer morbid curiosity. The scene? A shark leaping high enough into the air that it bites into a passenger plane!

The trailer gained over two million views between MTV.com and YouTube in the weeks leading up to the movie's release, with viewers questioning whether it was merely a publicity stunt for the MTV awards or some kind of joke, the punchline of which would eventually be revealed. It was one of the most watched trailers of 2009, counting more views than James Cameron's *Avatar*.

Who would make a film like this…
The Asylum is an American independent film company, founded in 1997 and originally specialising in low budget horror films before finding its niche in 'mockbusters'; movies that closely resemble current hits but remain on the legal side of the line between copyright infringement and artistic license … just. Many of their films are shot very quickly (*Mega Shark vs Crocosaurus* (2010) was thought to have been shot in just twelve days) and released within days of the movie that provided the original inspiration. For example, Asylum movie *Transmorphers* (2007) was released two days before big-budget movie *Transformers* (2007). Sending out films entitled *Titanic II* (2010), *Dino Croc vs Supergator* (2010) and *2-Headed Shark Attack* (2012), people know roughly what to expect from the studio: action and silliness, which could go in any direction at all.

Multiple film companies have threatened The Asylum with lawsuits over similarities between their own titles, themes and subject matter; Universal Pictures claimed copyright infringement on their film *Battleship* (2012) after The Asylum announced the title of their next film would be *American Battleship*. The Asylum renamed it *American Warships* (2012).

The makers, production studios and producer of *The Hobbit* movie trilogy went to copyright infringement war with The Asylum over their film title *Age of the Hobbits*, amid fear that The Asylum's movie (which includes an extinct species of human in battle with flesh eating dragon riders) could be confused with their own adaptation of J.R.R. Tolkien's book *The Hobbit*. Warner Bros. studio sent a 'cease and desist' letter to The Asylum, who refused to take the word 'hobbit' out of the title, citing scientific use of the term. A judge later found that The Asylum's hobbit title did violate Warner Bros.' trademark, so the film was temporarily blocked from release and its title was changed to *Lord of the Elves*, or alternatively *Clash of the Empires* (2012). This appears to be the first successful attempt to take legal action over an Asylum mockbuster.

20th Century Fox threatened legal action over the similarity of The Asylum's *The Day the Earth Stopped* (2008) to Fox's *The Day the Earth Stood Still* (2008) but the case appears to have been settled out of court.

... and who reads reviews anyway?

Unsurprisingly, *Mega Shark vs Giant Octopus* did not get good reviews, but in general B-movies, or 'Z-movies' as the Asylum's creations have been called, or indeed any movie designed to be both self-aware and bad, don't. Still, for a movie exhibiting what has been described as fairly awful acting, dreadful CGI, ludicrous science and fewer shots of the warring beasts than expected from the trailer, an eighteen per cent rating on reviewing site Rotten Tomatoes isn't actually that bad! At the time of the film's release, Debbie Gibson (credited as Deborah Gibson) was already telling interviewers that she would love the idea of a sequel.

The fans of 'bad' movies and B-movies tend to find the sheer ridiculousness a selling point; discrepancies, obvious continuity errors, budget cuts and all! As The Asylum is the undisputed king of the B-movies, they can recycle footage both used and unused across several of their films. In order to make *Mega Shark vs Giant Octopus* longer, the editors used footage of the shark attacking a submarine from the left, mirrored it and then repeated it so the shark was now attacking from the right!

Behind the scenes

Debbie Gibson talked about her experience filming *Mega Shark vs Giant Octopus* in an interview with MTV, saying that once she had read the script she was on board as it sounded too much fun to pass up, and just as she expected filming was a fun, informal whirlwind where it was impossible to take things too seriously.

Vic Chao (Doctor Seiji Shimada) posted an Ask Me Anything invitation to the forum website Reddit, giving a lot of insight. Echoing Gibson's account of her positive and slightly surreal experience, in response to a question asking how seriously the production was taken, he described witnessing an actor who hadn't learned his lines having to read them from a post-it note stuck to a wall while the camera crew focused on Chao's reaction instead! He also noted that it was extremely unusual to have an Asian character ending up 'getting the girl' in the end and yet this is what happened, possibly for the first time in a US-produced monster B-movie.

Giving a very interesting piece of behind-the-scenes B-movie insight, Chao answered a fan's question asking whether he would root for the mega shark or the giant octopus. He explained that while he would personally vote for the octopus outsmarting or outmanoeuvring the shark, in the context of an Asylum movie with a low budget, his allegiance would change to the shark. Being easier to create using CGI, the shark would get a lot more screentime.

Mega Shark vs Giant Octopus **fact file**

Released: 2009
Directed by: Jack Perez (as Ace Hannah)
Starring: Deborah Gibson, Vic Chao, Lorenzo Lamas, Mark Hengst,
    Sean Lawlor, Russ Kingston, Stephen Blackehart
Creature: A mega shark and a giant octopus
Effects: CGI
Legacy: *Mega Shark vs Crocosaurus* (2010); *Mega Shark vs Mecha Shark*
    (2014); *Mega Shark vs Kolossus* (2015)

In what was almost certainly a deliberate casting choice, Debbie Gibson's former 1980s music rival, Tiffany, was cast as a lead in the Asylum's 2010 film *Mega Piranha*, which also played her song *Frozen Skies* in the end credits. While The Asylum may draw mixed opinions of their worth and ethical approach as a film company, the success of their concepts and strategy cannot be disputed. They would later go on to make *Sharknado*.

Writer, Travis Beacham, contributed an early screenplay draft for a remake of the 1981 swords and sandals fantasy *Clash of the Titans*. When it was eventually made, it included a cast of well-known action stars including Sam Worthington as Perseus. The team wanted a darker, less whimsical feeling to the movie, allowing Worthington to keep his trademark close-cut hair, making Perseus look more like a soldier than a romance novel cover model.

Of course, remaking the last film to feature Ray Harryhausen's stop-motion work would require an entirely new Kraken for Perseus to defeat and while Harryhausen was approached with an offer for involvement in the film, he had always stated that he never felt that his films needed to be remade and he wanted no involvement in *Clash of the Titans* (2010) whatsoever. Taking the Kraken design back to the descriptions from earlier legends told by sailors, the team gave it tentacle-like appendages and added grasping clawed arms, a distinct head and the mouth of a shark. Director Louis Leterrier is uncredited for the role, but he put on a green suit for the green screen sequences in order to play the part!

This Kraken was criticised for being a grey mass with tentacles while Harryhausen's original stop-motion creature had personality, and while the 1980s audience was given ample time to see the Kraken, many critics have complained that the various creatures in the *Clash of the Titans* remake appeared rushed and moved so quickly that their unique traits and individual horror factor was lost. This criticism was especially applied to the Medusa scene; some reviewers felt her movements were so smooth that her scenes resembled footage from a videogame, without the slow and creepy build-up of her scenes in the original film. The remake looks considerably less dated (understandable considering the money spent on it) but the creatures have none of their original charisma and instead we're left to watch a big spectacle with all of the effects but none of the attraction.

The world was still waiting for a genre-changing kaiju battle, but in the meantime monster movie fans were given a few more offerings from The Asylum and other studios. Here are a few, and not all of them were bad....

2010 Moby Dick (2010)

If *Jaws* is the most copied deep water monster movie out there, then *Moby Dick* is surely the most remade, so when The Asylum had a go in 2010, it was never going to be a high budget epic (that version would come a few years later). Remaking a movie about whaling can be a risk; whales are not generally considered good villains for a film, but still The Asylum had some 'you won't believe this' tricks up its sleeve. Captain Ahab was given an updated metal leg and the whale was allowed to move on land too (which is scientifically impossible, but nobody watches a film called *2010 Moby Dick* for scientific accuracy). Most of the critical responses agreed that the film was better than it had any right to be.

Mega Shark vs Crocosaurus (2010)

Not done with their water monsters yet, The Asylum gave fans another that year. *Mega Shark vs Crocosaurus* was not the viral sensation that the first movie in the *Mega Shark* series had been, but it still had a witty marketing department and produced another viral advertisement. The Asylum participated in a competition to make the next Doritos commercial for Super Bowl XLV, showing a mega shark attacking a naval fleet as the captain wonders what could possibly satisfy the hunger of such a beast. The answer, of course, turns out to be Doritos. A helicopter carries a 'mega Dorito' over the ocean, which is taken by the mega shark in a spectacular jump like the one in the first movie's viral advert, and the crew celebrate. As expected, the movie was not well received by critics but as expected, The Asylum did not lose money from it.

Sharktopus (2010)
Surprisingly, *Sharktopus* is not a movie produced by The Asylum but by veteran producer, Roger Corman, for the Syfy channel, but it also did not fare well in spite of its shark-octopus hybrid. (Neither did *Piranhaconda* (2012), also not an Asylum production.)

Bait (2012)
Set in the aftermath of a tidal wave, against the backdrop of a flooded underground car park and coastal supermarket mid-robbery, *Bait* had enough interest going for it that the sharks that appeared provided an added bonus to a concept that could easily have worked on its own as a survival thriller. Still, the inclusion of sharks turned the movie into a horror-comedy with a little more horror than comedy, though the expected comedy staples like a particularly annoying dog (and owners) in a subplot were either loved or hated by audiences. *Bait* was fun; sharks lunged toward the screen, particularly unsavoury characters were killed off satisfyingly brutally, a character died in a manner both heroic and utterly ridiculous (full body armour made of shopping baskets) and the visuals were very similar to the many viral faked photographs of displaced sharks swimming around flooded streets and shopping centres after various storms.

The dialogue and chemistry were heavily criticised but the (mostly animatronic with a touch of CGI) sharks held up considerably well and with a forty-seven per cent positive review score on Rotten Tomatoes, *Bait,* while not reinventing the shark movie, was not a total flop either.

Grabbers (2012)

The plot for *Grabbers* sounds like a no-budget movie concept thought up by method actors on a night out: a remote Irish island is playing host to an infestation of tentacled sea monsters – or possibly aliens – that appear to have fallen from the sky. When the town drunk manages to survive a direct attack from what the locals have called 'grabbers', the island's marine ecologist suspects that the alcohol in his blood might be toxic to the creatures. There's only one solution: get drunk! With one sober volunteer keeping an eye on the rest of the population, the party starts.

Though the plot sounds as though the team were aiming for a 'so-bad-it's-good' review at best, the movie received rave reviews with a seventy-two per cent positive score on Rotten Tomatoes. *Empire* magazine, *Dread Central*, *The Daily Telegraph*, *The Guardian* and *The Irish Times* all gave *Grabbers* reviews that ranged from good to excellent.

Grabbers even won awards! At the Edinburgh International Film Festival 2012, it was announced as one of the 'Best of the Fest'. At the Strasbourg European Fantastic Film Festival (which focuses on horror, fantasy and science fiction) it won the Audience Prize for Best Film, and it won both the Audience Award for Best Film and the Titra Film Award at Swiss film festival NIFFF. *Grabbers* was nominated for seven more awards and Ruth Bradley won Best Actress at the 2013 Irish Film and Television Awards.

Mega Python vs Gataroid (2010)

The Asylum brought out the warring monsters again with *Mega Python vs Gatoroid* and in a nod to previous movies, also brought old rivals Debbie Gibson and Tiffany together; this time in a swamp.

2-Headed Shark Attack (2012)

Deciding to bring something new to the shark movie genre, they offered two bites for the price of one in *2-Headed Shark Attack*. The original two-headed shark design had, if possible, been even sillier than the finished monster, with one head on top of the other, but just as with most two-headed mutations, the heads were eventually placed side by side.

Stranger than fiction

2-Headed Shark Attack sounds utterly implausible as well as inevitable. (How much further can filmmakers take the shark attack genre before needing to add extra heads?). Still, the creature design isn't as implausible as it might appear, for two-headed sharks have actually been found!

The presence of an extra head on an animal is called bicephaly and the shark in *2-Headed Shark Attack* is a textbook example. Bicephaly is usually caused by the incomplete splitting of an embryo, causing twin animals that are fused side by side with the outward appearance of two heads on one body, though some bicephalic animals can have multiple organs. Among many species, snakes, kittens, pigs, cows, sharks (yes!), tortoises and even humans can be bicephalic.

Two-headed sharks have been reported since the 1960s and in 2008 a fisherman caught a baby blue shark with two heads, taking photographs of it before throwing the shark back and sending the photographs to *National Geographic*. This led to a study examining the phenomenon in sharks, which found evidence to suggest that bicephaly is increasing among embryos. It appears more common in blue sharks but bull sharks, Atlantic sawtail sharks and dog sharks have all been found with bicephaly.

As of yet, sharks with more than two heads have only been found in movies made by The Asylum.

In this lull between true genre-changers, many of the deep water monster films offered appeared relatively samey, getting middling reviews at best (an effect produced by a virtually equal number of five star reviews and one star reviews) with the exception of the unexpected hit *Grabbers*. In the meantime, another screenplay by Travis Beacham (from the *Clash of the Titans* remake) about giant warring creatures, robot pilots and survivors' guilt had been taken on by Legendary Pictures.

The idea for Beacham's story had been based on a chance walk along Santa Monica pier, where he imagined a giant monster and a giant robot fighting, and instead of leaving things with that spectacle, he developed it further. What if the robot needed two pilots to operate it and what if one of them died? Could the robot still function and how would the other pilot be affected? Just as *Godzilla* represented more than a monster and *Jaws* represented more than a shark, Beacham's idea represented more than a fight between titans.

Meanwhile, film director, Guillermo del Toro, was reportedly working on an adaptation of the H.P. Lovecraft horror *At the Mountains of Madness* with James Cameron as producer, but when he met with the team at Legendary Pictures who had taken on Beacham's twenty-five-page film treatment, he was so intrigued by the premise that he made a deal; he'd work on both movies at the same time, producing and co-writing the small project based on Beacham's idea while also directing *At the Mountains of Madness*. However, if the latter were cancelled, he would step in to direct the former. Due to various conflicts, *At the Mountains of Madness* was indeed cancelled and del Toro signed up to direct the Legendary Pictures film.

Pacific Rim (2013)

Rather than focus on a kaiju attack in the same way as *Godzilla* and its copycats and tributes, *Pacific Rim* moved the timeline onward. Set years after an initial and devastating kaiju attack during which San Francisco, Sacramento and Oakland were decimated, the world's military pooled its resources for the first time to defend the rest of the world against repeat attacks. The Jaeger Program, in which colossal robots were created with the purpose of fighting the kaiju, was initially a success. Each robot contained two pilots who would work in synchronicity in order to operate it, and in public opinion these Jaeger pilots became celebrities; treated like a combination of rockstar and astronaut. The world was saved and life moved on. Now, however, the Jaeger Program is failing. Amid unsuccessful attempts at keeping the kaiju attacks at bay by building a giant wall, the scientists and core military group behind the initial Jaeger Program are setting up one final attempt to destroy the portal known as 'the breach' at the bottom of the Pacific Ocean that the kaiju are using to enter earth in the first place … and they need a pilot. Cue Raleigh Becket, a former Jaeger pilot plagued by survivor's guilt after the death of his brother during a kaiju attack. Back in action and fighting the less-than-welcoming attitudes of other pilots as well as his own self-doubt, while assisted by bickering scientists, mathematics genius Gottlieb, and kaiju expert Newt, as well as rookie Jaeger pilot Mako Mori (adopted daughter of the chief ranger with a revenge mission of her own), he prepares to go back into battle.

The genre changer

For a movie that is, at its core, a great action spectacle with fighting robots and kaiju, *Pacific Rim* has achieved very positive reviews as well as a closer analysis than usual in both social media and academic articles. Why? Yes, *Pacific Rim* had a budget of over 180 million dollars but an enormous budget does not necessarily make an excellent movie. Some of the entries in this book have been panned even while attracting an enormous audience for their advertised spectacle alone. So, what made *Pacific Rim* so appealing?

The team and cast were proven talented creators in their respective fields. Del Toro creates distinctive visual effects and excels at creature design. As a lifelong fan of kaiju movies, he introduced ideas he wanted to see, including a kaiju birth and an attack from a child's perspective, which would become a central plot point for one of the characters.

Writer, Travis Beacham, had a winning concept, and even though not all of his projects have gained critical success (the television series *Carnival Row* for example), his ideas have generally been praised and respected.

The team cast the characters well. Charlie Hunnam, at that time most famous for his portrayal of conflicted biker, Jax Teller, in the award-winning series *Sons of Anarchy*, brought the same earnest and well-meaning, if troubled, demeanour to his character Raleigh Becket. Rinko Kikuchi's character, Mako Mori, drew wide praise for her competence, character arc and writing. After Tom Cruise's scheduling conflicts meant he had to turn down the role of Marshal Pentecost, Idris Elba was cast after del Toro watched his performance in the *Luther* TV series, recognising that his presence held the same weary authority that the character he envisioned butting heads with Charlie Hunnam's character would. Elba watched footage of both politicians and actors in roles that required a commanding presence and the knowledge of an unbearable weight on their shoulders, like Mel Gibson in *Braveheart* (1995).

Del Toro made a deliberate choice to circumvent stereotype and write his characters as flawed humans, with a stubborn but morally admirable Black leader, who is not early cannon fodder, a Japanese heroine who is not sexualized or submissive and does not fade into the background while the hero has his moment, and a tattooed scientist with a big personality whose mutual frustration and reluctant affection for his more reserved colleague contributes a lot of the comic relief moments. Del Toro said in an interview that every casting and characterisation decision was made in order to play against the usual stereotypes.

Yes, there are popular tropes; the science team, the money-grabbing character you just can't trust, the character who sacrifices themself and more than one spectacularly ludicrous fighting moment (one entails an entire oil tanker being used as a baseball bat), but less beloved tropes, like the military saving the world by going to war rather than looking for a more peaceful solution, are all absent. Guillermo del Toro is a pacifist, who successfully aimed to avoid promoting war in any way in the making of *Pacific Rim*. Rather than naming his ranks after military titles like Private and Major, he gave them titles like Ranger and

Marshal in a similar manner to a western movie. He even shows the streets being evacuated before a kaiju attack so that when modes of transport get thrown, there is no need to worry about people inside them.

Rather than making the kaiju predatory animals acting in the name of their own survival or displaced creatures to be shot at and blown up, he wrote the kaiju as an invading force from another dimension. This is not a matter of finding an animal out of its usual territory; these are bioweapons used by an invading colonising force behind the scenes, so fighting back is perfectly reasonable.

The overarching message del Toro has said he wanted to convey was that people must work together and only by working together can they heal themselves. Both Becket and Mori are flawed from their past traumas, but as Jaeger pilots they must open up by necessity, allowing each other to share in their memories and by doing so they can begin to heal. It is a message that is repeated throughout the film, from the two fundamentally different scientists finding a way to collaborate, to the teams that do not get on but must immediately set their differences aside to battle an enemy. Unlike many monster movies, the final takeaway from *Pacific Rim* is not one of war but of peace.

The Mako Mori test

The Bechdel test is not designed to rate films as good or bad but to make viewers think about the absence of women of substance in films. It was originally illustrated in a 1985 comic strip by American cartoonist, Alison Bechdel, who credited the idea to her friend, Liz Wallace, and the writings of Virginia Woolf. The strip entitled '*The Rule*' shows a character telling her friend that she will only watch a film if:

1) It includes more than two named female characters
2) They talk to each other on screen …
3) … about something other than a man.

The test is certainly not foolproof and nuance must be taken into account (for example *The Shawshank Redemption* (1994) is set in a male prison and does not pass, while *Sex and the City* (2008) occasionally features conversations about shoes and therefore does) but it is a starting point for discourse about the roles offered to women. Women have traditionally played either no role or an extremely sexualised role in action movies, and many action movies do not pass the Bechdel test. This includes *Pacific Rim*.

However ...

Tumblr user, Chaila, coined the term 'The Mako Mori test'. Mako is in a very male dominated environment but has a character arc of her own that does not revolve around a man and his story. While *Pacific Rim* may not pass the Bechdel Test, writers have pointed out that it should not be written off for this reason. A film passes the Mako Mori test if:

1) It contains a named female character
2) Who has a character arc of her own ...
3) ... that does not revolve around supporting a man's plot arc

Del Toro chose to create a female character with a backstory and her own motivations. While it could be implied that she and Becket might form a romantic relationship after the events of the film ended, the central point of the storyline they shared was one of building mutual trust and chemistry which was not essentially romantic. The character, Mako Mori, still has a passionate fanbase and is often referenced in critical texts discussing characterisation in movies.

The stars of the show

The kaiju and Jaegers were created in homage to monster movies like *Godzilla* and his robot co-stars (a genre known as 'mecha'), and not a direct copy. Not known for ripping off source material, del Toro wanted to create something different.

The kaiju come from an alternate dimension (sometimes referred to outside the film as the 'anteverse'), travelling up from the sea to cause terror. Each kaiju looks completely different despite being a genetic clone, though many appear to be based on deep sea creatures.

There were around one hundred kaiju and Jaegers designed for consideration in the film and every week the filmmakers would do an *American Idol* style presentation and 'vote off' their least favourites. Many were designed using a real creature as inspiration, which would emerge as an otherworldly monster by the end of the design process.

In homage to earlier kaiju films in which a person in a suit did most of the action, the designs were created to look as though they could have been made for an actual actor who could wear the kaiju suit.

One problem to get around was the science of movement. In general, something as enormous as the kaiju and Jaegers would move much more slowly than they needed to in the film. VFX supervisor, John Knoll, explained to *Gizmodo* magazine that his family background in both science and engineering served him well, allowing him to achieve as much realism as possible but while also pushing the boundaries. The trade-off between speed and weight was an obstacle to get around. Moving fast could give the kaiju and Jaegers a weightless appearance, the exact opposite of what would be required for the film, so the team focused on the impact of their movements even if the action would be a little slower; displaced air, particles and flying debris. Special attention was given to the battles in the water: the way in which both a kaiju and Jaeger would move and the way the water would react.

Pacific Rim is an action movie so the kaiju aren't scary in the same way that a horror movie would make them, but they are awe inspiring, fun and fascinating to watch … and maybe a little scary too.

A global hit

But not a domestic one, by any means. In fact, *Pacific Rim* was considered a flop in the US box office!

On 22 July 2013, it was reported that the film had reached #1 at the international box office over the weekend. Extremely successful in China, it was the sixth largest Chinese debut of all time for a Hollywood film, the sixth highest grossing American film in China, ever, and grossed over 100 million dollars in China alone! In Japan, it was in the top five films on opening weekend, initially earning three million dollars.

Pacific Rim holds a seventy-two per cent positive rating on Rotten Tomatoes and was nominated for twenty-one awards, going on to win three.

Pacific Rim fact file

Released: 2013
Directed by: Guillermo del Toro
Starring: Charlie Hunnam, Idris Elba, Rinko Kikuchi, Charlie Day, Rob Kazinsky, Max Martini. Ron Perlman
Creature: Kaiju of many types
Effects: CGI and animatronics (for the smaller creatures)
Legacy: *Pacific Rim* videogame (2013); the sequel *Pacific Rim: Uprising* (2018); anime series *Pacific Rim: The Black* (2021); 3D theme park ride in Indonesia —*Pacific Rim: Shatterdome Strike*; The Mako Mori Test; … and The Asylum's inevitable mockbuster *Atlantic Rim* (2013).

You cannot make a kaiju movie without at least thinking about Godzilla so it would feel like a disservice to the king of the monsters and partial influence on *Pacific Rim* not to mention the fact that in 2014, *Godzilla* was remade by an American studio … for the second time.

1998's *Godzilla* was panned by audiences, critics and, most damning of all, Toho Studios, but 2014's *Godzilla* (also produced by Legendary Pictures) emerged to positive reviews, many of which stating that it 'made up for' the failure of 1998's effort, which most fans have 'disowned'.

Director Gareth Edwards specifically wanted to impress Toho Studios enough that they would consider the movie part of the *Godzilla* franchise but initially had trouble casting it due to the last adaptation's failure. His film *Monsters* (2010) impressed actors Elizabeth Olsen and Bryan Cranston enough that they agreed to star. The character Godzilla was designed to look similar to the original Toho design and was a mixture of CGI and motion capture, played by stuntman T.J. Storm. While many Japanese critics have criticised the lack of dedication to the nuclear theme of the original, the special effects were widely praised. Godzilla only appears onscreen for around eight minutes, but the scenes in which he swims generate the same fear and awe any good water monster does; his back scales sticking up from the surface like a line of terror-inducing dorsal fins, attached to a creature that moves like a crocodilian. *Godzilla* (2014) was nominated for fifteen awards, winning six, and none of them were Golden Raspberries!

Pacific Rim was not a 'deep water monster movie' in the same way that *Jaws*, *Lake Placid* and even *Megashark vs Giant Octopus* were, but the genre is ever moving, looking for new novel settings and creatures, and if these ideas didn't evolve then neither would the movies.

Pacific Rim not only takes a lot of inspiration from deep water monster movies but it combines the best ideas from the genre with big budget action. It would not be the last film to do this.

Would everyone consider the kaiju in *Pacific Rim* 'sea monsters', considering they originate in another dimension? Maybe not, but we can agree that their comfort in the water and resemblance to sharks, crustaceans and other familiar sea monsters places them in the same family at least.

The next chapter debates even stranger creatures: just what counts as a sea monster?

SHIPWRECKS,
SCANDALS
AND AN ICON...

CHAPTER NINE

ARE MERMAIDS
MONSTERS?

Virtually every culture has some kind of mermaid legend in its history, from Syrian tales in 1000 BC to Hans Christian Andersen's popular and much-adapted fairytale *The Little Mermaid* (which was considerably gorier than Disney's musical take on the story).

Mermaids have been appearing in movies for over a century now and although historically they and their cousins have a darker side, it is only relatively recently that this has been shown in the movies. Before this, film pioneer Georges Méliès' 1904 silent film *The Mermaid* was the first time the creature had been portrayed on film. A magician (played by Méliès himself) turns himself into a fisherman and conjures up an undersea landscape which includes a mermaid, before placing himself on a throne as a sea king.

A most scandalous mermaid

From around 1911, one woman was the face of mermaids. Annette Kellerman was the first woman to rebel against the cumbersome swimming outfits women were expected to wear at that time and dared to put on a one-piece bathing suit. For today's viewers it resembles a modest catsuit but at the time this was revolutionary … and so popular that Annette started her own swimwear range!

Growing up with leg weakness, her parents enrolled her in swimming classes in order to strengthen her muscles and she did so well in her classes that by age 15 she was winning races and giving diving displays. She began to perform mermaid themed acts and would swim with fish in a glass tank. At age 19 she attempted to swim the English Channel but did not succeed. Still, she was generating more than enough publicity for other opportunities to be offered to her.

Scandal struck after she was reported to have been arrested for her one-piece swimming costume but no record of this incident has been found, and in 1916 she became the first major actress to perform in a nude scene in a movie. The film, entitled *Daughter of the Gods*, has now been lost but there are still images found online in which she appears as a water nymph.

Annette continued to use her swimming talents to portray mermaids in movies, even making her own costumes, until her final film role in *Venus of the South Seas* (1924). Her legacy includes having streets, swimming venues and even a racehorse named after her, books she had published on both swimming and beauty, and a 1954 movie, *Million Dollar Mermaid*, based on her life.. After her death, her ashes were scattered in the Great Barrier Reef.

The romantic comedies *Miranda* (1948) and *Mr Peabody and the Mermaid* (1948) both show mermaids as being mischievous and seductive, capturing the attention of all the men in the vicinity. Miranda even holds a man captive until he agrees to take her on a sightseeing trip to London.

Disney's *Peter Pan* (1957) also shows mermaids to be mischievous but with a slightly mean streak not dissimilar to Neverland's Lost Boys and Pan himself.

While sirens were historically portrayed as dangerous and seductive in a similar way to vampires (though sirens were traditionally part bird as shown in Greek mythology and the epic tale *The Odyssey*), with the exception of some moody short films in which they are doomed and tragic figures, mermaids have been considerably better treated by the film industry.

Did You Know?

Daryl Hannah's mermaid portrayal in the romantic comedy *Splash* (1984) popularised the name 'Madison'. The scene had been a joke in the movie; unfamiliar with human names, the mermaid saw a sign for Madison Avenue and chose Madison to be her human name. The word wasn't even on the radar as a potential first name at the time – this was the point of the joke – but by the year 2000, Madison was the third most popular girls name in the US.

The lovable, rebellious and human-obsessed Ariel in Disney's adaptation *The Little Mermaid* (1989) is far from monstrous; she's one of the most beloved Disney princesses in the franchise, with a continuing legacy today. On the other hand, Ursula, the villainous part-octopus bad-bargaining sea witch in the film, grows to gigantic size and starts attacking ships in one scene. Now, *that's* a sea monster!

Most of the 1980s and 1990s films featuring mermaids were aimed at children and teenagers and usually involved characters hiding a mermaid best friend, though *The Thirteenth Year* (1999) gave a traditionally 'teen girl' plotline to a teen boy, who finds he is turning into a merman. Still, the films were mostly coming-of-age or adventure comedies, so what happened to the little mermaid between then and now? She's had quite a transformation....

She Creature (2001)

Two horror movies apparently featuring mermaids were released in the same year but in *Dagon* (2001), the character was part of a vision and more closely resembles *The Little Mermaid's* Ursula than the creature most people would think of when hearing the word 'mermaid'. *She Creature* is possibly the first film in which a mermaid appears as a true monster doing monstrous things, though the human characters' actions are considerably less forgivable – a group of sideshow workers show off their mermaid exhibit but reveal that they have a real mermaid in captivity too. The mermaid appears to make friends with one of the workers' wives, defending her from the actions of men who are prepared to harm her, before taking gory revenge and engineering her escape.

The movie itself got mixed reviews; the editing looked choppy but the practical effects from the Stan Winston Studio were gruesome. *She Creature* was also praised for the portrayal of female friendship (or possibly romance) and camaraderie as the mermaid and the wife of one of the carnival workers begin to protect each other from the generally unpleasant male characters. *She Creature* is, for a horror movie in the early 2000s, surprisingly ahead of its time.

She Creature fact file

Released: 2001
Directed by: Sebastian Gutierrez
Starring: Rufus Sewell, Carla Gugino, Rya Kihlstedt, Jim Piddock, Reno Wilson, Mark Aiken
Creature: Mermaid
Effects: Prosthetics by Stan Winston Studio
Legacy: None… yet

Mermaids grew more sinister in the movies released over the following years. They get a spooky scene in *Peter Pan* (2003) in which Wendy is new to Neverland and risks getting too close as an incredulous Peter warns her that the mermaids intend to drown her. The unnaturally smooth-looking, black-eyed and webbed-handed mermaids try to do just that. The scene lasts for just one minute but it's a haunting piece of film, helped by the blue lighting and eerie music.

Later, *Pirates of the Caribbean: On Stranger Tides* (2011) would show a very similar scene in which singing mermaids surround a boat and attempt to drown its inhabitants, though there is also a subplot involving a love story between a mermaid and a missionary.

While not specifically a deep water monster movie, *The Cabin in the Woods* (2011) needs a mention here because it's a good parody about almost every cliché and stereotype the horror genre has, while including a merman. Explaining away the generic characters, their incomprehensibly stupid behaviour, varying monsters and even order of death with a hilarious Lovecraftian twist and a new take on the 'military coverup' idea (a trope in itself), one of the many running jokes is the long-held ambition of one character to see a merman. Throughout the film, he reiterates this, even coming close to his dream once ... until, at the end, he gets closer than he could ever wish for as the longed-for merman squelches inelegantly toward him, looking like an ungainly webbed cross between a flabby whale and an amphibian with a shark's mouth. The ensuing scene is both gory and hilarious, partly because the merman was designed to be the absolute opposite to any 'attractive merfolk' design ever used in any movie, ever!

A true mermaid horror movie of the exact type parodied in *The Cabin in the Woods* wasn't released until 2014, when *Killer Mermaid* aka *Mamula* (named after the island filming location) hit the screens in a B-movie resembling a slasher movie and creature horror combination. Set partly in an abandoned building on a remote island, *Killer Mermaid* brings a boat of couples and simmering tension together when they see what looks like an imprisoned young woman in a dungeon. She is actually a trapped mermaid who uses a siren-like call but never speaks, held captive by an unhinged sailor wielding a hook. The special effects make up and CGI combination is spectacularly awful and in an incredibly optimistic move that hints at a sequel, the UK title is *Killer Mermaids*, though the presence of more than one mermaid is only suggested in the last few seconds of the movie. Depending on the audience's individual preferences, this might just be considered 'so bad it's good' due to the ridiculous action sequences and the terrible mermaid design!

When writing a monstrous mermaid character, the potential is virtually limitless. Mermaids can potentially speak, as well as move around on land resembling a human and there is always an opportunity for body horror in a tail. Mermaid movies aimed at an older audience have followed a pattern in recent years, taking full advantage of prosthetics, blood and sea slime! In a tale more closely adapted to Hans Christian Andersen's original than it appears at first glance, the genre was offered something completely different in Polish horror musical *The Lure*.

The Lure (2015)

Two mermaid sisters, Silver and Golden, leave the water and begin performing as singers in a Polish nightclub. Silver falls in love with a man and loses her singing voice in the process. Meanwhile Golden is warned by another sea creature out of water that if her sister's new-found lover does not return her feelings, she will turn into sea foam; the original fate of Hans Christian Andersen's Little Mermaid character. The lengths the lovesick mermaid goes to in order to try to keep her man makes her eventual fate doomed from the start.

It is probably the most faithful adaptation of the original, even with its rock bands and strippers, visually portraying the body horror described less graphically in the original fairytale. Director, Agnieszka Smoczyńska, called her debut feature film a coming-of-age story, echoing parts of her own growing up; experimenting with alcohol and falling in infatuation for the first time. Smoczyńska's mother ran a nightclub and she grew up with this environment as her 'normal'. Not wanting to make an obvious biographical film or to show things too close to her heart, she used the mermaids as a metaphor. Writer, Robert Bolesto, had a similar familiarity with the club environment but seen from another perspective: two of his friends parents belonged to a music group which played in the same type of bars that Smoczyńska's mother ran. Finding common ground, they began to work on the film and as soon as the mermaid idea was placed on the metaphorical table, the idea for an adaptation of the fairytale was set into motion.

The film twists and turns, mirroring the way in which the mermaids move in the water, or perhaps the strangeness of growing up in an ever-changing environment with a rock music soundtrack, or even the immigrant experience that Smoczyńska has said highly influenced her work. Always a new obstacle at each corner, a new area of unfamiliarity to navigate among people who may or may not be trusted. The mermaids want to go to America, which they imagine to be full of opportunity, reflecting the desire of many Polish people at the time, looking to travel to America for the chance of a better quality of life.

Cultural insights and differences add multiple layers to most film creations; look at the way in which *Godzilla* was perceived by its Japanese audience versus its American audience. *The Lure* is a Polish film by a Polish director and when asked why she did not emphasise the film's 1980s setting, Smoczyńska told Dorota Hartwich at *Cineuropa* that as the 1980s were a very specific period in

Poland (there was great political unrest and mass protests), she didn't want the time period to overshadow the focus of the movie, which was the relationship between the mermaid sisters and their journey.

The Lure got a mixed reception in Poland (where Warsaw's mascot is a sword-wielding mermaid) but still ended up with an eighty-nine per cent positive score on Rotten Tomatoes, winning eight awards.

Bodies

Smoczyńska has made it clear in many interviews that the mermaid form was her representation of the messiness of growing up female; the mermaids are fetishised and abused, their bodies used as a commodity, expected to draw people in through fascination and lust, while at the same time repulsing them. Beautiful young women from the waist up, their tails are in no way 'sexy' or in the least bit proportional. Enormous, cumbersome-looking slimy grey-green appendages more similar to eels than the colourful and slender fins of Disney mermaids. The prosthetic tails were nearly seven feet long, weighed more than sixty pounds each and were operated by the actresses using pedals. They were instructed not to attempt to be elegant; their awkwardness moving through the human world was a deliberate choice by choreographer Kaya Kolodziejczyk.

Smoczyńska has said that while she appreciates that any audience will come up with their own interpretation, she did not intend to write a feminist film and still does not see *The Lure* in this way.

The tragedy of either loving somebody entirely wrong for you, or watching a loved one make that mistake, is something many can relate to and as one of the mermaid sisters falls in love with a man who tells her that he will always see her as a fish, we all can guess that this is not going to end well for her. Most of the men who intend to harm the mermaid sisters live (or not) to regret their actions; a cathartic spectacle for many women who have either dreamed of being mermaids or of seeing justice done to those whose actions are portrayed in *The Lure*. (Or both!) The audience perception of this movie as a feminist story is understandable.

The glittering, grimy world

The Lure press kit is compelling and detailed, containing clips from rave reviews from the Sundance Film Festival where the movie premiered, information on the cast and crew, soundbites from the sisters who inspired the film and an interview with the director. Growing up in one of the 'dancing restaurants' which were very popular in Communist Poland, the director had a glimpse into what she called 'a world of lost souls and warm vodka'. In these places the food was better, there were entertainment acts and people could dance in pairs.

She worked with cameraman Jakub Kijowski to show a contrast between the lurid glittering world of the club and the drab grimy world outside. From the perspectives of the mermaids, the onshore world is a tumbling kaleidoscope of opportunity, while their home world is flat and monotonous.

Real sisters

The mermaids were based on real sisters known by the writer Robert Bolesto. Sisters Barbara and Zuzanna Wrońska wrote the songs for the film and grew up in a similar world to Smoczyńska, having parents playing in bands which performed for the crowds in these clubs. While their insight inspired the story, Bolesto did not want to make it too personal by revealing unnecessary details. The nightclub scenes were filmed at the abandoned Club Adria in Warsaw, where the Wrońska sisters' parents often performed.

> ### *The Lure* fact file
>
> **Released:** 2015
> **Directed by:** Agnieszka Smoczyńska
> **Starring:** Marta Mazurek, Michalina Olszańska
> **Creature:** Mermaids
> **Effects:** Prosthetics and a little CGI
> **Legacy:** A lot of analytical articles!

Hans Christian Andersen wrote of the mermaid attending the prince's wedding to another woman: 'She laughed and danced with the thought of death in her heart'. Interestingly, while the original tale has been thought to be Andersen's attempt at coming to terms with his homosexuality, the transition from human to mermaid has been used as a coming-of-age metaphor several times.

If *The Lure* captured the frenetic energy of growing up in a place many would see as bizarre but which was everyday normality for the narrator, *Blue My Mind* released two years later would capture the everyday highs, lows and risks of being a normal human teenage girl … with the added problem of turning into a mermaid. As if a teenage girl doesn't have enough problems!

Blue My Mind (2017)

Mia is fifteen and has just moved to a new city. She is the new kid in class and instantly singled out by a group of girls who are both popular kids and rebels. Led by queen bee Gianna, they don't quite know what to make of Mia and alternate between hazing and tentative friendship. Gianna and the group experiment with sex, drugs, shoplifting and more. So far, so teenager. Except that one day Mia finds her toes growing together and soon more changes come as her actions grow more extreme in order to escape the transformation keeping pace with her.

There are some vividly uncomfortable moments, both in the realm of body horror (Mia separating her toes with nail scissors) and teenage behaviour going further than wanted or planned (a house party scene near the end is extremely graphic and disconcerting as Mia finds herself blindfolded and out of her depth with a group of young men at the party) but the overriding feeling throughout much of the movie is one of discomfort instead of pure fear. Mia clashes with her parents, finds herself in situations simmering with danger and explores some of the current 'moral panic' discussions often seen in tabloids discussing the latest bad influence on TikTok. Mia watches explicit videos with her friends and plays games involving choking each other until they pass out.

Blue My Mind is occasionally reviewed as a horror film, while other reviews describe it as 'coming-of-age', 'dark fantasy', or 'art house', transcending genres. Mia is not necessarily a monster-, it's the changes to her body that seem monstrous. Still … who knows? She has not fulfilled her potential yet and the film leaves what exactly that might be as an open-ended question. Perhaps Mia does not know either.

The movie has been praised for its excellent performances by the actors and criticised for its ambiguousness. The parallels to many issues plaguing teenage girls, especially regarding sexuality, body image and friendship, are well done and while some reviewers felt the film lost its way as Mia's transformation became more obvious, others felt that the friendship and support between the two girls was a positive and beautifully done piece of character building which is often lacking in young adult and coming-of-age films, in favour of 'mean girl' dynamics. The friendship does, at times, border on a potential romance, but this is left to the viewer to interpret and never presented as trivial or baiting the LGBT+ community.

Mia's tail is giant, slimy, cumbersome and flops around on the floor as she drags herself through her flooded house to reach the bath, but the full transformation doesn't take place until near the end of the movie. At the beginning, there's nothing as obvious as even a stray scale; instead, Mia begins gulping salt water and eating her mother's pet fish before the physical changes begin and don't stop. The assault on her body more closely resembles an infection or rash. This eventually leads to excruciatingly painful public embarrassment; another teenage staple.

Blue My Mind has been described as anticlimactic for its meditative and bittersweet ending; as Mia's comfort in her body and new state of being grows, she takes control of her own life and makes the decision to leave home – a decision most college-aged teens will be familiar with – and her story is no longer for the audience to spectate. Rather than crashing down on her, the turbulence of Mia's story does not end at the break of the wave, but at the ebb of the tide.

Blue My Mind fact file

Released: 2017
Directed by: Lisa Brühlmann
Starring: Luna Wedler, Zoë Pastelle Holthuizen
Creature: Mermaid
Effects: Prosthetics and CGI
Legacy: None yet…

Mermaids have been seen as transitional creatures throughout history, but why has the mermaid image captured this feeling in so many people? Phoenixes, werewolves and other shapeshifters exist in the world of myth and legend and may seem better suited to the idea of physical change, so why do we recognise the symbolism of change and transition in the mermaid?

The mermaid has been used to represent many things throughout history. Once used to symbolise escorting as a profession, Mary Queen of Scots was compared to one on an unflattering placard implying that she murdered her husband. Not long afterward, the symbolism changed again; this time, the mermaid represented power over the sea. Queen Elizabeth I of England was painted seated on a chair featuring carved mermaids, in celebration of her defeat of the Spanish Armada.

Perhaps this is exactly it; the mermaid has been such an attractive and adaptable symbol that she can take on any meaning assigned to her, becoming anything we want her to be!

Mermaids have never been far from the public eye. From ancient depictions in pottery and pre-Raphaelite art, to Barbie and similar toys, to every remake of *Peter Pan* and the *Pirates of the Caribbean* franchise; the image of the mermaid has been unforgettable.

Mermaids on the small screen

In 2018, two television series put mermaids at the front and centre of the action. Both were aimed at young adults and both emphasised the sexuality of the creatures, but the similarity ends there.

Siren follows mermaid, Ryn, as she leaves the water to look for her abducted sister. Over its three seasons, it grew a passionate fanbase but its viewers opinions were divided over its inclusion of a polyamorous relationship which was intended to be positive and romantic but featured an enormous and disturbing power imbalance.

On the other hand, *Tidelands* was more salacious; of the sex, blood and betrayal variety. Calliope has returned from prison, having possibly been framed. Discovering that the family business her brother has inherited from their father might not be exactly legal and following an encounter with the mysterious local community of 'Tidelanders', she sets out to find out the truth about her family history and the crime she was blamed for. Predictably, Calliope is revealed to be a Tidelander herself – half-human, half siren – belonging to neither community comfortably. The brutal potential of both sides shows itself in different ways but the Tidelanders probably win the title of 'most monstrous' in a scene involving their leader punishing a child by taking one of his eyes.

The sirens themselves are barely shown in *Tidelands* though their presence is a mysterious shadow over all actions taken by the characters. *Siren* doesn't shy away from showing the mermaids but feels more like a teen drama in which some of the protagonists happen to have tails.

Mermaid sisters: Rusalka and Sirens

Rusalka

The English title of the Russian language film *Mermaid: The Lake of The Dead* (2018) is slightly inaccurate; Russian culture has its own very specific version of the mermaid, the rusalka, which the film's Russian title names.

In *The Lake of the Dead*, legend tells that drowned unmarried women become mermaids. Marina is due to be married but is unaware that her fiancé, Roman, met an evil mermaid on the shore of their local forest lake and he has fallen in love with her. The mermaid intends to keep him away from Marina by holding him prisoner in her underwater world. Marina has one week to battle the mermaid, save her man and overcome her fear of the water. There was an excellent but untaken opportunity for a twist in the tale: Marina is the name of a famous rusalka in Slavic legend and as the character was not yet married, the movie could have become an alternative origin story.

Reviews were generally negative, relying on standard horror tropes without using the water to its best advantage. Part of the allure (pun intended) of mermaid movies is the setting; a few shots of a tail, bad CGI and easy jump scares are no match for a film which uses the often-eerie underwater atmosphere well.

Soviet historian and scholar, Vladimir Propp, claimed that before the nineteenth century the rusalka were associated with crops and fertility but by the end of the nineteenth century the legend had taken on a darker turn, perhaps due to a negative change in the perception of 'witchy women'. Now, a rusalka is considered malicious and connected with an 'unclean spirit'. Rusalki share one aspect of the mermaid mythology in that they are able to seduce and kill men by luring them to the water with their great beauty (often shapeshifting to reflect the personal taste of their victim) before drowning them. According to Russian and Soviet ethnographer, Dmitry Zelenin, the rusalki were made through several very specific circumstances; young women whose unhappy marriages drove them to drown themselves or who were murdered by drowning (especially after experiencing an unwanted pregnancy) would become rusalki. The fate of the men who drowned them or made them unhappy is not mentioned.

Though the rusalki are often said to each own a comb made of fish bones, in most legends they still have long, loose and very tangled hair. According to *Dal's Explanatory Dictionary*, the expression 'walks like a rusalka' (Russian: *Ходит, как русалка*) is applied to girls with unkempt hair.

Sirens

Part woman, part bird. In Homer's myth *The Odyssey*, the sirens beautiful and haunting singing would cause men to crash their ships and die. When having to pass by their island, Odysseus had his sailors' ears plugged with wax so that they couldn't hear the song and had himself tied to the ships mast so that he could do the impossible: hear their song and live. As in the *Tidelands* TV series, there is often crossover and confusion between the attributes belonging to a mermaid and those that belong to a siren. Descriptions that give the siren a fish tail appear in the *Liber Monstorum*, a seventh or eighth century catalogue of marvellous creatures (and some humans too!), and over time the sirens became more mermaid-like until the two creatures were often considered the same species.

Trends and patterns behave like waves; we've seen shark horror rise, fall, then rise again with *Jaws*. We've seen the trend for horror-comedy reach a peak in the 1990s before slowing into a more serious and self-aware pattern. It stopped being fashionable to portray real creatures as deliberately malevolent and instead the surge of 'based on a true story' animal horror took its place. The way in which mermaids are written is no different; away from the world of children's cinema the mermaid is no longer a romantic heroine or magical friend. She is a lot more interesting!

Mermaid Down (2019) was made from an award-winning script, deals with exploitation as a theme and can easily be considered a commentary on the shark finning practise still going on.

This mermaid is pulled aboard a boat and immediately has her tail severed. She is experimented on and kept in an asylum for the mentally ill where nobody believes that she is a mermaid, and she is isolated, aware she will die if kept from the water too long. The film then brings in a supernatural element as a friendship grows between the mermaid and a ghost.

Mermaid Down was crowdfunded through an Indiegogo campaign! The success of crowdfunding has meant that to an extent, audiences can choose to control what they want to see. 716 backers raised over £82,000 in order to make the film independently.

The advertising campaign was haunting and emotive, with artists impressions on posters announcing the 'last day to set her free', implying that the backers had a hand in the mermaid's situation and outcome, and the mermaid was described as 'the most believable mermaid ever to be captured by movie cameras'. This is not necessarily a commentary on special effects but has a double meaning as a reference to the fact that the mermaid is imprisoned in an asylum where nobody believes her.

Different levels of monetary donations got the backers perks, such as being the first person to see what the mermaid looks like, or even being awarded a mermaid tail of their own for donations over $9,000.

Many audiences love a good woman-driven revenge movie – on land examples being *Kill Bill* (2003) and *Peppermint* (2018). The ability to witness a wronged mermaid getting spectacular and bloody revenge is an opportunity that had not yet been screened. A review claimed that the mermaid was designed as a metaphor for the entire ocean and its fate at the hands of humans. The film was co-created by director, Jeffrey Grellman, and clinical psychologist, Dr Kelly Lauren Baker, who has worked extensively with assault victims.

Just as a memorable movie can spark a wave of copycats or end a trend by being either terrible or unbeatable (*Mermaid Down* has generally good reviews and a seventy-six per cent positive rating on Rotten Tomatoes), this was the last of the main character mermaids … at least, for a while.

One of the most disturbing recent movie mermaids is without a doubt a brief appearance in a black and white psychological horror.

The Lighthouse (2019)

A psychological horror-thriller in which two lighthouse keepers – a veteran and a newbie – spend a long period of time isolated together on a small island, descending into madness. The new keeper (Robert Pattinson) starts to see the older one (Willem Dafoe) behaving in a strange manner, while also hallucinating disturbing sights. Are the men what and who they seem? What is happening on the island, and what is the significance of the mermaid?

Despite the movie's sheer strangeness and willingness to take madness, symbolism, and mermaid genitalia (described by Kayleigh Donaldson in *SYFY* as 'speculative gynaecology') to entirely new levels, *The Lighthouse* was named in many listicles and reviews as the best movie of 2019, nominated for an Academy Award, and to date has won thirty-four awards in total. It has an approval rating of ninety per cent on Rotten Tomatoes.

A cliff-hanger ending?

The Lighthouse was based on Edgar Allen Poe's apparently unfinished short story (also called *The Light-House*) – his last work before his death. But …

was the story actually finished? Written on just two pages and taking the form of diary entries, it details the story of a lighthouse keeper who is looking forward to having some alone time manning the lighthouse with just his dog for company. He begins to hear noises in the walls and starts to worry that he isn't safe or alone in his lighthouse. The next entry notes that he is looking to reassure himself by inspecting the lighthouse and island. The final entry mentions that the structure appears to be set on a bed of chalk … and the story ends there, Poe having died.

Chalk is a very soft crumbly rock, making it a risky foundation for a building and the story could in fact be there on the page; the man is concerned about noises, which could be made by the unstable structure shifting. He notices the chalk foundation and within the next day he is buried in the falling lighthouse. Certainly, Poe often buried people alive in his stories, it was a very common theme for him, but we will never know what his intention was for the ending of this tale. Was the story really unfinished, or just very short?

The mermaid

The mermaid in *The Lighthouse* appears human above the waist, but instead of revealing a compelling siren call, she mockingly screams at Pattinson's character (who had previously had another rather disturbing scene involving an image of a mermaid). Both beautiful and grotesque in a similar manner to the mermaids in *The Lure*, her appearance is one of the most memorable in the film though her scenes were some of the most challenging to shoot. The actress, Valeriia Karaman, was unable to walk wearing her prosthetic tail, so she had to be carried to the water's edge then filmed quickly before the waves could come and wash her away!

This mermaid can be perceived in the same way a siren would, leading lost sailors to their death. Though neither of the men in the lighthouse are sailors and they know exactly where they are physically, they are lost in every way both mentally and spiritually. The tale does not end well for either man and so it is up to the viewer to determine if the mermaid was a hallucination on the part of a man losing his sanity or a real creature fulfilling her role.

The Lighthouse fact file

Released: 2019
Directed by: Robert Eggers
Starring: Willem Dafoe, Robert Pattinson, Valeriia Karaman, Logan Hawkes
Creature: Mermaid
Effects: Prosthetics
Legacy: Many analytical articles!

The 'Hollywood mermaid' is still the defining public image for the mermaid and it will take more than a few creepy or murderous portrayals to change that. Disney has remade *The Little Mermaid* as a live action film with Halle Bailey starring as Ariel and there will be more aspects added to Ariel's story for this generation of young children (and adults too). The tale of a mermaid as a transitional coming-of-age figure may just be getting started. But is there more? We are now perhaps more than ever recognising that there are other cultures outside of Hollywood and other stories that could be told. Other people with something to say.

Brazilian fairytale-fantasy-meets-cop-drama series *Invisible City* (2021) was released to Netflix and created by a largely Brazilian team, acted mostly by Brazilian actors. Many of the characters, demi-gods and forest spirits are unknown to US and European cultures but are well-known and familiar parts of Brazilian folklore, much of it centred around the rainforest and its otherworldly inhabitants.

When environmental police detective, Eric, finds what looks like an endangered pink river dolphin washed up on the beach, it turns out to be something else entirely, placing Eric in the middle of a murder investigation involving characters who are not quite human. Their attitudes to life and humanity ranges greatly; some want nothing more than to be left alone while others greatest ambition appears to be to cause mayhem. Amid the investigation and widening of his world, Eric discovers something about himself in the process. It is a predictable discovery in terms of the plot but the characters and setting are something that many people in the show's audience will not have seen. Camila is an Iara – the Brazilian equivalent to a mermaid. According to the oral tradition of Brazilian folklore, Iara was a once a beautiful woman whose two brothers were so jealous of her that they tried to murder her. She fought back and killed both in self-defence but her father refused to listen to her version of events and drowned her in the river. Now, she sings beautifully, luring men to either come to the water and live with her forever or to their deaths (there are similarities to the rusalka here) depending on the version heard. Eric survives Camila's own attempts to drown him and later she tells him that she became an Iara after her lover drowned her, but she was resurrected and cursed to drown men.

Though the series being in Portuguese might be expected to count against its potential popularity (in general, English language films perform better with an English-speaking audience) despite Netflix never publishing data about its series and viewing figures, *Invisible City* received good reviews online and released its second season in 2022. Reviewers found this second season a little rushed but praised its message about the value of protecting the land.

Whether mermaids and all their sisters and cousins count as deep water monsters or not, the fascination they inspire is not going away any time soon and as opportunities are offered to a wider range of diverse people, settings and legends, filmmakers are finding that there are many stories left to tell.

CHAPTER TEN

SHARKNADO

OR *HELL, NO!*

STARRING: EVERYONE, APPARENTLY

A waterspout over the sea picks up a large variety of sharks, then becomes a raging tornado over Los Angeles. Suddenly a city full of beautiful people is contending with a swirling, building-ripping vortex full of sharks. Our unlikely hero, conveniently named Fin, finds himself on a rescue mission as sharks fall from the sky. That sounds terrible. Or brilliant.

The movie that merely used the words 'enough said' as a tagline and has been described as 'so bad, it's good', 'one and a half hours of your life you'll never get back' and 'utterly terrible' has been mentioned on national news channels, still sells merchandise, trended on Twitter, became the most watched original movie encore in Syfy channel history and spawned five sequels. An impressive legacy!

How did this happen? How was this *allowed* to happen? What does the cult status of the *Sharknado* franchise say about the world of the deep water monster? And ... if you like *Sharknado*, what other movies are out there for you?

Sharknado (2013)

Back in 2006, a *Cow and Boy* webcomic episode was published, joking about the worst movie idea of all time ... sharks blowing around in a tornado. Later, *Leprechauns Revenge* (2012), (a Syfy film about bloodthirsty leprechauns) was released, in which a character makes a joke about a town that was 'never the same after the sharknado hit'. Just a year later, the same year their mockbuster *Atlantic Rim* was released, The Asylum (who else...) also released *Sharknado*. Described as both a 'trash fire' and 'a work of cinematic genius', *Sharknado* was like nothing shown before. The envelope was no longer being pushed, it was whirling around and around in a shark's jaws while people below ran about screaming.

Sharknado originally looked to be another piece of B-movie silliness helped along by a good marketing campaign, attracting slightly fewer viewers to Syfy than average on its first airing ... but celebrities who had watched the movie began to tweet about it, including actors Wil Wheaton and Olivia Wilde. The last two tweets from actor, Cory Monteith, before his death in 2013 were bemused posts about the movie. The Syfy channel showed the movie again twice more that month and each time the viewer count increased dramatically. The next month, *Sharknado* even began playing in cinemas, though box office numbers were relatively low.

Production

So ... the plot of *Sharknado* is really all in the title. It is a ludicrous concept that most filmmakers would have laughed off as a joke, except for director Anthony

C. Ferrante and the team at The Asylum, already responsible for *Snakes on a Train* (2006) and *Abraham Lincoln vs Zombies* (2012).

Even the actors involved approached the project with a mixture of self-deprecating humour and willingness to sacrifice their dignity. At the time the first movie was being cast, the filmmakers disguised how ridiculous the plot sounded. The original title had been *Dark Skies* and lead actress Tara Reid was horrified when the real title emerged, but she later began to get recognised positively for her recurring role in the franchise. Echoing Debbie Gibson's sentiment about life on the set of *Mega Shark vs Giant Octopus*, Reid said in interviews that it was impossible to be too serious when creating such a silly, fun film.

On the other hand, Ian Ziering who plays Fin said that he had serious reservations about the 'unwatchable' script but with a family and new baby to support, he took on the role in order to earn enough to qualify him for the Screen Actors Guild health insurance! He said in an interview that he had been afraid the movie would end his career but by the time it became a cult hit he had already signed on for the sequels.

The initial reluctance of many cast members is now one of several running jokes about *Sharknado*. An episode of *The Big Bang Theory* TV series shows regular guest star, Wil Wheaton, commiserating with aspiring actress Penny over being fired from a terrible movie set, before Wil's agent calls to offer him an audition for *Sharknado 2*. Wheaton excitedly rushes off. In real life, Wheaton did have an uncredited role in the sequel, playing 'dead passenger'.

That chainsaw scene

Aside from the sharks-in-a-tornado image, the scene in which Fin dives into a shark's mouth while holding a chainsaw is probably the most iconic in the franchise and has been reproduced on merchandise many times. But it almost didn't happen. After the movie wrapped, Ian Ziering received a call from director Ferrante asking him to come back in for just one more scene. Though there was no budget left, Ziering agreed and with the help of dubious CGI and a harness, the scene was shot, edited, aired, printed and now appears on t-shirts the world over.

Legacy

The sequels only got stranger, ending up in locations all over the planet, in space, and eventually involving robots, time travel and quotably terrible lines.

Celebrity cameos got more obvious and self-aware, while people with all kinds of claims to fame were requesting a cameo. Just a few of these across the franchise: Jerry Springer gets attacked; Bo Derek plays Tara Reid's character April's mother; David Hasselhoff plays Ian Ziering's character Fin's father … called Gil (of course); *Game of Thrones* creator, George R.R. Martin, was decapitated, echoing one of his own characters shock deaths; Margaret Cho has her wedding ruined; and *Star Trek* star, Nichelle Nichols, plays the NATO general secretary.

How did this film achieve such success? Well, sheer daring was a start and clever promotion helped. The original was released to coincide with *Shark Week* so that people searching online for *Shark Week* or other related terms could not help but find it by accident. It was an inspired marketing tactic!

At one point, discussion on Twitter reached about 5,000 tweets per minute and *Sharknado* still has a surprising seventy-four per cent positivity rate on Rotten Tomatoes! The typical scenes expected in shark or disaster movies were there and the creators struck the right balance between pleasing the audience by providing the expected shots (and gory deaths) and being so unpredictable that the audience would wait to see what the franchise would do next. The Syfy channel began to run a 'Sharknado Week' in tribute and parody to Discovery's *Shark Week*, and against all odds *Sharknado* has become a cult success.

Sharknado: **fact file**

Released: 2013

Directed by: Anthony C. Ferrante

Starring: Tara Reid, Ian Ziering, Cassie Scerbo, Jaason Simmons, John Heard

Creature: Many species of shark in tornadoes

Effects: CGI

Legacy: *Sharknado 2: The Second One* (2014); *Sharknado 3: Oh Hell No!* (2015); *Sharknado 4: The 4th Awakens* (2016); *Sharknado 5: Global Swarming* (2017); *The Last Sharknado: It's About Time* (2018); two spin-offs involving Lava Tarantulas and taking place in the *Sharknado* universe; *Sharknado: The Video Game* (2014); book *How to Survive a Sharknado* by Andrew Shaffer (2014); comic book *Archie vs Sharknado* (2015); and three documentaries: *Sharknado: Feeding Frenzy* (2015); *Sharknado: Heart of Sharkness* (2015); and *The Real Sharknado* (2021)

The way people treat bad movies – perhaps even movies in general – has changed. *Sharknado* is fun, and sometimes that is enough. *Sharknado* is widely considered the defining bad movie in the 'bad movie' genre in which the goal appears to have been to make the worst movie possible; incredulity can keep an audience in their seats and the old saying that all attention is good attention has been known to hold true. Unless a film is outdated or outright offensive, a bad movie can still be a successful one.

In general, filmmakers have moved away from portraying sharks as malevolent by default. *The Reef* showed characters genuine terror exacerbated by their situation – being lost at sea – but the shark was not a threat for a large part of the movie. In a total reversal from the realism trend in the late 2000s, *Sharknado* gave viewers a movie with a situation that could be laughed at. This does not mean that sharks can't add the fear factor to other movies but that our approach to them has changed, there's so much more potential! As the horror-comedy genre began to trend and CGI became more accessible, it was only a matter of time before a movie like this would be made.

Going viral

It has been said that social media and the rise of the 'viral' success has led to the making of movies that would not normally have been given the green light. Before the internet and social media were a part of everyday life in the way they are now, the success of a movie was generally measured on its box office performance. While money is still a huge indicator today, a film performing badly in cinemas does not automatically indicate its failure as it may still become a cult success. Similarly, viral reach is often the goal. Just as *Mega Shark vs Giant Octopus* chased viral recognition, a good social media campaign can lead to public interest just as well as an in-cinema advertisement, if not more, as we're more likely to see it.

Trends influence other trends and evoke responses. Amid the yearly release of *Sharknado* films and other movies with similarly ridiculous plotlines, some filmmakers responded by making character-driven and sombre creature movies, giving fans something more serious to watch and somebody to root for.

In 2015, Ron Howard's epic *In the Heart of the Sea* told the story of the sinking of the *Essex* through a young Herman Melville's interview with survivor Thomas Nickerson. It was an ambitious project with a well-known and very dedicated cast (Chris Hemsworth lost eighteen kilos to play the starving first mate Owen Chase) and a story told through excellent visual effects and cinematography. Yet, it flopped at the box office. The director's way of introducing more modern and enlightened viewpoints (like 'whaling is wrong') through scene cuts and time jumps does not translate to the screen. The movie was described by many as disjointed and so full of ideas that it constantly interrupted itself. Still, many acknowledged that *In the Heart of the Sea* was worth a watch and recommended that the audience judge for themselves.

Away from the epic stretch of the sea and marooned on a claustrophobic rock, a monster horror film became more popular than expected despite the director's insistence that this is a survival film and not, in fact, a creature feature at all.

The Shallows (2016)

Experienced surfer and medical student, Nancy, is on a personal mission: to find an island of sentimental value to her family. While surfing in the vicinity she comes too close to a whale corpse, attracting the attention of the great white shark feeding on it. Dealing with a bite to her leg and the circling shark, Nancy pulls herself onto a rock. She is safe for now but running out of time; the rocky area is tidal and will be completely covered by the sea in hours. Sooner or later, she will have to swim for her life.

Nancy is played by Blake Lively, who was inspired by her husband Ryan Reynolds's performance in the movie *Buried* (2010) which also focused on a person in a situation in which they are trapped and alone. While Lively's character is trapped in paradise, the movie feels claustrophobic. She cannot leave the rock she is on without risking the shark attacking her, but it is only a matter of time before she has to.

Horror and survival movie characters often act in ways entirely counterproductive to their predicament and it is an enduring trope which often ruins movies as far as reviews are concerned. Nancy is smart and unlike many protagonists in survival movies, she begins with a fighting chance and a self-preserving demeanour, making her an easier character for an audience to support. Nancy sensibly tells somebody where she is going, keeps a wary distance from the two strangers surfing nearby, attempts to warn other surfers about the shark, attracts attention from a man on land (though his intentions are so far from honourable it's almost cathartic when he gets bitten in half) and finally uses all of the tools at her disposal, including the knowledge she has gained as a medical student, in order to perform basic surgery on herself, though not all of the scenarios she faces are in any way realistic.

The science or lack of it. How realistic is *The Shallows*?
There are several memorable scenes in *The Shallows*, the first being Nancy's predicament in the first place, but how realistic are they?

Being bitten: Sharks bite if they feel threatened, if they are investigating something they are unsure about (like a human toddler putting everything in their mouth) or in a case of mistaken identity – assuming the person is a creature they can eat. Nancy is near an enormous rotting whale carcass which the shark is eating. With an abundance of food in front of it, pursuing Nancy as prey would be unusual behaviour but it is possible that she could be perceived as competition for the food source. Many sharks are territorial and would send other animals a clear 'go away' message if one approached something it was eating.

Being trapped: The idea that a shark would circle her while there is an easier meal right in front of it plays into the unfair 'evil shark' trope. Shark expert, Chris Lowe, spoke to *Smithsonian Magazine* about known shark behaviour compared to *The Shallows*. He explained that while they do patrol areas looking for food, the behaviour it shows in the film (circling Nancy's rock having 'chosen' her as its next meal) is inaccurate. This has been a criticised aspect of the film due to The *Jaws* Effect and the outdated trope in which sharks act more like a vengeful person or serial killer than an animal. In this situation, despite Blake Lively's line acknowledging the animal is not at fault and interviews given by the director where he explains that she entered its territory, this has been considered contradictory to the events shown in the plot.

Swimming race: Nancy times the circling shark in order to figure out how much time she will have to retrieve something from the water, but while she is a competent surfer and certainly a strong swimmer, the fact is that the top speed of a great white shark has been monitored at 40 kilometres per hour and the average human being swims at around 3 kilometres per hour. Even the top speed of Olympic swimmer Michael Phelps is under 10 kilometres per hour. The idea that this circling can be timed as though it is a toy train going around and around a track is ludicrous. It is possible for a shark to change direction and speed up!

Serial killer: Later, the shark appears to attack anyone who enters the water. In 2021, there were just nine shark-related fatalities deemed 'unprovoked', out of a total of eleven fatalities recorded around the world. The one in *The Shallows* attacks four people, killing three of them, in around forty-eight hours!

The jellyfish shield: Later, Nancy shields herself by hiding in a swarm of jellyfish after noticing the shark being hurt by coral which she was warned about earlier. The coral is described as stinging like a jellyfish, so when the jellyfish arrive, Nancy holds her breath and sinks down to hide among them. Shark skin is so tough that a jellyfish would not be able to cause damage to it – even a whole swarm of them. It is a compelling scene to watch but utterly fictional.

Shark cage: Finally, in the 'showdown' scene used in most of the promotional material, Nancy has pulled herself onto a buoy which the shark attacks several times. Nancy then uses it as a makeshift shark cage before using gravity and excellent breath-holding capabilities to escape. None of this is even remotely practical or possible, but it makes a hell of a spectacle!

Reviews

Most magazines and reviewers appear to have an unspoken agreement that all articles ranking shark movies place *Jaws* in the first spot, but in May 2022 *Cosmopolitan Magazine* made what may be the most controversial move in shark movie history and placed it in second place … below *The Shallows*!

It performed much better than expected at the box office and in general the public loved it. *The Shallows* still places highly in shark movie ranking lists, either as a worthy runner up to *Jaws* or in third place behind *Deep Blue Sea*. Rotten Tomatoes lists a seventy-eight per cent approval rating for it and of the four awards it was nominated for, two were public choice awards.

Critics have mostly offered great praise – both for surpassing the usual shark movie clichés and for Blake Lively's performance in carrying an entire movie almost alone. Still, the reviews which criticise it have used strong words to make strong points.

Staci Layne Wilson's review published in *Dread Central* had mild praise for the shark but criticised the unnecessary sub plot involving Nancy's deceased mother (death not shark-related) as well as the writer's choice to have Nancy do much of her planning by thinking out loud – describing 'Anthony Jaswinski's intelligence-insulting screenplay'.

The family subplot is also criticised by *The A.V. Club*'s Ignatiy Vishnevetsky, who disagreed with Staci Layne Wilson's praise for the shark, calling it an 'elastic looking digital monster'. He ended his review asking if a heroine could just survive a shark attack without the unnecessary baggage.

The effects

The vast majority of the movie is shot on blue screen with Blake Lively in a tank. Director, Jaume Collet-Serra, said in an interview with *WeGotThisCovered* that just one shot out of every scene is 'real'. The real location scenes were filmed on the protected Lord Howe Island in the Tasman Sea between Australia and New Zealand. For Nancy to have her rock, the team had to transport and place an enormous boulder into the sea while taking care not to harm any local wildlife, including the endangered muttonbird population. Ever since the disastrous aftermath of the filming of *The Beach*, which destroyed large areas of the natural beach setting of Ko Phi Phi Le, filming locations have needed extra layers of protection from crews and post-movie tourism.

Collet-Serra claimed he did not want the film to be a typical creature feature, preferring to take inspiration from survival films. *The Shallows* does show this influence; there are shots of Nancy dealing with the isolation, the concept of saying goodbye to her loved ones and also the psychological torture coming from the fact that safety is just a few metres away but she cannot reach it. However, there is a giant shark in the movie and this is the reason she's hurt, trapped and unable to reach the shore in the first place. Some may well class the movie as both survival horror and creature feature on that basis.

Chris Lowe felt that the shark itself looked realistic but in fact it is entirely CGI, with Collet-Serra feeling strongly that his vision could not be achieved by using animatronics. In fact, so many of the props broke in the water that he told *WeGotThisCovered* that he was often just pointing Blake Lively in the direction she needed to be looking in, instead of having her look toward a physical object.

On the other hand, the injured seagull sharing Nancy's rock is very real! Originally, the idea had been to use an animatronic or CGI bird but the producers were very much against the idea and as Collet-Serra said, they would work around a real bird because nobody can act the part of a seagull better than a seagull. There were three cast in the movie. The one filmed most was named Sully and he lives in an Australian sanctuary. Blake Lively named his character 'Steven Seagull' for the movie.

There is comparatively little gore compared to the blood-splattered affairs many creature horror movies have become. This was a deliberate choice from Collet-Serra, but there are still some brutal scenes involving Nancy performing surgery on herself, which was done with a prosthetic that Lively stitched up on camera – very realistically. There was no CGI involved and shooting this scene even disturbed the cameramen!

Did You Know?
Isabella Nichols, the number one junior champion surfer in the world, was Lively's surf double for the more complex surfing scenes, but Lively still did most of her own stunts. During a scene near the end in which Nancy gets yet another injury, things get a little more real than the crew would have liked; the blood coming from Lively's nose was the result of an actual mishap!

The Shallows **fact file**

Released: 2016
Directed by: Jaume Collet-Serra
Starring: Blake Lively, Sully the Seagull
Creature: Great white shark
Effects: CGI
Legacy: Almost certainly the only film to ever be ranked above *Jaws* in a shark movie list!

The Shallows **vs** *47 Meters Down*
In 2017, *47 Meters Down* went for the same kind of realism and claustrophobia used in *The Shallows*, but this time at the bottom of the sea. Two characters end up trapped in a shark cage which has broken off from the boat, which is still above them but out of range of communication … unless somebody leaves the safety of the cage and swims upward, risking both nitrogen narcosis and the sharks. There are some truly unsettling sights and clever use of light as well as a shock twist ending that for once does not revolve around, or even include, the death of a single shark, but it did not do especially well at the box office or

in the eyes of critics. This did not prevent a poorly received sequel from being made. *47 Meters Down: Uncaged* (2019), was a sequel in name only as none of the characters are the same and the unusual setting is very different.

Part of the reason for both *47 Meters Down* movies' lack of success could be due to *The Shallows*! Blake Lively's character was smart, resourceful and likeable. Compared with the lying sisters and unsafe boat crew in *47 Meters Down*, and the gang of school-skipping teen girls who sneak into a dangerous location, dive too deep and irritate local wildlife in *47 Meters Down: Uncaged*, it is a little more difficult to root for anyone but the sharks!

More from The Asylum

In between The Asylum's *Age of Tomorrow* (2014) and *Android Cop* (2014) (absolutely, totally different creations to *Edge of Tomorrow* (2014) and *RoboCop* (2014), of course), the production company knew that they'd have to keep the *Sharknado* juggernaut going, while also releasing the next instalments in the *Mega Shark* series and reviving the *Shark Attack* series that began with *2-Headed Shark Attack* and would eventually end up with a 6-headed shark. This book cannot go into detail about every single deep water monster film released by The Asylum simply because, with the exception of a standout concept, viral success or catastrophic failure, there are simply too many to cover and they all do exactly what is said in the title (though Chapter Thirteen is a checklist of one hundred monster movies from the deep for the die-hard fan to tick off).

Even as the world of film moved on and around *Sharknado* (and there were plenty of other monster movies released which were not influenced in any way by the franchise) there was one more major effect caused by the *Sharknado* phenomenon. Its success attracted the most unlikely people to the most unlikely films. Cameo roles in the *Sharknado* franchise had become so sought after that now even B-movies and 'made for TV' specials were seeing well-known and talented actors in the cast list. When the made-for-TV sci-fi horror *Bermuda Tentacles* (2014) starred the action megastar, Linda Hamilton, (best known for *Terminator 2* (1991)) it was an unexpected move, yet the film also starred several other actors known for much more critically acclaimed movies. How these veteran actors were persuaded is anyone's guess; maybe it was the influence of *Sharknado*'s stream of celebrity guests? Suddenly the B-movie, while never destined for Academy Award success, was becoming less of a showreel embarrassment and more of a fun stopgap between more serious projects. Writer, Jose Prendes, was convinced to write for *Mega Shark vs Mecha Shark* (2014) based on the success of *Sharknado* in spite of the writer acknowledging he had not enjoyed previous films released by The Asylum.

In *The Guardian* newspaper's farewell article to the *Sharknado* franchise as the sixth and final movie was released in 2018, writer Stuart Heritage acknowledged that without *Sharknado*, summer action blockbuster *The Meg* (2018) would never have been released. A B-movie concept, but with A-list actors and an enormous budget.

The Meg (2018)

Rescue diver, Jonas Taylor, is on a mission to save the crew of a damaged nuclear submarine, when he sees an unidentified but enormous creature ramming the hull and makes the decision to save the people he has already rescued from the submarine, losing some of his own team in the process. He is plagued by survivors' guilt and frustration as his account of what happened is blamed on pressure-induced psychosis. Nobody believes him until an underwater research lab funded by a billionaire discovers what could be the same creature. Reluctantly, Taylor comes to offer guidance and work with the team to decide how best to kill the creature, revealed to be a megalodon and thought to have been extinct. Of course, there's an escape, technology, self-sacrifice, a tiny dog and a giant prehistoric shark hunting unsuspecting swimmers.

Based on the 1997 novel by Steve Alten, teams had been trying to make the film ever since the book's publication but instead it had hit 'development hell' in which the concept was bounced between writers and studios until finally the rights reverted to Alten. In 2015, he announced that a film adaptation was back on track. Over the next two years, big names would enter and leave due to either budgetary issues or creative differences, including Eli Roth and Guillermo del Toro, but then names began to stick. Action star and former Olympic diver, Jason Statham, was announced in the starring role, before Ruby Rose, Li Bingbing and Jessica McNamee were confirmed to have signed on too.

International relations
The Meg was an American and Chinese co-production, featuring well-known Chinese actors and paying attention to culture. Jason Statham also happens to have a huge following in China.

To be formally recognised as a co-production with Chinese production companies, a movie must meet three guidelines: be at least partly set in China; be backed with significant financing from China; and feature Chinese people cast in main roles. Most of *The Meg* was filmed in New Zealand but it was still awarded the co-production status for scoring well on the other criteria.

In compliance with the Chinese rule that movies be suitable for audiences of all ages, *The Meg* focuses on the action parts of the story rather than the potential for shark-related horror and gore.

Chinese censorship checks look out for anything that has the potential to make the country look bad and making a movie that set shark attacks in Chinese waters was taking a big risk, but it paid off.

Creating the shark and its world

The megalodon was created using CGI, but as the team required a very fast turnaround the visual effects team made very, very rough drafts of the shark shots and sent them for approval before continuing with effects and realism. No more joints, hinges and uncooperative rubbery animatronic sharks; now, a computer programme worked with muscle and bone structure to allow the team to make the shark move in a realistic way, muscle by muscle if required.

In addition to the main character – the megalodon – more work needed to be done. The idea that an entire previously unknown ecosystem existed needed to be clearly conveyed; which entailed creating an entire previously unknown ecosystem! Over thirty different kinds of seaweed, fish, jellyfish and less complex organisms all needed to be created from scratch, as well as the ocean floor and terrain itself. Bubbles were important too, and the tiny movements of nearly-microscopic debris in the water. The things that are easy to overlook are usually the elements that make the difference between real-looking and not, and as much as critics like to tear *The Meg* apart, the special effects impressed nearly every critic reviewing the movie.

What happened?

Casting big action stars like Jason Statham in a movie with an enormous budget and a formula often associated with a summer blockbuster, made by a team that had clearly been carefully honed over many years, *The Meg* was set to be a monstrous success across two countries known for being huge consumers in the movie market and with a love of monsters. So why was it released to such a mediocre reception?

While the performances of the lead actors have been praised and the action sequences have been seen as fun and well done by most audiences and critics, the movie itself has only a forty-six per cent rating on Rotten Tomatoes. It appears that with the money spent and serious treatment of the material, filmmakers were hoping to make a movie with the same kind of cultural impact as *Jurassic Park*, but *The Meg* had very little originality and contained frustrating 'red herring' elements that appeared onscreen and were yet never actually used (like a small child's shoes with flashing lights which at no point played a role in finding her, luring the shark anywhere or giving away a hiding place). It has mostly been described as unoriginal, no matter how big the shark, the budget or the stars are.

The concept for *The Meg* is undoubtedly B-movie fodder, and yet it was not treated with the same self-aware silliness found in a B-movie. Many of the tropes an audience would expect from this kind of film were missing. For example, the teasing shot in which a helicopter makes its way over the open ocean. The camera follows it … and follows it … and yet no shark jumps out of the ocean to take it down, or even appears at all. *The Meg* contains many scene set-ups that we have come to expect from B-movies, so when these kinds of events do not happen the audience is not necessarily satisfied. Moving away from these predictable but fun elements was probably not the best idea when there was nothing to replace them with.

The Meg was even nominated for a Golden Raspberry award for 'Worst prequel, remake, rip-off or sequel' (referring to *Jaws*). Even then, it failed to rise (or sink) to a winning entry here, losing out to *Holmes and Watson* (2018). Owen Gleiberman of *Variety* published an excellent review of the movie, concluding that it wasn't good enough or bad enough to make any kind of significant impact.

The Meg did actually make a profit despite mediocre reviews and a sequel was almost immediately announced for release in 2023, based on Steve Alten's second Meg book: *The Trench*.

The Meg fact file

Released: 2018
Directed by: Jon Turteltaub
Starring: Jason Statham, Li Bingbing, Rainn Wilson, Ruby Rose, Winston Chao, Cliff Curtis, Shuya Sophia Cai
Creature: Megalodon
Effects: CGI
Legacy: *Meg 2: The Trench* (2023)

Suffering a worse fate with not only mediocre reviews but outright outrage was *Pacific Rim: Uprising* (2018). The decision to minimise the iconic character, Mako Mori, by killing her shortly into the movie and to all intents and purposes replacing her with a younger version, was a decision that went down very poorly with viewers.

The monster action genre would move onto land with movies like *Rampage* (2018), but while the release of *The Meg* brought the big-budget shark silliness to a grinding crawl, there was one more extremely silly cult movie yet to come; the ultimate parody of a parody....

Bad CGI Sharks (2019)

Estranged brothers, Matthew and Jason, are unexpectedly reunited and when a terrible shark movie script they once worked on together takes on a life of its own, they find themselves being hunted by a variety of poorly rendered CGI sharks which appear in snapchat filters, pause attacks in order to buffer and (along with Jason's ludicrous man-bun) become the stars for the right reason: they're hilarious.

The team started attracting attention before the film was released; the reviews from people who hadn't watched it were scathing. The reviews from those who had were generally very positive including *Film Blitz*, *The Daily Jaws* and YouTuber Decker Shado. Even IMDB reviewers joined in on the comedy, with one parody review barely taking about the actual movie, just comparing it favourably with *The Godfather*.

Many low budget monster-themed B-movies are let down by a single-minded focus on fairly awful looking monsters, leading to a neglected script and interchangeable character templates. *Bad CGI Sharks* was working with a shoestring budget of $6,257.34 and a crew of five people. There is not much that can be done with that kind of money and so the team decided to play to the strengths they had: you can write a good plot and create interesting characters with no money at all. The movie was shot in just twenty-one days but editing took a full two years.

Bad CGI Sharks has won six awards to date at the Golden Wheat Awards, 'Only The Best' International Film Awards and The Gladiator Film Festival.

Bad CGI Sharks fact file

Released: 2019
Directed by: MaJaMa
Starring: Matthew Ellsworth, Jason Ellsworth, Matteo Molinari, Jenn
   Liu
Creature: Sharks
Effects: (Bad) CGI
Legacy: A music video by mostly shark movie niche YouTube creator
   FLOSHARK 3D, featuring the song *Higher* by the band Dark Signal

You probably can't beat *Sharknado* for big budget horror-comedy but in terms of self-aware parody and great intentions, *Bad CGI Sharks* might just come out on top. After this final laugh, eventually the creature horror genre would take a new direction. Far, far away from whirling freak weather conditions, 'meta' interpretations of CGI monsters and accidental prehistoric creature releases, romance would blossom in an underground laboratory between a woman and a character who has already appeared in this book....

WHAT'S NEXT...?

CHAPTER ELEVEN

CTHULHU   THE CREATURE   LOVE   DEATH   AND ROBOTS

In 2011, writer, Daniel Kraus, collaborated with film director and supporter of both underdogs and monsters, Guillermo del Toro, to write a piece of work inspired by *Creature from the Black Lagoon*. Del Toro, already having a soft spot for the Gill-man, had imagined him having a happy ending and getting the girl a long time ago, while Kraus had also been sitting on an idea of his own: what if the Gill-man was in a laboratory, and what if the janitor broke him out and made him a safe haven in the bathtub at home? Their resulting collaboration became both a book and a movie.

The Shape of Water (2017)

It is 1962 and Elisa Esposito is a janitor at a secret government laboratory. She is orphaned and although she can hear, she cannot speak, having been found lying by a river as a baby, with strange wounds on either side of her neck. She communicates using sign language and has two friends: her next-door neighbour and her co-worker. When a captured, amphibious man known as the Asset is brought to the laboratory, Elisa is fascinated by him, and the feeling is mutual. Her sympathy for him becomes a bond which eventually turns into love. When Elisa overhears plans to euthanise the Asset, she plans to break him out and return him to the water.

The movie's 1962 setting provided some interesting talking points for the actors. Octavia Spencer who plays Zelda, Elisa's co-worker and friend, pointed out that Elisa had gravitated to marginalised communities (Zelda is Black and Elisa's neighbour, Giles, is gay) as she herself was both disabled in a way and constantly underestimated. The tendency of outsiders to assume that Elisa is stupid or deaf is something that Elisa uses to her advantage; she is able to listen in on plans and obtain information while being apparently 'invisible'. In one scene she tells the lab directors exactly what she thinks of them in very explicit terms using sign language while keeping a polite expression on her face, leaving Zelda to formulate a more acceptable answer.

Though she cannot speak using her larynx, Elisa is far from voiceless; she even gets a powerful monologue though in an unusual but very effective writing decision, her words are spoken by another character. She tells Giles to repeat the words she is signing back to her as she fights to defend the life of the Asset. It's a speech that anybody in love could make, talking of how he listens, he loves her just as she is, he's happy to see her – all the little things that together comprise being 'in love'.

Michael Shannon played Colonel Richard Strickland, the man responsible for capturing the Gill-man, aka Asset. He also weighed in on the modern shift in perception, noting that in both the original 1950s film and the 1960s setting of *The Shape of Water* (which can be seen as a direct sequel), his character would have been seen as the hero while to a modern audience he and his actions were unquestionably villainous, and more chilling for the fact that Strickland would have seen himself as the hero too.

Creature design

The creature designers took a big risk with the look of the Gill-man. They could have taken a potentially easier route and made him more physically and romantically appealing to the audience in the same way as mermaids and sirens, but they stayed true to the original concept from *Creature from the Black Lagoon*, updating him with elaborate costuming and CGI for the final touches.

As with most of del Toro's films, the creature design would centre around a 'man in a suit'. The Gill-man suit was made by Legacy Effects and included animatronic parts that would be enhanced digitally by effects company Mr X to emphasise aspects like subtle facial muscle movements that wouldn't have been visible under the prosthetics. This was especially important as the creature needed to be believable and beautiful on land and in water where most of the shots were recreated digitally.

The suit itself was made from a foam rubber base, with silicone for details like the gills. The aim was to recreate the look of a fish swimming through water, with translucent membranes and scaly textures. Much of the face was created with make-up and partial masks so that the actor could still emote, and it took an average of three hours each day to get him into the full suit and makeup.

The Asset is played by experienced creature actor, Doug Jones. Jones also plays the Faun and the Pale Man from *Pan's Labyrinth* (2006) – a del Toro fantasy horror film – and said in an interview with NPR that he felt 'utter terror' upon being told that the Gill-man was going to be the romantic lead! He discussed his character's body language with del Toro, who had a very specific idea; part hero, part god, very regal, with elements of a matador's confidence and sensuality … and yet remaining definitively 'not human'. Jones visited dance studios to practise a way of moving distinctly differently from other monsters he had portrayed in the past. Del Toro clarified the nature of the Asset to help Jones's inspiration: he is not a monster or mutation but a river god, and therefore he acts accordingly, with immense dignity.

Building a romance … without speaking

One big challenge with showing the romance unfolding onscreen was that both characters were unable to speak, needing distinctly different ways of communicating both with the outside world and with each other. Elisa's sign language would only take her character so far, as the Asset did not share her language and Doug Jones's Asset needed to convey sentience, emotion and intelligence if a budding romance with a human character was to be believed. Seeing these two characters learning to communicate with each other, and find common ground takes place amid a great deal of mystery surrounding Elisa's origins. The scars on her neck were never explained – are the two characters more closely connected than first meets the eye? Is Elisa human at all? Are the scars gills and was she unable to speak because she had never learned to breathe through them? All this gives us more to think about than a one-dimensional villain and creature designed to elicit nothing more than sympathy.

The book Daniel Kraus wrote alongside the film was able to show us the perspective of the captured Gill-man as he could write from the point of view of multiple characters at once without the need for extra exposition.

Elisa uses musicals and old lavish films as escapism. While eating dinner with the Asset she grows increasingly, tearfully frustrated that she cannot express the depth of her feelings in a way that he will understand. We see her fantasising about the two of them in a musical dance number in which she is finally able to sing, before the colour returns to her world and she loses the ability, communicating her love for him through sign language that he is unable to understand at that time. It is an interesting directive use of colour. Usually movies do the opposite, showing fantasies in brighter colours which lose their vibrance when the characters return to their drab everyday world. Del Toro had originally considered making the entire movie in black and white to resemble the original but eventually decided against it.

An unlikely success

There have been many, many films which had the right plot, the right actors and seemingly the right everything, and yet somehow don't impress and are not remembered. *The Shape of Water* is completely and utterly bizarre yet people fell in love with it, audience and critics alike. But why?

To start with, Elisa is *weird*. She's also endearing, smart and lonely. We're rooting for her, even if her love story happens to be with an amphibious creature!

Many films set in the past are rightly criticised for a lack of diversity and inaccurate representation of the demographics of the age, and the makers of these often cite a more bigoted time period as the reason for this. *The Shape of Water* effortlessly shows that setting a film in a past era does not have to be a barrier to casting a diverse range of characters, and some film writers with varying disabilities have commented on the rarity of seeing a disabled person cast as the romantic lead, making Elisa a positive representation.

It's a love story, but more than just a romance. Even the love between friends is placed in the foreground with Elisa enlisting the help of her friends, who show various degrees of reluctance but at the core of their actions is the love they have for her. In order to allow her the opportunity for romance, they act in unexpected ways. In *The Shape of Water*, love is strange, but love also conquers all.

Del Toro would work on both book and movie at the same time but Kraus did not want to be influenced by del Toro's visuals and end up writing a copy of the film, so he never visited the set, or even looked at production stills. They had decided that they wanted to turn the initial idea – a happy ending for the creature – into these two distinct pieces of art, but without making them so different that one would look like an alternative ending for the other.

If a monster has no intention of eating or harming humans at all and is a character in its own right with the ability to communicate, is it still a 'monster movie'? *The Shape of Water* crossed genres; a feat that Guillermo del Toro has mastered, earning him the trust of producers, which is a battle he admits has been hard won. Although it is a fantasy, a drama and a romance – though with one or two horrific scenes involved – it *has to* also count as a monster movie; there's one walking around onscreen! But *The Shape of Water* rose above the usual monster movie tropes by portraying a human character as convincingly monstrous while giving the creature a trait rarely seen in movie monsters: humanity.

Did You Know?

The Shape of Water has a ninety-two per cent positivity rating on Rotten Tomatoes, grossed over 195 million dollars, received 264 award nominations, and won 93 of them- including 4 Academy Awards: Best Picture, Best Director, Best Original Score and Best Production Design.

The Shape of Water **fact file**

Released: 2017

Directed by: Guillermo del Toro

Starring: Sally Hawkins, Michael Shannon, Richard Jenkins, Doug Jones, Michael Stuhlbarg, Octavia Spencer

Creature: Gill-man, aka the Asset – a river god

Effects: Prosthetics and animatronics enhanced using CGI

Legacy: *The Shape of Water* book (2018)

The way we consume media has changed; the COVID-19 pandemic kickstarted several new waves of creativity. The idea that our attention spans are getting markedly shorter has been discussed in multiple articles, think pieces, academic studies and worried conversations the world over. Many studies have 'proven' this to be the case while a 2021 article in *Psychology Today* clarified that it appears to be our ability to take on new concepts and ideas that has decreased rather than our attention span (which does not magically disappear after the allotted time, it just needs a 'reset' break). This is potentially a result of the continuous stress of the COVID-19 pandemic, though people have blamed the rise of short-form video platforms like TikTok (with Instagram and YouTube following suit with their own versions of the short-form video) as a factor exacerbating the problem.

TikTok's allotted video time was originally sixty seconds long, though the platform now allows people to post three-minute videos. While many people are quick to disparage the platform, dismissing it as being for 'teenagers lip syncing to music', the truth is that it has been a genre starter all of its own.

Explorers, educators and enthusiasts use short-form video to talk about their areas of interest from period fashion to specific creature behaviour, giving people the facts in bitesize form, which can spark a new interest for viewers. As the TikTok platform is algorithm-based, the more content a viewer consumes dealing with a particular niche or theme, the more the app will offer the viewer similar content.

Short stories of around 1,000 words or less are known as 'Flash Fiction'. The original silent movies were only a few minutes – even seconds – long. It was only a matter of time before the 'short story' format re-entered the movie world. Telling an entire story in short format takes skill. For example, the first few minutes of the Pixar film *Up* (2009) documents several decades in the life of a couple from first meeting to death and is often listed as one of the best and most emotive works of storytelling of all time. A short movie can showcase the talent and creativity of its makers and allow people to trial new ideas without committing to making and editing several hours of footage. When taking this to social media like TikTok, the short-form video has provided a way for creators to be seen more immediately and build a fanbase without needing to follow the traditional and often fruitless path of submitting work to agents and publishers.

'LIGHTS ARE OFF' is a name well-known on TikTok, Instagram and YouTube for short-form horror videos which regularly go viral. These videos sometimes rely on jump scares and sometimes on a creepy and disturbing factor that viewers cannot always pinpoint. The hashtag #thalassophobia often features in the captions to these videos and some of the most viewed and shared videos feature tiny divers and gargantuan sea monsters.

TikTok is sometimes criticised for a lack of originality; once people find what works in the algorithm, it is often easier to try and replicate that success than risk an entirely new concept, especially with a small budget. After all, what is described as samey in one context can be considered a trademark in another. The work of LIGHTS ARE OFF involving deep water monsters tends to either feature slow-moving creatures which keep the viewer's attention, until their perspective is changed and they find the jaws of another creature looming toward them, or gives the viewer a sustained sense of unease before a jump scare seemingly comes out of nowhere. Dominating this format still requires originality and continued creativity; the videos created by LIGHTS ARE OFF attract millions of views per video on TikTok alone.

Shortly before the pandemic made TikTok creators out of many of us, a new and experimental but much anticipated short-form series emerged on Netflix. Episodes lasting no longer than seventeen minutes and with different storylines, characters and even animation styles showcased myriad futuristic worlds. The series was modelled on previous animated stories in the 1970s but was more ambitious, thought provoking, occasionally controversial, and very successful. Two more series were later released. A cyberpunk universe is generally the last place many would expect to find deep water monster stories but even *Love, Death and Robots* was not immune to the allure of the sea monster.

Love, Death and Robots (2019, 2021, 2022)

Fish Night

Season One of *Love, Death and Robots* aired in 2019, with eighteen episodes. *Fish Night* told the story of two bored salesmen whose car breaks down in the middle of the desert, which used to be an old sea bed, as the older man explains to the younger one. They have to spend the night in the desert and the two discuss the idea that if human ghosts can haunt their old homes, what if the ghosts of the sea could haunt theirs?

This appears to be a new setting for the Greek tale of Icarus, who wants to fly to the sun but forgets the danger, but while *Fish Night* was not the most critically praised or memorable of the episodes, it has been the subject of many discussions from a symbolic point of view. The relationship between the two men has been questioned; they seem comfortable enough with each other to not only complain and argue but to lay claim to sleeping spots without the forced politeness two strangers might exhibit, and the younger man takes his clothes off to swim without a second thought.

People have suggested that there is no younger man after all; he's a metaphor for the loss of the older man's youth. The two men are wearing almost exactly the same thing and their dialogue could be interpreted as an inner monologue. Others have taken a more literal interpretation, seeing it as a simple commentary on the fact that humans have not been the worlds apex predators for nearly as long as we like to think and that if we really were to go back in time, we'd find the world a considerably more dangerous place. After all, the episode is based on fact; many deserts were seas once. Meaning and symbolism aside, some viewers loved it for its animation while others found the abrupt ending very frustrating. Either way, it is a story that makes you think, and demonstrates that even in the most unlikely places, filmmakers will find a way to include a monster of the deep.

Not all of the episodes had been written with animation in mind, in fact, most were adaptations of short stories from accomplished and respected writers. In the original story by Joe R. Lansdale, the team were a father and son and it was the old man who went into the sea, provoking a different interpretation about the old man choosing to die on his terms.

Fish Night fact file

Directed by: Damian Nenow
Original story: Joe R. Lansdale
Creature: Shark – presumably a megalodon
Effects: Animated
Length: Ten minutes

Love, Death and Robots took a break for the year 2020 but returned in 2021 with significantly fewer episodes. The series was well-received again, though to less fanfare than the original. There appeared to be no standout episodes this time but the makers still found a way to include a sea monster or several.

Ice

In the episode *Ice*, a family of four have moved from Earth to an ice-covered planet. The eldest son, Sedgewick, is 'unmodded'; he moves like a normal human being and has the senses of a normal human being, while his younger brother Fletcher has the gymnastics ability and fluid motions of a dancer, lightning-fast reflexes and the ability to heal quickly. Sneaking out of the house at night, the brothers join a group of modded teenagers in a game of 'chicken' across the ice, where Frostwhales breach and speed is everything.

The episode didn't get rave reviews but it's a nice tale about brothers supporting each other when push comes to shove, literally. Modded Fletcher falls from an apparent injury to his leg, while unmodded Sedgewick helps him to safety, gaining him acceptance in the group. In the story that this short was based on, the brothers fall out over Fletcher faking the injury- a considerably less peaceable ending than the one we are given instead.

The game could have been played with machinery, guards or even shifting icebergs but the fact is, sea creatures are just that bit more exciting. The Frostwhales are luminous, gravity defying and add an extra element of danger to the water. The freezing temperatures mean humans can't enter, giving the creatures' world an extra dimension of mystery.

> *Ice* **fact file**
>
> **Directed by:** Robert Valley
> **Original story:** Rich Larson
> **Creature:** Frostwhales
> **Effects:** Animated
> **Length:** Thirteen minutes

In 2022, Season Three arrived, back on form and containing at least one standout episode and arguably three deep water monsters. For a series of just nine episodes, that is really quite impressive!

Bad Travelling

The longest of the episodes this season appears to go back in time, setting the story on a hunting boat in a *Moby Dick* style seascape, with shark hunting ships travelling to and fro across the ocean, occasionally never to return. The phenomenon, the audience learn, is known as 'bad travelling'. A giant crablike creature attacks the ship and while it cannot speak, it uses dead members of the crew as its mouthpiece just as a ventriloquist would use a dummy and gives the ship's navigator Torrin a horrible choice. The moral dilemma threatens to tear the crew apart … literally!

Despite the cyberpunk setting that *Love, Death and Robots* is known for, *Bad Travelling* feels like a tale from long ago, just with a different monster and a very modern animation style. But it is actually based on a short story by Neal Asher from an anthology entitled *Space Pirates*, so these are space sharks, a space crustacean and a space ocean. Still, it reads like an old time-y whaling horror complete with a *Here Be Monsters* atmosphere. We even get our gratuitous shot of seals leaping out of the ocean, one of which meeting its death in the jaws of one of the immense Jable sharks the crew are hunting. Too tough for leather and too greasy to make good food, the Jable sharks do, however, have oil in them.

According to the subtitles, the invading crustacean is called a thanapod. The Greek translation could mean death-foot or 'death on legs', and it lives up to its name. The episode is gory and involves pulverized dead bodies and zombie-esque imagery.

The episode was very well received for its visuals which were extremely disturbing, as well as for the debate-worthy moral dilemma: the crew must choose between allowing the thanapod to run riot kaiju-style onto a well populated island, leaving them all unharmed as part of the bargain, or to risk their lives by tricking the creature and setting it down on an uninhabited island. Torrin takes matters into his own hands and a debate raged on Reddit over whether he or the crew were the most monstrous.

The animation was done with motion capture – filming the actors on a set and mapping their facial expressions. The animation studio then exaggerated and caricatured their features. A lot of the story was told using light; the lead character's dual nature hinted at throughout by having him appear half-lit for much of the time. This was director David Fincher's first animated project. Having already directed horror and thriller movies like *Alien 3* (1992) and *Se7en* (1995) and TV series like *Mindhunter*, Fincher is no stranger to suspense, gore and morally complex disturbing characters.

Bad Travelling fact file

Directed by: David Fincher
Original story: Neal Asher
Creature: Thanapod, Jable shark (one shot)
Effects: Animated and motion capture
Length: Twenty-one minutes

One of the upcoming trends in horror has been sitting under our feet and possibly at the bottom of the ocean for years, slowly unfurling a tentacle occasionally, until it decides to unleash the full scope of its unnamed horror on the world. The Deep Ones. The Old Ones. The unknowable Lovecraftian monstrosities. The episode *In Vaulted Halls Entombed* featured an imprisoned monster that bears a striking resemblance to H.P. Lovecraft's creation, Cthulhu, but as most of the action takes place in the titular vaulted halls and the desert, we cannot be sure. If he is indeed Cthulhu, he is supposed to be under the sea, and the makers have been very quiet on the subject of his identity. While the CGI effect on the characters enters 'uncanny valley' territory, the creature itself has been praised as a good example of using the technology at hand to visually describe the (apparently) indescribable.

As the series has continued, the water monsters in *Love, Death and Robots* have grown more complex. From a dangerous memory in *Fish Night* to a fascinating spectacle in *Ice*, Season Three gives both of its monsters (three if you count the Lovecraftian horror) the ability to communicate.

The thanapod used its terrifying corpse puppet to make its feelings very clear. The Lovecraftian monster was less of a complex character but finding out what a Lovecraftian horror likes for breakfast and how its last relationship ended tends to take away the mystery of Lovecraftian horror … so this leaves us with the siren.

The Emmy award winning episode that made even non-sci-fi fans stop and look was the final episode of Season Three: *Jibaro*. Just like *The Shape of Water*, here are two characters with a barrier to communication, but unlike our Gill-man and his happy ending, these two destroy themselves and each other.

Jibaro

Conquistador Jibaro comes across a lake which contains a dangerous but mesmerising siren, aka the Golden Woman. She uses her screams to drive his comrades to madness and they run into her lake to their deaths, but her voice has no effect on Jibaro; he is deaf. When her attempt to kill him fails, her fear and anger turn to fascination. The feeling is mutual and soon a dance between them begins … but one of them has another agenda.

On one level, the siren is as unfathomable as any other horror. What she wants appears to be nothing more than for people to stay away from her lake, but she looks human, albeit covered in beads and jewels which we find out later are a part of her body – like fish scales.

Known to dislike motion capture, the director and writer, Alberto Mielgo, preferred using animation to create the characters. The deliberately disconcerting style is a mixture of 2D and 3D, and the Golden Woman's dance was modelled on movements by dancer and choreographer, Sara Silkin. The dance was filmed from multiple angles, then the footage was sent to the animation department.

The way the siren moves is more fishlike or snakelike than human, leading with her head and swaying almost bonelessly. Her song is not the enchanting, seductive sound often described in stories about sirens; it is a wild and tortured-sounding scream.

The use of sound is jarring. There is no verbal dialogue in the episode and when shot from Jibaro's point of view the sound is often muffled, but when the perspective shifts to third-person the effect is that of overwhelm. Clashing sounds from all the armour and metal, jingling from bells and chains on the horses, the sounds of leaves and trees in the forest and a nearby waterfall all compete for attention. Speaking of overwhelm, Jibaro appears at home in his deafness so when a twist of consequence caused by his greed enables him to hear, assaulted by so many unknown sounds he panics. For him, the gaining of an entirely new sense is not a source of wonder as many fantasy and science fiction works portray, but a confusing and frightening phenomenon.

Jibaro is by far the most discussed and analysed episode of *Love, Death and Robots*. Originally written as an allegory for toxic relationships and greed (confirmed by Mielgo), many people have interpreted it as a commentary on colonisation and the act of invading a culture, taking its resources and unique aspects, and leaving the culture poorer for it. The siren's lake is shaped like a heart; the implication that she and her perceived riches are the heart of the place and by the end of the episode they have both been broken is clear. In this interpretation, Jibaro and his men are unquestionably the villains, while in Mielgo's writing, neither character is 'good'. The episode has even been described as 'a dance between predators'.

Jibaro **fact file**

Directed by: Alberto Mielgo
Original story: Written for the series by Alberto Mielgo
Creature: Siren aka the Golden Woman
Effects: Animated
Length: Seventeen minutes

The recent success of the short-form video format does not necessarily mean that longer form media is dying out. For people who enjoy being immersed in a world for longer, *Avatar: The Way of Water* (2023) has a running time of 192 minutes – over three hours!

Water monster related media for virtually every taste out there is being created all the time, though there will always be trends in theme and a 'monster of the moment'. One appears to be waking at last from its slumber, deep at the bottom of the sea....

Lovecraftian horror

The works of H.P. Lovecraft will always have to deal with significant hurdles before adaptation. Lovecraft was known to be generous when allowing people to borrow his ideas but there has been controversy over who now owns the copyright and if, in fact, all of his works are considered 'in the public domain', making them available for adaptation without obtaining permission from his estate. American laws are a little more tangled than EU laws which made Lovecraft's works public domain in 2008, but while a direct adaptation may require a closer look at the law, the 'cosmic horror' concept is for all to use.

Matt Ruff's 2016 novel *Lovecraft Country* was adapted for television in 2020 and featured Jonathan Majors, Jamie Chung, Michael Kenneth Williams and other acclaimed actors, with plotlines involving monsters both human and cosmic. Both book and series made Lovecraft's notorious racism into a significant plotline throughout. Lovecraft's views have historically and understandably put people off working with the source material but the *Lovecraft Country* TV series proved that it could be done, working with the author's best concepts and combining them with commentary on the values of the time while giving well-written character parts to Black people, who have often been limited to comic relief or cannon fodder in past genre movies. Though the series attracted 1.5 million viewers for the finale and has an eighty-eight per cent positive rating on Rotten Tomatoes, *Lovecraft Country* was not renewed for a second season.

While attempts have been made to take the Cthulhu mythos into the wider public recognition, the first movie to succeed entered the water, the domain of the slumbering god himself....

Underwater (2020)

A team of marine researchers and workers are drilling in the Mariana Trench, the ocean's deepest spot, until an earthquake of unknown cause shakes their facility, causing massive ruptures and leaks. The small team of engineers, the captain and a biologist appear to be the last survivors and they decide to try a last-ditch attempt to save themselves, by putting on pressure suits and walking for a mile along the ocean floor to the next facility in order to get help or use an escape pod there. But of course it soon transpires that they are not alone.

Being trapped in a body of water without a way of sending a message and with something lurking below – whether that's the deep ocean, a shallow sea, a drifting boat or a tiny island – can be both agoraphobia- and claustrophobia-inducing at the same time!

Underwater brings out our claustrophobia as the protagonists escape through crawlspaces while also wearing restrictive diving gear and occasionally venturing outside with the enormous agoraphobia-inducing void above their heads.

Most reviews were not unkind to the movie, but none had strong praise either. The direction, acting and use of the underwater setting have all been commended, but the plot itself has been described as derivative of the film *Alien*, with many reviewers saying that it all feels very familiar. The use of light and dark, the claustrophobic setting and the glimpses of immense facilities and escape pods are all there. In addition, the capture of an apparently infant creature and subsequent examination looks very similar to *Alien*'s most famous scene, just without anything happening. One reviewer suggested that it might have worked better as a video game. Another felt that the plot needed an 18 certificate in order to include the gore that would have livened things up. While gore is not a necessity for a successful horror movie of this kind, ensuring there are memorable deaths that enhance the plot surely must be.

For a movie with a largely good cast and a running time of an hour and a half, *Underwater* has been commended for not dragging its runtime out and people more used to mockbuster movies or lazier attempts at scares would find *Underwater* better than many offerings out there.

Cinematography

Roger Ebert praised the actors' believable performances and the cinematography. Wide shots of the sheer size of the underwater projects – glowing beacons of hope at first glance – contrast with claustrophobic filming from inside the helmets of the submerged people. The shots of the creatures are murky though, and that is not always the best strategy for an audience that often wants a payoff with a monster reveal at the end. The final monster is never even shown in full. We see teeth but only get the impression of wings and its true size and shape.

Cthulhu

Horror fan website *Bloody Disgusting* gave *Underwater* a rave review for the ending in which the monsters faced by the survivors throughout the film don't even register on the true scale of the potential hell about to rain down on the world! Director, William Eubank, has confirmed that the enormous monster shown in the final act is Lovecraft's most iconic creation: Cthulhu himself. (Though according to Lovecraftian canon, the Elder God is apparently sleeping in the Arctic at the point of human inaccessibility and not in the western Pacific Ocean, where the Mariana Trench is.)

Casting Cthulhu as the monster of the deep had not been the original plan. A creature they called The Behemoth and which resembled a giant whale had been intended as the final monster of the film, but Eubanks changed his mind. As production had not yet reached that point in the movie, they were able to change the creature quite easily, with Eubanks calling it 'a secret Lovecraft love story'. While it has been criticised for its very late reveal, others have called this the only unexpected part of the movie.

Cthulhu has been represented in feature length movies before, but never with the budget and talent represented in *Underwater*.

Underwater **fact file**

Released: 2020
Directed by: William Eubanks
Starring: Kristen Stewart, Vincent Cassel, Jessica Henwick, John Gallagher Jr, Mamoudou Athie, T.J. Miller
Creature: Cthulhu and other monsters the 'Clingers'
Effects: CGI
Legacy: Only rumours so far …

Next, in movie monsters of the deep …

As we saw with the announcements of *Pride and Prejudice and Zombies* (2016) and the 2023 slasher movie *Winnie-the-Pooh: Blood and Honey*, as soon as a creation enters the public domain you never know what might be coming next. Guillermo del Toro has made it very clear that he still intends to adapt *At the Mountains of Madness* and in the meantime his horror anthology *Cabinet of Curiosities* (2022) is on Netflix and partly adapted from Lovecraft's work. Could he be a step closer to the movie he has wanted to make for so long? Giving a creature as iconic as Cthulhu to talented writers and filmmakers who will keep the best bits and work to a standard we expect today, could the Old Gods be waking at last in a new trend for Lovecraftian horror?

Sometimes all it can take is the seed of an idea to inspire other directors. *Jaws* spawned the modern 'shark movie' phenomenon and *The Blair Witch Project* (1999) showed filmmakers that minimal budget did not have to mean minimal impact, undoubtedly influencing *Open Water*. *Underwater* is the first big budget, feature length film to introduce Cthulhu and by association the Lovecraftian Universe. While *Underwater* itself was thought to be derivative with a few good highlights, it may just have set the scene for an entirely new world.

There will always be monster movies starring creatures from the deep. Alongside the next giant-finned or tentacled B-movie and the next inevitable shark bite adventure, maybe one day the great Cthulhu will fall in love, the Loch Ness monster will be a family pet in a 1980s homage, or a gritty survival story will be set in an ocean infested with malevolent rubber ducks. (The Asylum? Are you reading this?)

No matter what trends are on the horizon for the deep water monster movie, it is clear that there's still more to be explored … much more, down in the depths.

We haven't seen it all yet.

Chapter Twelve

MOVIE MONSTERS OF THE DEEP AWARDS

Not everybody is destined to become a film star. It isn't always about an individual's looks or even their talent; sometimes they were just in the right place at the right time or had a certain 'something' – an X-factor that fascinated people. Life is thought to have begun in the ocean and out of the estimated one trillion species of living organisms on this planet, around seventeen per cent live in the water. Of course, not all of these are animals and not all of them have movie star power. This is a collection of some of the most well-known and memorable water monster movie stars, and some creatures that haven't yet had their chance to shine.

The Lifetime Achievement Award: The giant squid

In the 1990s, a magazine series called *Bugs!* was on the shelves of almost every newsagent in the United Kingdom. It came every fortnight with the tagline 'uncover the creepy-crawly world of minibeasts' and included a small part for a plastic beetle that the reader could assemble themselves over time until eventually they would have a fun ornamental sculpture for their room (or bunk bed with pull-out desk, next to their glow-in-the-dark stickers and lava lamp; it was the 1990s, after all!). The magazine occasionally had a very broad definition of the terms 'bugs' and 'minibeasts', as a giant squid is in no way a minibeast and yet the writers couldn't resist featuring it in Issue 029. An article discussed its known behaviour, size, habitat and its epic battles with sperm whales that could even be commencing under the sea at that very moment. But if it wasn't strange enough that a magazine known for its macro-photography of tiny creatures would feature one of the largest animals on earth, things got stranger; there were no photographs in the article at all. The giant squid was illustrated by artists because it wasn't until 2004 that scientists captured photographs of a live giant squid in its natural habitat!

Photographing the giant squid was an incredible achievement. After centuries of description by sailors and disbelief by people on shore, the giant squid was only recognised as a living species in the mid-twentieth century. A small portion of one was captured by the crew of a French ship in 1861, but the first whole giant squid sightings happened when many were found stranded on Newfoundland beaches between 1870 and 1880. One was also caught near to death in March 2004. This specimen, named Archie (after the giant squid's Latin name *Architeuthis Dux*), is on display in a custom-made tank in London's Natural History Museum.

In September 2004, a five-tonne fishing boat with two crew members (Tsunemi Kubodera, from the National Science Museum of Japan and Kyoichi Mori, from the Ogasawara Whale Watching Association) set out on a mission which had taken two years to plan. While epic battles between sperm whales and giant squid have been depicted in art and literature for many years, the battle is far from equal. Sperm whales prey on giant squid (even though some whales have scars from the encounters) and so the two travelled to a known sperm whale hunting ground in the hope that the whales would lead them to the squid. They dropped baited lines to 900 metres with a camera and flash attached and waited. (And waited and waited – this was their third trip and twentieth try!) Eventually, a giant squid measuring nearly 8 metres attacked the line and was snagged. In the four hours it took the squid to break free, Kubodera and Mori captured over 500 images of it: a world first!

The first ever video of a giant squid was captured in November 2006, by explorer and diver, Scott Cassell. Rather than baiting a line, his team clipped a specially designed camera to the fin of a Humboldt squid. The unwitting photography squid captured what was claimed to be a giant squid of around 12 metres long!

Still, the giant squid isn't the biggest cephalopod in the sea. That title goes to the even larger *colossal squid*. Only discovered in 1925, the first full living specimen was caught and photographed in 2005, though the entire creature was simply too big to bring onboard the boat!

Squid (whether giant, colossal or regular size) may have not been featured in as many movies as could be expected but their contribution to art, creature design and monster movies of all kinds gives them the Lifetime Achievement Award here … and the fact that these creatures are real sheds a new light on those ancient tales attributed to drunken sailors!

Honourable mention to the Kraken- one of the first sea monsters in the world.

The All-Star Award: The shark

The iconic deep sea monster movie is of course *Jaws*, but just how many shark films are there? One person lists a collection of 183 titles on IMDB but this list has not been updated recently and therefore does not include more recent titles like *The Requin* (2022) or made-for-TV movie flops like *Shark Huntress* (2021). Taking mockumentaries and the regular release of B-movies made by The Asylum into account, a conservative estimate would be at least 250 movies in which a shark is the star.

Even kids' media has embraced the shark! The recovering fish-eater with the familiar name of 'Bruce' seems fearsome but turns out to be a friend in Pixar's huge hit *Finding Nemo*. Soon afterward, *Shark Tale* was released, full of references to shark-themed horror and multi-layered jokes that appeal to adults as well as children. In one of the first scenes a shark is humming the *Jaws* theme because according to him it's his theme song. In 2016, the viral success of a video by South Korean education brand *Pinkfong* covering the old campfire song *Baby Shark* made it the most watched video on YouTube and spawned toys, games, a musical, a kids' television series and countless parents left clinging to sanity with *Baby Shark* playing on repeat!

Cuddly plush shark toys aside, there are 537 shark species known to exist and out of these, around 12 have been deemed dangerous to humans with 3 considered responsible for the most attacks: the great white, the tiger and the bull. The great white is arguably the most intimidating looking fish in the world. It is almost instantly recognisable due to its distinctive colouring and large triangular teeth, but the species does not necessarily deserve its notoriety.

While great white sharks have apparently been responsible for the most attacks and fatalities, this may not tell the whole story and context is very important. Other sharks may bite more people but with less force meaning less damage and therefore less likelihood of the bite being fatal. In terms of which is more dangerous, an initial bite from a great white is likely to do more damage as they are the more powerful of the three, but great white sharks tend to be quite shy, while bull sharks are known to be aggressive and more likely to continue attacking after an initial bite. Most shark attacks occur in warm tropical waters where great whites are less common than tiger and bull sharks. The three 'most dangerous' sharks are distinctive, so it is easier for many to correctly identify them, meaning that the lists of shark attack statistics skews towards these species, leaving the unidentified sharks a mystery. Oceanic whitetip sharks are often a likely candidate as they eat almost anything and can be both territorial and aggressive. Still, when it comes to casting a monster in the movie world, great whites just have the right look for the part.

Great white sharks have usually been the starring species in shark films but filmmakers searching for something scarier have looked to the extinct megalodon which is making a comeback. Unlike the infamous megalodon, the shark movie is far from extinct.

The Versatility Award: The crocodilians

Accepted by the well-known crocodile and alligator movie stars, as the other, lesser-known members of their species – caimans, gharials and tomistomas (aka the 'false gharial') – have barely reached the audition stage.

Once worshipped as gods and existing on earth for at least sixty-five million years, their death rolls, sheer size, powerful jaws and potential for explosive jump scares can all be used as selling points for a movie. Crocodiles and alligators are able to attack both in the water and on land, though their preferred hunting method is adapted to target land creatures attempting to enter or drink the water. Crocodilians have been filmed hiding motionless in watering holes with just the tip of their snouts visible above the surface, moving closer to animals like wildebeest that have let their guard down in order to take a drink. When they come into reach, the predator strikes, taking the animal into the water and going into a 'death roll' designed to incapacitate prey.

IMDB users have made comparatively few lists of movies starring crocodilian species and these have not differentiated between crocodiles and alligators, but they are almost certainly second in line behind the shark in terms of the number of movies they feature in. While they do star in films in which the action takes place almost exclusively on land, this book focuses on the ones that make use of their watery setting. After all, this book concerns deep water monsters and anybody who has watched the ambush scene in the first *Planet Earth* documentary can see just how scary the thought of these creatures waiting in the water can be.

As crocodilian species are reptiles and spend a lot of their time conserving energy by lying motionless on the shore or the water's surface, they are often underestimated – unlike a swimming shark. Perhaps this apparently calm demeanour is why crocodilians have been cast in creature features fewer times than sharks-, though they have had a surge of popularity over the last two decades and not just in Australia but in America too. The film *Crawl* (2019) received many positive reviews, especially for its 'double danger' aspect. Set in a flooded house in the middle of a hurricane, swimming champion, Haley, finds her unconscious and injured father in the crawlspace … along with several alligators which soon block her only way out.

The Untapped Potential Award: Nessie the Loch Ness monster and all her relatives

What *is* Nessie? Are there more Nessies in the loch? Renowned British naturalist, Sir Peter Scott, was shown photographs of the Loch Ness monster and was so impressed that he decided to legitimise the creature in 1975 by giving Nessie a Latin name: *Nessiteras Rhombopteryx*. This was Greek for 'Ness inhabitant with a diamond-shaped fin'. Naming a creature not yet proven to exist was considered a very impressive and unusual move but accepted solely based on Scott's respected status and excellent reputation in the field of natural world discovery … until politician, Nicholas Fairbairn, pointed out that the name was an anagram for 'monster hoax by Sir Peter S'. Unfortunate coincidence or private joke? We may never know. The truth is out there….

Whether they are really enormous eels, otters swimming in a line, flocks of birds photographed from an odd angle or a rare survivor of a prehistoric species, lake monsters are easy subjects to base a story around – from spooky cryptid-based horror like *Incident at Loch Ness* (2004) to family movie *Magic in the Water* (1995) and any other children's film in need of a touch of mystery.

With the exception of a couple (and I do mean around two) very low budget horror movies, lake monsters tend to feature more as characters in children's films than in horror and have been considerably better received by younger viewers. We give lake monsters cute names like Nessie (of Loch Ness) and Champ (of Lake Champlain) and they tend to either resemble a 'living fossil' plesiosaur (Nessie) or a sea serpent (Naitaka of Lake Okanagan). Until the eponymous *Baby Shark* song went viral, it was easier to give a sweet and charming personality to a newly invented or historic lake monster and make a children's film about that than a real-life apex water predator, and probably always will be. The 1980s had the kids' cartoon *The Family Ness*, the *Pokémon* series has Lapras and Gyarados (resembling a plesiosaur and a water dragon respectively), and there is even a *Scooby Doo* movie in which the 'lake monster' turns out to be a man-made hoax (or is she…?).

Considering the dramatic improvements in CGI and the success of *Jurassic Park* (less successful but still entertaining later instalment, *Jurassic World*, features a mosasaur and a shark in a Seaworld-inspired water show), it is surprising that lake monsters and even plesiosaurs do not star in movies more often.

The Best Comeback Award: The megalodon

The name literally means 'big tooth'. This shark is thought to have gone extinct around 3.6 million years ago and was one of the most powerful predators to have ever existed on this planet. As they have only been found in fossilised fragments so far, we still don't know exactly how big they were or what they looked like in detail. Most scientists have estimated them to have measured around 20 metres long and though there is still debate over which shark it more closely resembled, most filmmakers have decided that the megalodon looked exactly like a bigger, scarier great white shark and gone with that.

In 1997, science fiction author, Steve Alten, wrote the novel *Meg: A Novel of Deep Terror* with the premise that the megalodon species has survived in the Mariana Trench, separated from the rest of the ocean by a layer of cold water. The novel contains many of the 'monster movie' tropes like the disbelieving government and the accidental release of the creature through human activity but appears to be the first work of fiction centred around the possible survival of the megalodon. Other works quickly followed suit: Alten wrote seven sequels beginning with *The Trench: Meg 2* (1999) and then the B-movie *Shark Attack 3* (2002) replaced its mutant great white sharks with a megalodon.

So, could it be true? Could the megalodon really have survived after all this time? After all, we are still finding new species and even the huge deep sea megamouth shark was only discovered in 1976. Fortunately (or unfortunately), while species that live further down in the still-mysterious deep ocean are likely to go undiscovered for longer, the megalodon has been linked to warmer waters nearer to the coastlines of all continents except Antarctica and these are very well explored areas. Are they still out there? The answer is 'probably not'.

The Contribution Award: The mutants and the kaiju

The kaiju genre is particularly popular in Japan where it originated. The first kaiju movie was of course *Godzilla*, closely followed by his monstrous enemies and allies, and Godzilla is still going strong as an official Japanese cultural ambassador! Not all kaiju are monsters from the deep; many come from the land, space and alternate dimensions. They are not, however, just 'big animals'. There is something about a kaiju that makes it stranger than merely its unnatural size. While the *Godzilla* franchise is wildly successful in Japan and there have been attempts to remake it for an American audience – some even moderately successfully – the kaiju film that received the most rave reviews by western audiences was *Pacific Rim*.

If a kaiju is not quite right for the part, what do you do when your fish, eels, octopuses and other potential monstrous creatures aren't big or scary enough? Just mutate them! Adding 'genetically engineered' in front of any species name generally allows filmmakers the artistic licence to do pretty much anything they want with their preferred creature. Change the behaviour of a species, alter its appearance and its hunting style or preferred food source and make it bigger. Much, much bigger. In the water we have *Alligator* (1980), *Monster* (2000) featuring an octopus, *Mega Shark vs Giant Octopus* and many more. Sometimes the strategy works but in general the 'mutated' angle is reserved for B-movies in which the most fleeting of explanation is passable. This works in a similar manner to the way any discrepancy or plot hole in the fantasy genre is often explained away with a shrug and the word 'magic'.

The Rising Star Award: The nameless horror

Writer H.P. Lovecraft's horror stories had a very distinctive style, focusing on the fear of the unknown and unimaginable. The way he wrote about unknown dimensions and deities has inspired creators for many years though the writer himself has fallen increasingly out of favour as time goes by, mostly because his fear and disgust for the unknown famously extended to races other than his own. Because he died in 1937, his writings are now in the public domain, so other writers can adapt his works and reference his characters in order to bring his better concepts into the modern age. Once known as 'Lovecraftian horror', the style is now often known as 'cosmic horror'.

More modern writers, John Langan and Jeff VanderMeer, have written works of cosmic horror which include water monsters, and VanderMeer's 2014 novel *Annihilation* was made into a movie starring Natalie Portman and Oscar Isaac in 2018. There's even the brief appearance of a mutated crocodilian creature. In the past five years, there has been a very interesting trend emerging from the dark unfathomable universe under the sea … watch this space.

The Controversy Award: The mermaid

No awards ceremony is without its share of controversy; who deserved to win and didn't, who deserved to be nominated and wasn't, and who stole the show at the ceremony whether they won anything or not. Controversy isn't generally awarded at a ceremony, but the papers the next day can't stop talking about it. Is there any water creature more visible, more represented in art and fiction and quite possibly more loved, than the mermaid?

When many people think of mermaids they think of Disney (all whimsy and wonder) and yet when it comes to horror movies, mermaids (and their relatives) are cast as monsters much more than they are offered the part of the hero (or, a little more accurately, the damsels in varying levels of distress).

So, are mermaids really monsters? Read Chapter Nine and make up your own mind....

Ones to Watch:

Deep water monster movies may be released all the time but their range of characters and creatures sometimes seems rather limited. Considering the enormous variety and potential in the creatures living in the water, there may be a few up-and-coming stars to watch in this list:

Top Choice: The leopard seal

Cute, cuddly and round, seals are universally adorable ... except for leopard seals. Also known as the sea leopard, the world's second largest species of seal has a varied diet but mostly eats penguins ... *and sometimes other seals*!

Leopard seals have long, sleek, streamlined bodies, larger heads than most other seals and jaws which can open extremely wide. Often measuring over 3 metres (around the size of an average male great white shark) with inch-long canine teeth, their wide jaws and violent manner of shaking their prey to tear off pieces as well as their potential to kill or injure a human make the leopard seal a formidable creature. Interactions between leopard seals and humans have been varied, with both aggressive and potentially maternal behaviour being reported over the years. In 2006, *National Geographic* wildlife photographer, Paul Nicklen, had a positive encounter while swimming with one, capturing never-before-seen behaviour on video as the seal appeared to offer him food as though he were a young seal learning to hunt. Contrastingly, biologist Kirsty Brown, was killed by one in 2003 while snorkelling, though whether it perceived her as prey or as a threat to its own life is unknown. In 2021 a leopard seal attacked three spear fishermen over the course of half an hour, inflicting multiple wounds, but again it is not certain if the seal felt threatened and acted in self-defence.

Leopard seals have not, so far, appeared as the deep water monsters in creature horror movies marketed at adults, but they have done so three times in movies made for children and families. *The Pebble and the Penguin* (1995) have their penguin protagonists meet an attacking leopard seal twice, computer animated *Happy Feet* (2006) includes a red-eyed and very disturbing leopard seal character and *Eight Below* (2006) gave its family viewers a jump scare as an animatronic leopard seal defended a whale carcass it was eating.

With no leopard seal themed horror movies yet, there's potential for a star to rise!

Second Choice: The sea snake

While the film *Dark Tide* (1994) (not to be confused with Halle Berry's shark thriller *Dark Tide* (2012)) does feature sea snakes, they mostly appear on a boat being studied, used as weapons in increasingly unlikely ways and against an outdated setting involving a lot of nudity and assault. Otherwise, the use of sea snakes (as opposed to land snakes on a boat or mutated snakes) has been surprisingly low. With numerous eye-catching species of sea snake from the banded sea krait, which is known to hunt in packs, to the unmistakeable yellow bellied sea snake, and with some of them boasting the most potent venom of all snakes, there's potential here for a sea monster movie.

An enormous sea snake with a taste for surfers? Sea snakes hunting in packs until the water resembles boiling spaghetti? Mutated, highly vicious sea snakes on a rampage? There are a lot of snake movie scenes that could be given an extra dimension in the water.

Factually, sea snakes tend not to be aggressive in the sea; fishermen catching them by accident have been known to throw them back into the sea using their bare hands. Sea snakes are more volatile on land, but this is understandable as they are out of their natural territory, making them clumsy and defensive. Still … when have facts ever got in the way of a monster movie?

Third Choice: The deep sea anglerfish

Around eleven per cent of adults are thought to be afraid of the dark (*nyctophobic*) and this fear factor has often been brought into deep water monster horrors; in fact, many have an 'in the dark' sequence. *47 Meters Down* uses a flare in near total darkness to create one of its best jump scare scenes, which was so successful that its sequel *47 Meters Down: Uncaged* was mostly set in the pitch black underground labyrinth of an ancient city.

Anglerfish, despite their fascinating biology and terrifying yet distinctive appearance, are rare in movies. One has a cameo as a minor threat in the children's film *Finding Nemo* and it is played as comedy. Now, imagine a deep sea dive, perhaps in a team with small submarines, a signalling system of occasionally blinking lights and radio communication that is sporadic at best. Is that light coming from one of the other submarines, or is it the infamous lure of a deep-sea angler fish, grown to colossal size through unknown biology, mutation or genetic engineering?

Highly Commended: The coelacanth [SEE-la-canth]

Coelacanths were enormous and bizarre-looking; more closely related to lungfish and other amphibious fish than any of the usual sea-dwelling species. They had small mouths, enormous eyes, extra sets of fins compared to most modern fish and they went extinct around 66 million years ago … or did they?

In 1938, a sailing vessel dredged up a live coelacanth from the Indian Ocean and it turned out that the species was already well-known to the local fishermen around the Comoro Islands. The fishermen called it *gombessa*. Known now as a living fossil, the coelacanth uses its sets of fins in the same way land animals use their legs for stability. They live in the area of the sea depths known as the twilight zone, where light is scarce and they drift with the currents, stabilised by all those fins and eating smaller marine animals.

In 1997, another species was discovered, this time in Indonesia and again, already known to local fishermen who called it *raja laut* – 'king of the sea'.

Both identified coelacanth species have a unique characteristic: there is an 'intracranial joint' at the top of their skulls, allowing them to turn their heads upward and open their seemingly small mouths extra wide for prey. This is not seen in any other kind of fish or any kind of vertebrate creature living in any environment on earth!

While the horror movie *Monster on the Campus* (1957) featured a coelacanth and some blood plasma-related gymnastics, no more recent 'killer coelacanth' movie has ever been made to my knowledge, but it is a strange enough fish to feature without mutating it and that extra head joint could give animatronics engineers a challenge.

Stick to the day job: no award here

There are other species that we just don't want to see in the movies as villains, even if we've seen them in the role before. Either they're too beloved to be recast as 'monstrous', they're already well-established as 'the good guys' or the movie was so bad it tainted the concept for all of us.

Top Choice: The Octopus

You'd think that octopuses or octopi (did you know that there's no agreed collective noun for octopus?) would feature either as an award recipient or at least one to watch. How many sea monster tentacles have we seen rising from the depths? The answer is 'a lot', but it seems that recently octopuses have been working with a publicist and are now considered more fascinating than fearsome. The critically acclaimed and moving documentary film *My Octopus Teacher* (2020) showed the shapeshifting, highly intelligent and self-sacrificing creature in a new light.

Perhaps the relative ease with which it is possible to turn an octopus into a sweet and funny character has made it a less attractive option for the role of a villain in a monster movie. Or perhaps it is the fact that real-life crocodiles and sharks can be filmed biting a lure for a bit of menacing and realistic footage, but an 'octopus attack' on a human is very difficult to make look real and frightening due to the fact that octopuses are not known to deliberately kill and eat people. Even the highly venomous blue-ringed octopus has been responsible for fewer than twenty recorded human deaths.

The last octopus-related monster movie to get a moderate amount of attention was the viral campaign advertising *Mega Shark vs Giant Octopus* and before that it was gory cult film *Deep Rising* (1998) and its 'octalus'. Octopuses are still in style; they've just cited 'creative differences' and moved on to other projects.

Second Choice: The orca

While *Moby Dick* was a critical success and its themes have been re-used in stories of any genre even today, the harm that humans have done to whale and cetacean populations makes turning them into any kind of villain an unlikely and unpopular choice for a monster horror film. The exceptions are *Moby Dick* remakes, but even they now tend to show Ahab in a less than flattering light and at the absolute worst portray the whale as righteously angry. Most monster horror involves the creature killing or injuring humans and somebody taking revenge, an act the audience needs to perceive as necessary if the 'monster' is to be the villain.

Captive Seaworld orca, Tilikum, killed his trainer, Dawn Brancheau, in a sustained and bloody attack. It was horrific but the multi-award-winning documentary film *Blackfish* offered an alternative point of view, exposing perceived corruption in the Seaworld theme park chain and presenting its treatment of its captive orcas as the true horror. Without demonising orcas, *Blackfish* found the balance between promoting a healthy respect for their strength and power, while providing a more sympathetic insight into their worrying behaviour in captivity. Villainising them now would be an unusual and risky move.

Third Choice: The selkie

Selkies are creatures from Scottish and Irish folklore; seals able to shed their skins and take on human form for a while. There are similar legends in Scandinavian mythology.

In most legends concerning selkies, human men (and occasionally women) steal a selkie's sealskin which prevents them from returning to the sea. Often the two would marry, but the selkie would always long for the sea and if given the chance, find and take their sealskin back, fleeing from their human spouse (and often their marriage's half-selkie children too). Some legends say that they are returning to the selkie spouse they were already married to.

A violent and murderous selkie would generally be pursuing revenge for the theft of their sealskin – and true form – if the movie stuck to legend. While that is not the best plot for a horror movie if the makers want the audience to sympathise with its human stars, there have been several popular and successful movies, books and songs in which a selkie and a human marry consensually, with a happy ending for both. With a world of other options out there, we can leave the selkie's sealskin alone!

Highly Commended: The sea otter

That's just not going to happen – they're fluffy and they sleep holding hands!

100 Monster Movies from the Deep

Horror, documentaries, comedies, family movies and total wild cards. How many of these have you seen, and why should you watch them?

Title:
Watch it for:
Key:

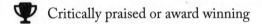 Critically praised or award winning

 Good for a movie night in

Bad, or 'so bad it's good'? You decide…

Brief monster appearance

(Mostly) family friendly fiction

✔ Documentary

☺ Fiction based on a true story

Historically significant

- *2-Headed Shark Attack* (2012)
A two-headed shark and silly fun!

- *20,000 Leagues Under the Sea* (1916)
The first motion picture to be shot underwater.

- *2010 Moby Dick* (2010)

The infamous Asylum studio's reimagining of the novel, with a whale that can move on land.

- *47 Meters Down* (2017)

A solid shark movie with a terrifying 'in the dark' scene.

- *47 Meters Down: Uncaged* (2019)

Blind sharks that hunt in a dark subterranean labyrinth.

- *Atlantis: The Lost Empire* (2001)

A fun adventure movie with guest appearances by coelacanths and a leviathan.

- *Avatar: The Way of Water* (2022)

Award winning visual effects and a lot of newly imagined water creatures.

- *Bad CGI Sharks* (2019)

Bad CGI sharks and a fresh take on the shark genre!

- *Bad Travelling* (*Love, Death and Robots* short) (2022)

Terrifying visual effects and 'nightmare fuel' monster.

- *Bait* (2012)

A fun 'bad' movie about sharks in a flooded shopping centre.

- *The Beach* (2000)

Possibly the most disturbing and realistic shark attack in a movie.

- *The Beast* (1996)

Based on *Jaws* author Peter Benchley's novel of the same name.

- *The Beast from 20,000 Fathoms* (1953)

Ray Bradbury's special effects in one of the most important monster movies of all time.

- *Blackfish* (2013)

A fascinating, if brutal, look at orca psychology.

- *Black Water* (2007)

An award-winning crocodile movie based on a true story.

- *Blue My Mind* (2017)

An unusual approach to the mermaid story, with some body horror scenes.

- *The Blue Planet* (2001)

Eight episodes showing different aspects of marine life in an award-winning series.

- *Blue Planet II* (2017)

More from the award-winning Blue Planet team.

- *Boss Croc* (2017)

Follow a crocodile's life journey from egg to adult.

- *The Cabin in the Woods* (2012)

A hilarious and inventive horror-comedy with a short but excellent merman scene.

- *The Cave* (2005)

Monsters in a creepy underwater cave setting.

- *Clash of the Titans* (1981)

Old-school swords, sorcery and stop-motion animation fun.

- *Clash of the Titans* (2010)

Curiosity. Which version of this story (and Kraken) do you prefer?

- *Cold Skin* (2017)

Unusual setting, creepy monsters and striking visual effects.

- *Crawl* (2019)

Tension, intensity and alligators.

- *Creature from the Black Lagoon* (1954)

One of the first and most influential monster movies, with iconic scenes and character design.

- *Dagon* (2001)

Lovecraftian tentacled monster horror.

- *Dark Tide* (2012)

Halle Berry in a shockingly zero per cent positivity rated movie.

- *Deep Blue Sea* (1999)

Groundbreaking horror-comedy with realistic animatronic mako sharks.

- *Deep Rising* (1998)

Seriously gory moments and an octopus-like creature.

- *DeepStar Six* (1989)

A movie similar to *Alien*, with a water monster.

- *Eight Below* (2006)

The terrifying animatronic leopard seal.

- *Fin* (2021)

Eli Roth's investigation into shark fishing. He calls it the scariest movie he has ever made.

- *Finding Nemo* (2003)

A family movie full of monster movie references and very quotable!

- *Fish Night* (*Love, Death and Robots* short) (2019)

Beautiful animation.

- *Frankenfish* (2004)

A diverse cast of semi-recognisable faces and a frankenfish. Based (very loosely) on real events.

- *From the Depths* (2020)

An unusual setting and monster twist ending.

- *Frozen Planet* (2011)

Award winning footage of marine life at the poles, including leopard seals hunting.

- *Ghost Shark* (2013)

A B-movie with a very unusual and shark-sympathetic plot.

- *Godzilla* (1954)

The original king of the monsters making history.

- *Godzilla* (2014)

Excellent special effects.

- *Gorgo* (1961)

A monster movie that spawned a comic book series.

- *Grabbers* (2012)

An unexpected award-winner and cult classic, with alcohol-sensitive aliens.

- *Great White* (2021)

A shark movie cliché bingo game. Who will survive?

- *The Host* (2006)

One of Quentin Tarantino's favourite movies – a mutated amphibian emerges in broad daylight.

- *Ice* (*Love, Death and Robots* short) (2021)

Interesting animation and exciting story.

- *Incident at Loch Ness* (2004)

A double-bluff! Are we watching a documentary or a story?

- *In the Heart of the Sea* (2015)

A cast of famous faces telling a true survival tale.

- *Jaws* (1975)

The must-see grandaddy of shark movies!

- *Jaws 2* (1978)

Roy Scheider returns as Chief Brody.

- *Jaws 3-D* (1983)

The sheer badness of it all, and one of the worst special effects scenes of all time.

- *Jaws: The Revenge* (1987)

To tick all the *Jaws* movies off your list.

- *Jibaro* (*Love, Death and Robots* short) (2022)

The award-winning special effects, sound and character design.

- *Killer Mermaid* aka *Mamula* (2014)

A fun 'slasher' movie with comedically terrible mermaid CGI.

- *Lake Placid* (1999)

Very convincing animatronic crocodile and excellent Betty White one-liners.

- *Leviathan* (1989)

Solid monster B-movie for movie night.

- *The Lighthouse* (2019)

Excellent performances and a mermaid. Robert Pattinson and Willem Dafoe go mad on an island.

- *The Lure* (2015)

A body-horror musical about cabaret mermaids!

- *Mako* (2021)

An Egyptian shark movie based on a real shipwreck.

- *Mako: The Jaws of Death* (1976)

An example of how not to shoot a monster movie.

- *The Meg* (2018)

Jason Statham versus a megalodon. A B-movie with an A-movie budget.

- *Meg 2: The Trench* (2023)

Jason Statham returns to fight another megalodon.

- *Mega Piranha* (2009)

Decide for yourself, just how bad is it?

- *Mega Shark vs Giant Octopus* (2009)

That viral shark-bites-plane scene; and Vic Chao.

- *The Mermaid* (1904)

The first mermaid movie!

- *Mermaid Down* (2019)

A crowdfunded movie with a psychology element and award-winning script.

- *Mermaid: The Lake of The Dead* (2018)

A rusalka (rather than a mermaid) and a lot of jump scares.

- *My Octopus Teacher* (2020)

A compelling story about the relationship between a diver and an octopus.

- *Open Water* (2003)

Based on a terrifying true story.

- *Open Water 3: Cage Dive* (2017)

Found footage element and jump scares.

- *Pacific Rim* (2013)

Giant robots battling kaiju emerging from the sea! And the character Mako Mori.

- *Piranha* (1978)

Entertaining and bloody 1970s horror movie.

- *Piranha II: The Spawning* (1981)

Sheer morbid curiosity.

- *Piranha 3-D* (2010)

'So bad, it's good' and possibly satirical. Gratuitous nudity and gore with a sense of humour.

- *Pirates of the Caribbean: Dead Man's Chest* (2006)

The Kraken.

- *Pirates of the Caribbean: On Stranger Tides* (2011)

Mermaids.

- *Pinocchio* (2022)

Guillermo del Toro's interpretation of the story, with stop-motion animation sea monster.

- *Planet Earth* (2006)

Stunning footage, especially the Shallow Seas episode with great white sharks.

- *Playing With Sharks: The Valerie Taylor Story* (2021)

The *Jaws* camerawoman's experiences and insights diving.

- *Red Water* (2003)

Rapper, Coolio, stars in this shark movie full of errors! Just how bad could it be…?

- *The Reef* (2011)

Critically acclaimed and terrifying survival story with real shark footage.

- *The Rift* (1990)

B-movie with low-budget mutated sea monsters.

- *Rogue* (2007)

Fun horror based on tales of a real crocodile.

- *The Sea Beast* (1926)

The first film adaptation of *Moby Dick*.

- *The Sea Beast* (2022)

Excellent animation and a sea-beast-sympathetic story for the family.

- *The Sea Serpent* (1985)

A sock puppet.

- *The Shallows* (2016)

Blake Lively carries this shark survival film, with the help of a real seagull actor.

- *The Shape of Water* (2017)

Multi-award-winning love story unlike any other monster movie out there.

- *Sharknado* (2013)

Sharks. In a tornado. The essential 'so bad it's good' movie!

- *Shark Night: 3D* (2011)

The range of shark species involved; some usual suspects, some very unusual!

- *Sharktopus* (2010)

A shark crossed with an octopus.

- *Sharkwater* (2006)

Rob Stewart's law-changing documentary, with stunning underwater photography.

- *Sharkwater Extinction* (2018)

The sequel and tribute to Rob Stewart's conservation work.

- *She Creature* (2001)

A mermaid's revenge.

- *Son of Godzilla* (1967)

Baby Godzilla!

- *Tale of Tales* (2015)

An unusual series of short, connected tales, with Salma Hayek and a sea dragon.

- *The Tank* (2023)

Claustrophobic monster horror to watch in the dark.

- *Tentacles* (1977)

Count the *Jaws* similarities!

- *Underwater* (2020)

Cthulhu's first movie outing in a long time….

- *Water Horse: Legend of the Deep* (2007)

Family fun with the Loch Ness monster.

Bibliography

Chapter 1

Andrews, Alfred C., 'Greek and Latin Mouse-Fishes and Pig-Fishes', in *Transactions and Proceedings of the American Philological Association*, 79 (1948), pp.243–244.

Avienus, R.F, *Ora Maritima* (6th century).

BBC News, 'Humpback whale gulps and spits out Cape Cod lobsterman' (*BBC News*, 12 June 2021).

English Standard Version Bible: Jonah: 1; Isaiah 27:1; Job 40: 15-24 (2001).

Eschner, K., 'The Real-Life Whale That Gave Moby Dick His Name' (*Smithsonian Magazine*, 18 October 2017).

Gilmore, David D., *Monsters: Evil Beings, Mythical Beasts, and All Manner of Imaginary Terrors* (University of Pennsylvania Press, 2012) p.150.

Granlund, John, & Crone, G.R., 'The "Carta Marina" of Olaus Magnus'. (*Imago Mundi Ltd*, 1951).

Homer, *The Odyssey* (The William Harvey Miner Co., 1895).

Kadane, L., 'Canada's mysterious lake monster' (*BBC Travel*, 2020).

Loxton, Daniel, & Prothero, Donald R, *Abominable Science!: Origins of the Yeti, Nessie, and Other Famous Cryptids* (New York: Columbia University Press, 2013).

Mayer, J., 'The Making Of The Octopus In "20,000 Leagues Under The Sea"' (*Science Friday*, 2018).

Melville, H., *Moby Dick: Or, The White Whale* (1892).

Meyer, R., 'No Old Maps Actually Say "Here Be Dragons"'(*The Atlantic*, December 12, 2013).

'Monsters, Sea-Monks, and Mermaids: Strange Creatures from the Sea from Antiquity to the Modern Age' (Leiden Arts in Society Blog: 23 September 2018).

Photoplay (Chicago, Photoplay Magazine Publishing Company, January–June 1926).

Seaburn, P., 'Mythical Aboriginal Bunyip Paintings Found and a Possible Recent Sighting' (*Mysterious Universe*, 2019). [Subscription required for full article]

Tikkanen, A., Essex History: *American Whaling Ship [1799-1820]* (Whale attack, survivors, and rescue) (*Encyclopedia Britannica*, 16 February 2023).

Verne, J., *Twenty Thousand Leagues Under the Sea* (Pierre-Jules Hetzel, 1887).

Chapter 2

Bradbury, R., *The Fog Horn* (Creative Company, 1988).

Clack, J., 'Eucritta melanolimnetes from the Early Carboniferous of Scotland, a stem tetrapod showing a mosaic of characteristics' in *Earth and Environmental Science Transactions of The Royal Society of Edinburgh*, Volume 92(1), pp.75-95. (2001).

Cotta Vaz, Mark, *Living Dangerously: The Adventures of Merian C. Cooper, Creator of King Kong* (Villiard, 2005).

Failes, I., *The History of Special Effects in Godzilla Movies* (Inverse, 14 October 2016).

Fandino, D., *The Origins of Godzilla: Castle Bravo and the Daigo Fukuryu Maru* (Journey to the (Wired) West, 21 March 2018).

Molloy, T., 'Dynamation: The Golden Era of Ray Harryhausen' (*MovieMaker Magazine, 2021*).

O'Meara, Mallory, *The Lady from the Black Lagoon: Hollywood Monsters and the Lost Legacy of Milicent Patrick* (Toronto, Ontario: Canada, Hanover Square Press, 2019).

Ryfle, Steve, 'Godzilla's Footprint' in *Virginia Quarterly Review* (2005) pp.44–68.

Ryfle, Steve, *Japan's favorite mon-star: the unauthorized biography of "The Big G"* (Toronto: ECW Press, 1998).

Tasker, A. *Ray Harryhausen Talks About His Cinematic Magic* (The American Society of Cinematographers, 23 February 2022).

The Unapologetic Geek, Sci-Fi Classic Review: *The Beast From 20,000 Fathoms* (1953) (YouTube Video, 22 December 2019).

Warren, Bill. *Keep Watching the Skies!: American Science Fiction Movies of the Fifties* (McFarland & Company, 2009).

Whalen, A., 'Godzilla Director Honda Ishiro Describes Seeing Hiroshima Firsthand In New Criterion Release' (*Newsweek*, 29 October 2019).

Wickliffe, Andrew, *Behemoth the Sea Monster* [1959, Eugène Lourié] (The Stop Button, 2006).

Chapter 3

1916 Shark Attack (page on Matawan Historical Society website).

Benchley, P., *Jaws* (Penguin Books, 1998).

Bratter, Steven, Tension Between Richard Dreyfuss and Robert Shaw in "JAWS" (YouTube video, 2012).

Burch, Tony B., *The life of Capt. Frank Mundus* (Talk Sea Fishing).

'Child actor who starred in Jaws becomes police chief where it was filmed' (*Sky News*, May 2022).

Copley, John Singleton, *Watson and the Shark* [1778] (National Gallery of Art, n.d.).

DeLong, W., *Shark Attacks Of 1916: Four Gruesome Deaths That Began Shark Mania* (All That's Interesting, 13 March 2019).

'DIES AFTER ATTACK BY FISH; C.E. Vansant Had Been Bitten While Swimming at Beach Haven' (*The New York Times*, 3 July 1916).

Dowling, D., *How the Creator of Jaws' Became the Shark's Greatest Defender* (Narratively, 2014).

International Shark Attack File (Florida Museum website, n.d.).

Kermode, M., 'Jaws, 40 years on: One of the truly great and lasting classics of American cinema' (*The Guardian*, 2015).

McCall, V., 'How America's First Shark Panic Spurred a Century of Fear' *(National Geographic*, 2019).

Mundus, J. M., Home Page of Frank Mundus, The Inspiration For Quint In *Jaws* (J. M. Mundus, n.d.).

Pepin-Neff, Christopher., 'The Jaws Effect: How movie narratives are used to influence policy responses to shark bites in Western Australia' in *Australian Journal of Political Science* (January 2015).

Nashawaty, C., 'Steven Spielberg talks about "Jaws" – the greatest summer movie ever made' (*Entertainment Weekly*, 9 June 2011).

Rowe, P., 'Saving WWII Indianapolis story from sharks' (*San Diego Union-Tribune*, 14 September 2016).

Spencer, A., 'The Woman Who Captured "Jaws", Then Worked to Undo the Damage' (*The New York Times*, 29 September 2021).

Villazon, L., 'How powerful is a great white shark's jaw?' (BBC *Science Focus* Magazine, 2012).

Wright, Michael, '"Monster Man" Frank Mundus Dies' (*East Hampton Press*, September 2008).

Chapter 4

Anderson, Rasmus B., 'Kra'ken' in *Johnson's Universal Cyclopædia* (D. Appletons, 1896) Vol.5 (new ed.) p.26.

The Associated Press, 'Andrew Kuehn, 66, Innovator In the Movie Trailer Industry' (*The New York Times*, 3 February 2004).

Bilbow, Marjorie, 'The New Films' in *Screen International* (21 May 1977), pp.16–17.

Eberhart, George M., *'Kraken'. Mysterious Creatures: A Guide to Cryptozoology* (ABC-CLIO, 2002) p.282ff.

Ford, Luke, *The Producers: Profiles in Frustration* (iUniverse, 2004) p.191.

Hayes, R.M., *3D Movies: a History and Filmography of Stereoscopic Cinema* (McFarland, 1998).

Healey, T., *The World's Worst Movies* (Conran Octopus, 1986).

Higgins, B., 'Hollywood Flashback: Bo Derek Was Chomped by a Killer Whale in 1977's "Orca"' (*The Hollywood Reporter*, 9 August 2018).

Milne, Tom, 'Tentacoli (Tentacles)' in *The Monthly Film Bulletin* (June 1977) 44 (521): p.129.

Parker, D., 'Roy Scheider Turned Down "Deer Hunter" To Star In This Hated Sequel' (*TheThings*, 31 August 2021).

Pulleine, Tom, *The Monthly Film Bulletin* (The Monthly Film Bulletin, December 1978) 45 (539): p.243.

Which Dennis Quaid Movie Had The Highest Cocaine Budget (Watch What Happens Live with Andy Cohen, YouTube video, 18 November 2018).

Chapter 5

Barton, S., 'Exclusive: Andrew Traucki Talks The Reef, The ABC's of Death, and More' (Dread Central, 17 July 2011).

Creature Features, To Build A Shark: The Shallows (YouTube video, 15 September 2020).

Ebert, R., 'Deep Blue Sea: movie review & film summary' (Roger Ebert, 28 July 1999).

The Evolution of VFX in Movies: The 60s Till Now (Pluralsight, 2015).

Failes, I., 'The sooner you kill me, the happier I'll be': a VFX oral history of Samuel L. Jackson's shocking 'Deep Blue Sea' departure (befores & afters., 2019).

'Gwen', Horror Rewatch: Deep Blue Sea (1999) (Horror Homeroom, 2015).

Howard, Jeff, 'Deep Blue Sea star Samuel L. Jackson goes swimming with the sharks' (*Las Vegas Sun*, 2 August 1999).

Jenkins, J., 'Deep Blue Sea': Screenwriter Duncan Kennedy Dives Deep into the Original Script for the 1999 Movie [Exclusive] (Bloody Disgusting!, 13 August 2021)

King, D., 'How "Avatar: The Way of Water" Solved the Problem of CGI Water' (*The New York Times*, 16 December 2022).

McCarthy, E., '17 Fun Facts About Deep Blue Sea' (Mental Floss, 2019).

Northrup, R., 'Avatar 2's CGI Is Ground-Breaking And You Had No Idea' (ScreenRant, 19 June 2022).

Chapter 6

The Best Shark Movies Of All Time (Ranker, 2021).

Biodrowski, S., 'The Host: Director Bong Joon-ho discusses his Monstrous Political Satire' (Hollywood Gothique, 2007).

Calvert, H., '7 Best Shark Movies Since Jaws' (Cultured Vultures, 17 March 2022).

Clough, R., 'The Top 25 Shark Movies' (Den of Geek, 25 September 2015).

Collins, A., *Lake Placid* (Empire, 1 January 2000).

Duncan, Jody. *The Winston Effect: The Art and History of Stan Winston Studio* (Titan Books Ltd. 2006).

Ebert, R. 'Lake Placid movie review & film summary' (Roger Ebert, 16 July 1999).

Ehrlich, D., 'Bong Joon-ho's "The Host" Is The Defining Monster Movie Of The 21st Century' (IndieWire, 5 May 2017).

Fickling, D., 'The Cruel Sea' (*The Guardian*, 23 July 2004).

Gilchrist, Todd, 'An interview with Blanchard Ryan and Daniel Travis' (Blackfilm.com, 2004).

Goldfarb, K., 'The Tragic Story Of Tom And Eileen Lonergan That Inspired "Open Water"' (All That's Interesting, 6 January 2023).

Goldin, M., 'Video shows animatronic puppet, not a real crocodile' (*AP NEWS*, 22 November 2022).

Lake Placid – Building The 30-Foot Animatronic Crocodile (Stan Winston School of Character Arts, n.d.). Blog with more information found on stanwinstonschool.com

Lee, Kevin B., 'The Han River Horror Show: Interview with Bong Joon-ho' (*Cineaste Magazine*, 2007)

'NatGeo team confirms Lolong the croc is world's longest' (GMA News Online & GMA News, 2011).

Weston, P., 'Meningitis killed Greenland shark found off coast of Cornwall, postmortem shows' (*The Guardian*, 12 April 2022).

Wixson, H., 'Stan Winston Week: Celebrating Lake Placid with Director Steve Miner & Exclusive Photo Gallery' (Daily Dead, 7 July 2014).

Chapter 7

Ashworth, James, 'Giant and colossal squid: revealing the secrets of the largest invertebrates' (Natural History Museum website, n.d.)

Black, Riley, 'Face-to-Face With a Leopard Seal' (*National Geographic*, 2010).

Bugs! Magazine (Orbis) Issue 029.

Naish, D., 'Photos of the Loch Ness Monster, revisited' (Scientific American Blog Network, 10 July 2013).

Osterloff, Emily, 'Coelacanths: the fish that "outdid" the Loch Ness Monster' (Natural History Museum website, n.d.).

Owen, J., 'Leopard Seal Kills Scientist in Antarctica' (*National Geographic*, 2003).

Pasley, J., 'Why giant squid, the once mythical kraken of the deep, are still mystifying scientists 150 years after they were discovered' (*Business Insider*, 19 October 2019).

Chapter 8

'BBC defends indoor lobster footage' (*BBC News*, 2001).

Claffey, J., '9-Year-Old Mass. Boy Who Loves Sharks Inspires Lawmakers to Ban Fin Trade' (Brookline, MA Patch, 24 July 2014).

Kettlewell, Julianna, 'Ancient sea monsters bite back' (*BBC News*, 2003)

Males, Jennifer & Van Aelst, Peter. Did the Blue Planet set the Agenda for Plastic Pollution? An Explorative Study on the Influence of a Documentary on the Public, Media and Political Agendas. (Environmental Communication, 2021) pp 40-54

McRae, Michael, 'Gustave, the Killer Crocodile – Update' (*National Geographic Adventure Magazine*, February 2008).

Snyder, S., *Mako: The Jaws of Death* (Madness Heart Press, 23 May 2021).

Tingle, Jamie, 'Review: Mako aka The Jaws of Death' (1976) (The Daily Jaws, 8 November 2022)

Wilcox, C., 'Fraud, Deception And Lies: How Discovery's Shark Week Became The Greatest Show On Earth' (*Discover Magazine*, 2014).

Chapter 9

Anders, C. J., 'Why Pacific Rim Doesn't Look Like Any Movie You've Ever Seen Before' (Gizmodo, 2013).

Belloni, M., 'Fox takes action against "Day the Earth Stopped"' (*The Hollywood Reporter*, 2008).

Cohen, D. S., 'Pacific Rim Visual Effects Get Operatic Twist' (Variety, 29 May 2013).

Collura, S., 'Clash of the Titans Creature Comparison' (IGN, 14 June 2012).

Fitzgerald, John, The Greatest Movie Scene Ever? – Mega Shark vs. Giant Octopus! (YouTube video, 22 May 2009).

Fritz, B., '"Hobbit" knockoff release blocked by judge' (*Los Angeles Times*, 2012).

Howell, P., 'Pacific Rim's Guillermo del Toro is a monster-loving pacifist' (*Toronto Star*, 5 July 2013)

Jacks, Brian, 'EXCLUSIVE: Door Open For "Mega Shark Vs. Giant Octopus" Sequel, Says Deborah Gibson' (MTV, 13 May 2009).

Katz, D., 'The Asylum: The Company Behind Sharknado, Snakes on a Train, and (a Movie Kinda Like) Pacific Rim' (*GQ*, 12 July 2013).

Kaye, D., 'Why Clash Of The Titans Was The End Of An Era' (Den of Geek, 20 June 2021).

Pacific Rim interview with Idris Elba (*Empire*, 2013).

Pickard, A., 'Mega Shark Vs Giant Octopus trailer: what more needs to be said?' (*The Guardian*, 22 February 2009).

Ryan, M., 'Clash of the Titans Director: "You Shouldn't Remake Clash of the Titans"' (*Vanity Fair*, 1 April 2010).

Seth, R., 'What Is The Bechdel Test, And Why Are Films Still Not Passing It?' (*British Vogue*, 15 July 2020).

Somma, Brandon, 'Masters of the Mockbuster: What The Asylum is All About' (The Artifice, 4 January 2013).

undeadbackbrain., Mega Shark vs Giant Doritos (YouTube video, 16 November 2010).

Weintraub, S., 'Guillermo del Toro Talks PACIFIC RIM, Creating the Massive World and Creatures, and More' (Collider, 19 June 2013).

Chapter 10

Andersen, H. C., *The Little Mermaid* (with Original Illustrations) (C. A. Reitzel, 1837).

Bacon, R., 'Blue My Mind (2017): Review – Better To Be A Fish Than A Teen' (Cultured Vultures, 12 November 2018).

Chhetri, P., '"Blue My Mind" director Lisa Bruhlmann reveals her inspiration behind the mermaid horror flick and why she wants to do sensual cinema' (meaww, 2018).

Donaldson, K., 'The Lighthouse, a film where Robert Pattinson gets it on with a mermaid, may be the best of 2019' (SYFY, 2019).

Ehrlich, D., 'Review: "The Lure" Is The Best Goth Musical About Man-Eating Mermaids Ever Made' (IndieWire, 25 July 2016).

Hartwich, Dorota, 'The Lure: An audacious voice in Polish cinema' (Cineuropa, 2 February 2016).

Ivanits, Linda J., *Russian Folk Belief* (M. E. Sharpe, 1989).

Jepsen, Philip, *On the Origin of Mermaids* (Mermaids of Earth website).

Peverley, S., 'Why We Can't Resist the Lure of Mermaids; (Blog: Professor Sarah Peverley, 11 July 2017).

Taylor, Beth, 'Annette Kellerman biography' (National Film And Sound Archive Of Australia website).

Chapter 11

'Blacktooth', Bad CGI Sharks (Review) (Horror Society, 29 September 2020).

Donato, M., 'Exclusive Interview: Jaume Collet-Serra Talks The Shallows' (We Got This Covered, 29 June 2016).

Frater, P., 'The Meg' Aims Big at China, but Will Audiences Bite? (*Variety*, 8 August 2018).

Gallucci, N., '"Phelps Vs. Shark", 5 Years Later: Shark Week's Biggest Scam Revisited' (Decider, 22 July 2022).

Gleiberman, O., 'Film Review: "The Meg"' (*Variety*, 8 August 2018).

Greco, Patti, '13 Crazy Behind-the-Scenes Facts About Blake Lively's Shark Movie, The Shallows' (*Cosmopolitan*, 23 June 2016).

Heritage, S., 'The end of Sharknado: saying goodbye to the silliest movie franchise ever' (*The Guardian*, 15 August 2018).

Kondolojy, Amanda, 'Syfy's "Sharknado" Hits Viewership Highs in Third Airing, Devours Additional 2.1 Million Viewers' (TV by the Numbers, 30 July 2013).

MaJaMa – https://majamaproductions.com/

Moraski, Lauren, 'Ian Ziering on a "Sharknado" sequel' (CBS news, 2014).

Thompson, E.; Bonner, M.; Igoe, K. J., & Sanwari, A., '15 Best Shark Movies of All Time, From the Bone-Chilling to the Ridiculous' (*Cosmopolitan*, 2023).

Vishnevetsky, I., 'The gimmicky survival thriller *The Shallows* is out of its depth' (The A.V. Club, 2016).

Ward, L.K, 'How Realistic Is the Shark Science in "The Shallows"?' (*Smithsonian Magazine*, 22 June 2016).

Wilson, S. L., *Shallows, The* (2016) (Dread Central, 24 June 2016).

Chapter 12

Arya, S., '"Jibaro is like a brutal disaster": Director Alberto Mielgo Explains The Toxic Relationship Featured In Jibaro' ('Love, Death + Robots' 3) (Netflix Junkie, 10 June 2022).

Beachum, C., 'Octavia Spencer (The Shape of Water): "Otherworldly and beautiful" themes are very relevant for today' (GoldDerby, 26 December 2017).

Colbert, S. M., 'Alberto Mielgo Interview: Netflix's Love, Death & Robots' (ScreenRant, 21 May 2022).

Failes, Ian, 'The Creature Fits The Suit In The Shape Of Water' (*VFX Voice Magazine*, Winter 2018 issue).

Lee, B., 'Underwater review – Kristen Stewart's soggy, silly monster movie' (*The Guardian*, 6 February 2020).

Lewis, S., 'Underwater Movie's Monster Is Cthulhu' (ScreenRant, 18 January 2020).

Miller, J., 'For Michael Shannon, the Clothes Made the Man in *The Shape of Water*' (*Vanity Fair*, 5 December 2017).

Miller, L., 'How Love Death + Robot's Eeriest Episode Was Brought to Life' (CBR, 8 June 2022).

Morgan, N., (Ph.D.) 'What's Happened to Our Attention Spans During the Pandemic?' (*Psychology Today*, 15 March 2021).

Navarro, M., 'Review: Nerve-Fraying Aquatic Nightmare "Underwater" is the Perfect Popcorn Horror Movie' (Bloody Disgusting!, 15 January 2020).

Potter, J., 'How an Evanston writer's boyhood idea inspired "Shape of Water"'. (Chicago Reader, 2018).

Spiegel, J., 'The Star Who Finally Gets His Due with "Shape of Water"' (*The Hollywood Reporter*, 8 December 2017).

Tallerico, B., 'Underwater movie review & film summary (2020)' (Roger Ebert, 10 January 2020).

Winchester, H., 'Behind-the-scenes of "Bad Travelling," part 1: Collaborating with David Fincher' (Chaos, 2022).

Yu, M., '"Shape Of Water" Creature Actor Doug Jones Understands The Monsters' (NPR, 3 March 2018).

Index

2-Headed Shark Attack, 110–11
20,000 Leagues Under the Sea, 9–11
47 Meters Down, 146–47, 180
   47 Meters Down: Uncaged, 181

Anglerfish, 180–81
Animatronics, 38, 63–4, 75–6
Asset (the), 155–7
Asylum (the), 104–11, 138–39, 147–48
Avatar: The Way of Water, 68

B-Movie, 66–7, 106–107, 123, 147, 150–51
Bad CGI Sharks, 151–52
Beach (the), 71–2, 145
Beast From 20,000 Fathoms (the), 16–18
Bechdel Test (the), 114–15
Behemoth, 3, 26, 168
Bible (the), 2
Bicephaly, 111
Black Water, 70, 81
Blackfish, 100, 183
Blue My Mind, 126–28
Blue Planet (the), 94–7
   Blue Planet II, 101
Brook Watson (*see* Watson and the Shark)
Bunyip, 7

Cabin in the Woods (the), 123
Cetus, 54, 56
CGI, 24, 58, 64–5, 67–9, 151–52
Clash of the Titans, 54–7
   2010 remake, 107–8
Colossal Squid (*see* Squid)
Coelacanth, 181
Creature from the Black Lagoon, 18–21,
   74, 154–55
   Revenge of the Creature, 25–6
   Creature Walks Among Us (the), 26

Creature suit, 24, 63
Crocodilian, 93, 175, 178
   alligator, 175
   caiman, 76
   crocodile, 3, 70, 75–7, 83, 92–3, 98,
      175
Cthulhu, 163, 166–9

Daigo Fukuryū Maru, 22–3
Deep Blue Sea, 63–4, 77–9
Dynamation, 17

Essex (sinking of the), 7–8, 141

Fiji mermaid, 18
Found footage, 69–70
From the Depths, 66–7

Galeophobia, 44
Giant squid (*see* Squid)
Gill-man, 18–21, 26, 154–58
Globster, 88
Godzilla, 22–5, 28–9, 80, 117, 177
   King Kong vs Godzilla, 28
   Son of Godzilla, 28
   Godzilla (2014), 117
Gojira (*see Godzilla*)
Gorgo, 26–7
Grabbers, 110
Greenscreen, 65–6
Guillermo del Toro, 65, 111–16, 154–58

Horror-comedy, 74, 104, 109, 152
Host (the), 84–6

Iara, 134–35
In the Heart of the Sea, 141–42
Invisible City, 134–35

Jaws, 31–48, 50–4, 58–9, 63, 78, 98, 174
Jaws 2, 50–4
 Jaws 3-D, 58–9
 Jaws: The Revenge, 74
 Jaws Effect (the), 44–5
Jersey Man-Eater (the), 32–6
Jonah, 3

Kaiju, 21, 104–17, 177–78
Killer whale *(see Orca)*
Kraken, 5, 54–7, 107–108

Lake Placid, 75–7
Leopard seal, 6, 179–80
Leviathan, 2–3
Lighthouse (the), 132–34
Loch Ness Monster, 6–7, 58, 176
Lonergan, Thomas and Eileen, 81
Lovecraftian horror, 163–64, 166, 168, 178
 H.P. Lovecraft, 111, 166, 168
Love, Death and Robots, 159–65
 Fish Night, 160–61
 Ice, 161–62
 In Vaulted Halls Entombed, 163
 Bad Travelling, 162–63
 Jibaro, 164–65
Lure (the), 123–26

Mako Mori Test (the), 114–15
Mako: The Jaws of Death, 89–92
Matawan Creek attacks *(see*
 Jersey Man-Eater)
Meg (the), 148–51
 The Trench: Meg 2, 150
Megalodon, 97, 99, 148–50, 174, 177
Mega Shark vs Giant Octopus, 104–107
Mermaid, 18, 120–35, 178–79
Mermaid Down, 131–32
Miniatures, 62
Moby Dick, 9, 12–3, 42, 108, 182
Mockbuster, 80, 105–106

Naitaka, 6, 101
Nautilus, 9–11
Nessie *(see* Loch Ness Monster)

Octopus, 11, 48–9, 56–7, 104–107, 182
Ogopogo *(see* Naitaka)
Open Water, 71, 81–3
Orca, 49–50, 100, 182–83

Pacific Rim, 112–17, 151
Peter Benchley, 35–8, 42, 45, 98
Piranha, 50, 60
 Piranha 2: the Spawning, 60
Pirates of the Caribbean, 2, 122, 129
Planet Earth, 97–8, 101
Primeval, 83, 93
Puppetry *(see* Animatronics)

Ray Harryhausen, 16–7, 54–7, 63–4
Reef (the), 70–1
Rhedosaurus, 17–8
Rogue, 83
Rusalka, 130

Scylla, 3
Sea Beast (the), 12–3
Sea snake, 180
Sea swine, 4–5
Selkie, 183
Shallows (the), 142–47
Shape of Water (the), 154–58
Shark, 3, 10–11, 13, 32–46, 49–54,
 58–60, 63–4, 66–7, 70–2, 77–9, 81–2,
 89–92, 98–102, 104–11, 138–52, 162,
 173–74, 177
 bull, 35, 111, 174
 great white, 33, 35, 36–42, 49–50, 58, 70,
  79, 98, 142–43, 174
 Greenland, 79
 mako, 77–9, 89–91
 megamouth, 177
 oceanic whitetip, 174
 tiger, 91, 174
Sharknado, 138–41, 147–48
Sharkwater, 101
Shark Week, 98–100, 140
She Creature, 121–22
Short-form video, 158–59
 TikTok, 101, 158–59
Siren, 129, 164

Squid, 98, 172–73
  giant, 172–73
  colossal, 173
Steven Spielberg, 36–9, 41–3, 50–1
Stop-motion animation, 17–8, 54–5, 64–5

Tentacles, 48–9
Thalassophobia, 19, 159
Typhon, 4

Underwater, 166–69
USS *Indianapolis*, 35, 40, 51

Walking With Dinosaurs, 96–7
Watson and the Shark, 32
Whale, 3, 8–9, 95, 108, 161, 173, 182

X-Files (the), 9, 88

Dear Reader,

We hope you have enjoyed this book, but why not share your views on social media? You can also follow our pages to see more about our other products: facebook.com/penandswordbooks or follow us on Twitter @penswordbooks

You can also view our products at www.pen-and-sword.co.uk (UK and ROW) or www.penandswordbooks.com (North America).

To keep up to date with our latest releases and online catalogues, please sign up to our newsletter at: www.pen-and-sword.co.uk/newsletter

If you would like a printed catalogue with our latest books, then please email: enquiries@pen-and-sword.co.uk or telephone: 01226 734555 (UK and ROW) or email: uspen-and-sword@casematepublishers.com or telephone: (610) 853-9131 (North America).

We respect your privacy and we will only use personal information to send you information about our products.

Thank you!